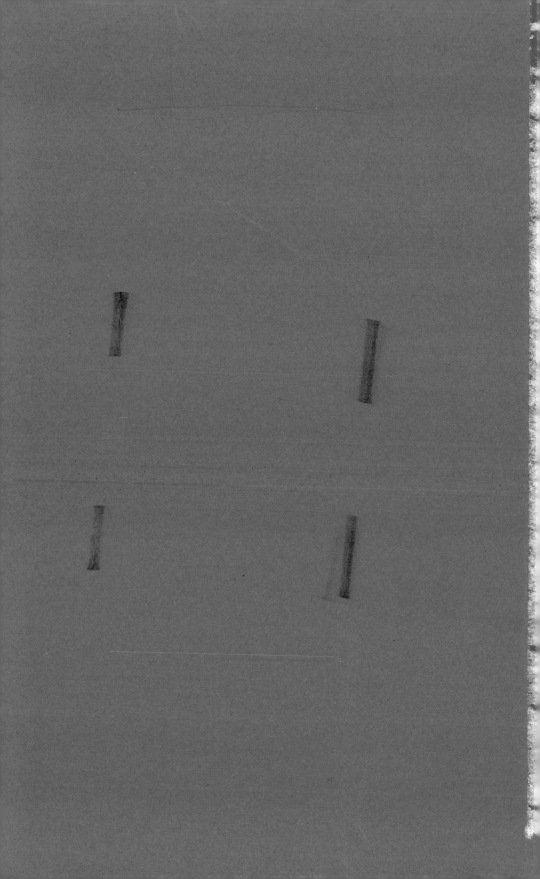

ACTING MY LIFE

ACTING MY LIFE

Ian Holm

with Steven Jacobi

BANTAM PRESS

LONDON · TORONTO · SYDNEY · AUCKLAND · JOHANNESBURG

TRANSWORLD PUBLISHERS
61–63 Uxbridge Road, London W5 5SA
a division of The Random House Group Ltd

RANDOM HOUSE AUSTRALIA (PTY) LTD
20 Alfred Street, Milsons Point, Sydney,
New South Wales 2061, Australia

RANDOM HOUSE NEW ZEALAND LTD
18 Poland Road, Glenfield, Auckland 10, New Zealand

RANDOM HOUSE SOUTH AFRICA (PTY) LTD
Endulini, 5a Jubilee Road, Parktown 2193, South Africa

Published 2004 by Bantam Press
a division of Transworld Publishers

The lines from *Moonlight* by Harold Pinter and *The Cocktail Party*
by T S Eliot are reproduced by permission of Faber and Faber Ltd

A catalogue record for this book is available from the British Library.
ISBN 0593 052145

Typeset in 11/15pt Palatino by
Falcon Oast Graphic Art Ltd

Printed in Great Britain by
Mackays of Chatham plc, Chatham, Kent

1 3 5 7 9 10 8 6 4 2

Papers used by Transworld Publishers are natural, recyclable products
made from wood grown in sustainable forests. The manufacturing
processes conform to the environmental regulations of the country of origin.

For my children: Jessica, Sarah-Jane, Lissy, Barnaby and Harry. With love.

CONTENTS

FOREWORD

I am an actor and this is the story of my life. However, I am not a writer. Steve Jacobi is. My story is therefore a collaboration. I lived the life and talked about it. He listened, replied, asked questions, talked to others, and slowly made his way into my skin, finding for my life an appropriate, characteristic voice. We talked for many hours, and soon the hours became days. By the end, Steve realized me as well as I understood myself. This book is the result of those times.

ACKNOWLEDGEMENTS

Thanks to everyone at the Royal National Theatre Archives and the Shakespeare Centre Library (at the Shakespeare Birthplace Trust) for their help in tracking down and providing photographs. To Carrie Brooke-Mellor at Rada, for information received. And to Brock Bogarde for giving permission for the use of Dirk Bogarde's letters.

The following gave generously of their time in jogging memory and making astute observations which have sometimes been incorporated into the text: Olivia Barker, Andrew Birkin, Dr Mike Coigley, Sir Richard Eyre, Hugh Hudson, Patti Love, Mike Newell and Sir Harold Pinter. We are in their debt.

We owe gratitude to Euan Thorneycroft at Curtis Brown and Sally Gaminara at Transworld Publishers, whose belief and enthusiasm ensured that the project never faltered.

Thank you to Sophie Baker, who was open-handed with memories and photographs. To Jessica and Sarah-Jane Holm, who helped fill many gaps and spoke with warmth and honesty. To Lissy Holm, who kept everyone happy and accommodated, in addition to supplying context for many reminiscences. And especially to Bee Gilbert, an indefatiguable and liberal dispenser of anecdotes, analysis, companionship, memorabilia and photographs. Love and appreciation to all of them.

1

CHILDHOOD

At some point, when actors – or probably most people – have made some kind of a name for themselves, they will seek to find the germ of their career in childhood. As Flannery O'Connor wrote, 'Anyone who has survived childhood has enough information to last him the rest of his days.' And, of course, it can be almost any kind of childhood. Childhood trauma, childhood failure, childhood misery, even (though rarely, it seems) childhood happiness. Maybe actors, like writers, need to be given a good going-over during their early years. I don't know. What I do know is that I did have some bad times (though not always perceived as bad at the time), an occasionally bizarre upbringing, and a mostly hateful time at school. Yet in the end, one accepted these things as normal.

Or, at least, normal for me. I know no other life. Who knows whether I was inordinately unhappy or not? Who can say whether those times in some way forged the man I became, the actor I was to become? Looking back, I suppose it is tempting to see each day as being part of some kind of metaphysical jigsaw puzzle, the relevance of each piece only becoming apparent as I was accepted at Rada, or went to Stratford, or featured in this or that movie, or played King Lear. But it never seemed like that. Nor should it. All lives are of a piece, though that piece is invariably fragmented and cracked.

Talking about my own life is a nervy experience, if only because it makes me feel that I've had one. On the whole, I prefer to ignore the past, or rather, to disown its obligations.

My life started in Ilford, at around two a.m. on 12 September 1931. I weighed just under eight pounds. I was a normal, healthy baby, whose birth occurred in a mental asylum. That's what I like to think, at any rate. It's what I've always believed. Barley Lane Mental Hospital in Goodmayes allegedly included amongst its facilities a room where mothers could give birth. My father, a doctor, was in charge of the place. When he was appointed, he and my mother had come down from Scotland, an exodus that only invited the rest of the family to look down on them, which they then did fairly often.

I have two early memories of my babyhood. One was being terrified by a face peering into my pram as I was being wheeled down Ilford High Street. The other was the dapper Mr Anderson, one of the inmates at the asylum. I don't know why or how I remember his name, or his oddly smart appearance, but Mr Anderson would spend his days filling a wheelbarrow with soil, and wheeling it from point A to point B, before picking each grain of dirt out and placing it carefully on the ground. At the time, it didn't seem such a strange or even unproductive thing to be doing. There were plenty of others who seemed worse off than him, and Mr Anderson even seemed quite adult by comparison. At least he got to use the wheelbarrow, a privilege denied to children, and indeed many of the other inmates, particularly those who had been infantilized by the asylum. In fact, one of the dominant, permanent overtones of the place was this back-to-childhood, back-to-the-kindergarten element. The inmates were handled as children – not as delinquent or bad children, necessarily, but, rather, as potentially decent, irresponsible children who didn't know what was good for them, and therefore frequently had to be told.

I knew how they felt; although, of course, I didn't *know* that I knew. And I suppose the fact that some of the inmates had been plucked from quite ordinary existences – as bank clerks, or dental assistants, or electricians – must have encouraged me to believe that there was a certain amount of pretence going on. Given the right circumstances, any one of them could pose as an average member of the public. In other words, people were granted two lives or sets of realities, in the same way, perhaps, that my father was not *merely* a father. As with the old saw that 'all the world's mad except thee and me, and even thee's a little cracked', I grew up thinking that one's identity wasn't fixed, and personality could be pretty fluid.

Naturally enough, I wasn't allowed into the asylum itself, and was restricted to observing the patients as they roamed or ambled hopelessly round the garden. It was easy to spend time watching the inmates as my own home was only a very short distance from the asylum. I don't know whether such proximity influenced the way my parents were thinking, but soon we moved into a big house partially designed, I think, by my father, who had been an architect's apprentice before he became a doctor. I would like to say it was a beautiful or homely place, but it wasn't. It was hideous. I remember it only as a spacious, square monstrosity set next to a golf course. I don't know which aspects of the house my father had a hand in, but all the evidence suggests that he made the correct choice in turning to medicine.

Although both he and my mother were sweet, harmless and almost entirely undemonstrative people, my father had the strange and perhaps dubious distinction of being an early pioneer of electric-shock treatment. He was good at shocks. Once, he hid underneath my bed as I tried to get to sleep. I didn't know he was there. Why would I? He never displayed any kind of emotion or showed an inclination to act out of the ordinary. Unaware of his presence, I lay on my front, quietly shuffling and obediently closing my eyes, thinking, no doubt, that this was how good boys behaved. Good boys kept quiet and tried with all their might to get to sleep when their parents told them it was bedtime. Maybe I was dropping off when I became aware that the bed was moving. At first, I thought it must be me, perhaps on the edge of a dream, certainly drowsy, my senses scrambled. I did another shuffle and tried even harder to go to sleep. The bed moved again. I thought about sitting up, this time convinced that something was not right. When the bed moved for a third time, this time more violently, I realized that I was apprehensive. My natural curiosity at wanting to discover the cause was being overwhelmed by a growing fear of the unknown. I sat paralysed as it shifted for a fourth time. Unable to bear it any longer, I leapt out of bed, only for a pair of strong, resistant hands to take a tight hold of my ankles. Anyone listening would have heard my wild screams being punctuated by the sound of my father's laughter. Not a man noted for his sense of humour, he nevertheless thought it the funniest thing. The result was that for several years after, I was traumatized and only able to lie on my back, afraid that if I took my eye off the room, the Bogeyman would surely get me.

This was the only time that my father played anything like a practical joke on me. He didn't mention the occasion again. We never discussed it at a later date. It was, as far as I can tell, entirely out of character. In all other departments of his life, he was a buttoned-up, cautious, austerely correct man. In perfect accordance with the standards of their day, my parents were not emotional people. I always suspected that from the point of view of those a little further down the social scale – maids, plumbers, and maybe even shopkeepers, for example – we must have seemed neither happy nor close. Now, I think we were probably as respectful towards one another as protocol, habit and character permitted, though we were never complicit. Still, whatever our collective imperfections, we did offer ourselves as some kind of 'unit', though a unit to which I never quite belonged nor was able absolutely to extricate myself from.

There's a framed photograph of my father hanging in my daughter's flat, which seems to encapsulate him. Naturally, it's in black and white – though not the modish glossy black and white of a Cecil Beaton, or even a Bill Brandt. No, this is an altogether murkier, paler affair. My father is looking down and to the left, almost as if he's afraid to look at the camera, as if it would be an extravagant surrender to vanity. Also, he looks slightly miffed, as if the camera had intruded on some important duty. He is neither old nor young, smiling nor unsmiling. The only thing you can be sure of is that the close-ness of the camera causes him discomfort. There's a photograph of my mother next to him, positioned at a different angle, probably to hint at a meaningful connection or dynamic between the pair of them. Alas, she is looking upwards and to the right, almost as if she couldn't bear the sight of him, which is an unfortunate distortion of an intimate if reticent relationship.

My father is wearing one of his many similar jackets, all of them a species of tweed, most on the heavy side. He might take his jacket off when pushing the heavy lawnmower across the grass on a sweltering summer's day, but that was as far as it went. And even then, the top button of his shirt would remain resolutely fastened.

If anything, my mother was even less demonstrative than my

father. Her family was quite wealthy. If her father didn't own White Horse whisky, he had some kind of significant stake in it. Mother was always talking about the 'South Africans', who weren't actually related to us but were great party-goers who always seemed to have a strange effect on her. At one point they suddenly arrived in Britain, coming over to Scotland en masse and by all accounts sweeping triumphantly through the country. Her five sisters and one brother resided in grand houses at places like Kilmarnock and Helensburgh, and the brother was talked of in almost reverential terms, apparently being something of a war hero. Inevitably, they thought that my mother had married beneath her, and referred to my father as 'the wee doctor'.

I don't think this was necessarily or simply a professional slight. My father was a small man. My mother was a small woman. I am a small man. Size, or lack of size, absolutely runs in the family. But whatever significance the patronizing references had, there was no doubt that the Holms looked down on the Cuthberts. To this day, I know nothing about my paternal grandfather, and never even met him. I have a suspicion that he was rather working class, precisely the rank of person from which I was to be shielded.

I don't know how much (if any) influence was exerted on my father by my mother's family, but there was a general air of severe, emotional restraint, occasionally challenged by the odd spasm of uncharacteristic behaviour, always on his side. Apart from moving the bed, he would often kiss me full on the lips, and, I think, rather liked the girls. You could tell that he had what was called 'a roving eye', though I don't believe he ever did much with it. He may have wanted to be a traveller, but he never strayed far from home. He knew what was expected of him and, by and large, kept his side of the bargain.

I can't imagine that my father had affairs. Literally can't imagine it. I never even saw my parents undressed, though obviously they must have had sex. There was a very middle-class, even Scottish, tightness about them. I'm not sure how much of that was really my father; I suspect my mother was the driving force.

When we lived in Worthing after the war, he was the one who walked me five miles to church every Sunday, while she stayed at home, religion not being something she felt inclined to bother with. My father, as ever, was playing his part, living up to expectations. It was the same when he died. My mother refused to go to the funeral, saying that it was 'up to others' to deal with things. It was as though his death had terminated some kind of contract. Another time, I remember her saying, 'I served your father for thirty years and never a cross word.' The idea of service, of duty, came naturally to her, while my father had to work at it a little harder. Had she died first, I'm certain he would have been fastidious in his mourning, solemnly grieving, gracing the funeral in a tight black suit, hinting at heartbreak but, bravely, holding anguish at bay.

I now have the feeling (though perhaps I would) that maybe he was acting a part, borrowing a certain style of behaviour, trying to be someone else, or at least not someone who may have been working class and had married above his station. There was, I suppose, the semblance of performance in his manner, though I didn't understand this at the time.

My own recollections of childhood performance are limited and scatological. I have heard of actors who talk of their childhoods as being extended opportunities to show off, which is what fired them to take to the stage in the first place. With me it is almost the opposite. I was too afraid, too fearful, to show off.

My first memory of putting on a show was while sitting astride a large, rather stained porcelain potty, straining, heaving with constipation while my nanny looked on, anxious for a tangible result. She fussed around the room, pretending to be busy with other things, while constantly checking whether my exertions had paid dividends. I knew that it was somehow necessary to show her that I was straining, that this was expected, a persuasive component in the matter of evacuating my bowels.

The other memory is hardly more sophisticated. While visiting my maternal grandparents in Scotland, I recall watching a huddle of mostly elderly people chatting and laughing amongst themselves. Compared to the undemonstrative, cocooned life I led at home, this surge of noise and abandon amongst adults must have seemed relatively raucous. Suddenly, I split the air with a loud farting noise. Without thinking, and aware of the pale old ghostly heads slowly turning towards me, like something out of a Sickert painting, I faced them and said, 'Who did that?' thereby denying the group its moment of courteous denial.

I guessed from the gales of laughter which followed that I had somehow said the right thing, that the indiscretion of bringing attention to the offence was outweighed by the levity with which I had accomplished it. It was my first inkling of the way that 'play' could be used to transform a moment. Of, perhaps, the way that putting on a show could bring reward.

I suspect the incident made such an impact on me because it was so alien to anything that occurred within my own household. The only time I can remember my mother showing uncontrolled emotion was when my elder brother, Eric, my only sibling, died in 1943. He was ten years older than me and died of cancer when he was twenty-two. I don't remember much about him other than assuming he was 'the bright one' (I was cute and fat) and feeling that I was being ignored, despite always doing my best to emulate him. I suppose it's classic sibling stuff, right out of J. M. Barrie, and Eric's death shattered my parents.

He died in Cairo. The night before we received the telegram, my father sat bolt upright in bed and exclaimed, 'Eric's dead.' When my mother received the news, she immediately vomited. It took my brother's death to whip my parents into an emotional lather. Afterwards, my father became intensely religious, as if even more duty was the answer, whereas my mother became, if anything, even less interested than she'd been before.

My main memory of Eric is of him walking into the sea with me on his shoulders. He waded through the waves, me terrified and screaming, him laughing. Having almost drowned in an Essex quarry pit when I was very small, I was terrified of deep water. He ducked me under the water, then brought me up again, gave me time to get my breath, then repeated the process. Not even my obvious fear could deter him from plunging me into the waves, again and again. No doubt time has exaggerated the number of times this happened, but it seemed an eternity. I connected his laughter with my father's odd and frightening behaviour when he ambushed me from underneath the bed. It all helped to create a culture of fear in me, a feeling that I wasn't quite up to it, not good enough. A bit of a disappointment. To this day, I haven't visited my brother's grave in Egypt.

It wasn't that home was a bad place to be. My parents were idiosyncratic, but essentially they were sweet, harmless people. Scrape the surface of anyone's childhood and you'll probably find all kinds of oddness and eccentricity that, at the time, you passed off as 'normal'. In many respects, I was well looked after. If anything, perhaps, I was too protected, and certainly wasn't prepared for school.

We moved to Mortehoe in Devon when my father retired, and were there 'for the duration'. He was only fifty-five, but apparently this was quite a normal retirement age for doctors in his line of work. The cottage – I guess it was a cottage, or at least a small house – was called Littlecote, and overlooked the

Atlantic. And that was where I spent the war, generally feeling sorry that it seemed so uneventful, watching Luftwaffe bombers droning overhead on their way to blitz Cardiff, where the real action was going on. Like so many things, it seemed tantalizingly out of reach. Sometimes they were so low that I could see the tail gunners and fancied that if I waved, they would return the gesture.

Otherwise, the war only made itself apparent in strange, discreet ways. We had been issued with gas masks, which we were supposed to carry everywhere. Mine was a Mickey Mouse mask with red rubber face-piece and bright eye-piece rims, though it still smelt of disinfectant and had the same gas-like odour as the grotesque, pig-snout monstrosities that had been given to my parents. The top of the local post-office pillar box was given a coating of yellowish gas-detector paint, the presence of which fascinated me and ignited strange, feverish expectations. And in rural Devon, at night and even in clear weather, the blackout often meant that there was not even a pinprick of light to be seen from the small farms and villages, or even upon the sea.

I suppose my experience of the war wasn't untypical of most people who lived outside London. It was even something of a glamorous sideshow. My father did the National Savings round, and would dutifully walk round the village collecting money. We had an Anderson shelter in the large back garden, only used once, when a bomber missed out on Cardiff and had to shed its cargo in order to get back to its own airfield. The bombs dropped in a field nearby and did nothing more serious than create a few holes and kill a cow. For most of the time, though, the shelter was unused, except as a place to play – or better, and perhaps more likely, to hide. There was also the coastguard station, from where we would spend hours watching the cargo and troop vessels head up the Channel.

School, however, was far more frightening. I was sent away to boarding school, even though the school was in the same village in which my family lived. It had been evacuated from Sussex, and was run by a Wackford Squeers clone (even down to the impaired eyesight) called Mr Tenant. He was an ogre with a taste for hitting small boys. He thumped everyone – using his hands, fists, cane, whatever was most convenient. Meanwhile, his dreadful wife was pouring a dreadful substance called Radio malt down our throats, no doubt convinced that it was doing us some good. And I was bullied. Being called Cuthbert didn't help – I was Ian Holm Cuthbert at the time, Holm being my mother's maiden name. And as I was stupid, or at least *felt* I was stupid, the only way I could keep up was to crib answers, which meant that I was often targeted by the other boys.

The effects of being bullied stayed with me for a relatively long time. Even several years later, at Chigwell Grammar School, I can remember lying in bed every morning, waiting patiently for the first sign of dawn through the thick, ugly curtains in our dormitory. I wanted to be the first up, not for reasons of health or nobility, but in order to slope off to the swimming pool. There, I would change into my trunks and carefully immerse myself in the cold water. All this despite my fear of water, but I knew that if I didn't, the other boys would at some point throw me in.

My education was a complete disaster. Convinced that I was the family dunce, self-conscious about my size, and grateful only that I had inherited my mother's perfect nose rather than my father's bulbous monstrosity, I was probably fair game. The only thing for which I ever got top marks was reading poetry. And even then, it got me into trouble.

Mr Tenant was ordinarily a Maths teacher, but for some reason he was taking us for English. He asked me to read a poem, which I duly did. I think I had an inkling that I had done it pretty well. He nodded approvingly, and even the rest of the class seemed impressed. Then he called me to the front, towering above me, smelling faintly of carbolic, smooth and menacing.

'You like reading, don't you?' he asked.

I nodded, expecting to be praised for my efforts.

I looked up, anticipating a smile of commendation, wondering what a smile from the ferocious Mr Tenant might actually look like.

As my eyes met his, his hand came down suddenly and sharply on the side of my face.

Bang!

As I staggered backwards, he told me I could return to my seat, and then proceeded with the rest of the lesson without offering a word of explanation, and acting as though nothing extraordinary had happened – which in retrospect, and considering the type of man he was, I suppose it hadn't. In the same vein, I also remember the volatile Mr Thurston who would suddenly explode into action by hurling his penknife at unruly boys.

Apart from reading poems, the only other vaguely theatrical experience I had in Devon was in the garage opposite our cottage, which was owned by Mr Gammon. His son, Ivor, was a simple soul, and was known locally as a boy who liked to dress in his mother's underwear. But he did fire my imagination, not necessarily through his strange dress sense, but because he told stories and acted out episodes from his own life for other kids. The garage became his stage, and surrounded by mysterious boxes, miscellaneous clutter, garden tools and dirty rags, and smelling of a mix of oil and rotting vegetables, he used it to spin colourful yarns about his family, thus acquiring an unconventional form of respect for being able to hold an audience in such unpromising circumstances.

It would be nice to say that, stung by my shyness and constant sense of fear, and then fired by the weird Ivor Gammon, I developed a passion for theatre and found a means of fulfilment and of bypassing my insecurities. Actually, it never happened like that. And any latent urges to show off or make an exhibition of myself were firmly quashed by Dr Hastings, the History master, who took me out to the 1st XI cricket field and showed me the biggest cock I've ever seen, before or since. He was, of course, an absolute screamer, and not necessarily untypical of the sort of man who bobbed up in education during and just after the war. The effect he had was to drive me further into my shell, to the extent that I carried a sheath knife with me for some time afterwards, and became (quite understandably, I think) mildly homophobic.

After the war, when the picturesque but insistent Devon hills became too much for my parents, we moved to Worthing and lived in a large house with an eyebrow window and sloping garden. We were joined there by Mr and Mrs Bottright, he as handyman/gardener, she as cook. I went to Chigwell Grammar School in 1946, where I stayed until I was eighteen, then did my National Service. It was a good school, founded by William Penn and run by the astoundingly wonderful Dr James, who was both scholarly and athletic, and, as if that wasn't enough, also a sleek, good-looking man endowed with charisma. Later, he went on to become High Master of Harrow. His very being reminded me of all the things I wasn't, and although my education continued to be a catastrophe (I failed School Certificate), thanks to him I did take my first tentative steps on to a stage. He encouraged me, perhaps even persuaded me, to try for a part in a farce called *Tons of Money*.

It was the first properly theatrical thing I did, and as far as school went, the only thing. Elsewhere, however, Worthing was proving to be an unlikely but relatively thought-provoking place. Our neighbours, Lance and Lydia Catermole, must have spotted something, and they tried to make me think in a lateral way about school. If I didn't like it and wasn't much good at it, then why did I stay? Why did I even have to stay at home? The idea of *not* staying had, of course, never occurred to me. And though I did stay on, the Catermoles offered me a glimpse of another world – one in which I wasn't bound to a place where I was destined to fail, or to a home where (despite my parents' qualities) I felt unappreciated, at times unloved.

I paid attention to Lance and Lydia. There was something exotic about them – he was a painter, and made a name for himself designing transport posters, and she worked in an embassy somewhere and told me she was a spy – though I now suspect that they were simply a little on the bohemian side. Whatever, aged fifteen, I read a part in a Hercule Poirot play for the local dramatic society, and was, I think, quite good.

Amongst the fleshpots of Worthing there was also a famous provincial actor called Henry Baynton – 'provincial' because he acted everywhere except London – who was introduced to me by my dentist, the aptly named Mr Pullford, who also serviced Baynton's teeth and thought we would have something in common. Here was the man who was instrumental in getting me into the business. He was a part of those sturdy touring companies which never went to the capital, knew Shakespeare backwards, owned the rights to Irving's *The Bells*, and had a fiercely loyal following at the venues he played.

Baynton was a tall, dapper, rather grand man, not averse to the odd cravat, which was considered quite daring in those days, especially in the suburbs, and he was so charming that he even conned my mother out of five pounds. He enchanted us all, occasionally managing to get his tongue down my throat. I didn't object. The experience was not unduly horrific or even uncomfortable, and I thought it a small price to pay for the theatrical know-how he was, I thought, handing on to me.

He tutored me for my Rada audition – a mixture of Shakespeare and a bizarre thing called *The Jewish Easter* by someone called Israel Zangwill. I don't know why he thought this was a good idea, but it must have made some kind of impression on Sir Kenneth Barnes (the Rada principal). Or perhaps he was so shocked at the choice that he let me in.

By the time all this was happening, I was more or less out of childhood – at least, in chronological terms. I must have felt, perhaps had been feeling for some time, that life was happening elsewhere. Although I was timid and was never particularly hopeful that life outside Essex would be much different, I must have had an inkling that just to be somewhere else might mean I could be some*body* else. My lifelong habit of forgetting the obligations of the past was already quite well developed. Like Larkin, who describes his own childhood as 'a forgotten boredom', I had the sense – and no more than the sense – that my life had so far been *un*spent and that not much had happened. Acting, at the very least, would be a change.

When I told my father that I wanted to be an actor – or rather, that I wanted to give it a try; I don't think I was ever either definite or passionate about it – he merely said, 'Prove it!' and I thought, 'I've been asked to do something now. So I suppose I'd better get on and do it.'

I now understand that this was a very middle-class response; vaguely aspirational, though ambitious without being passionate. In other words, it also involved a rather weedy need to please an authority figure; in this case, my father. It was also, I should say, the best thing he could have said to me.

Thus, my protected, cocooned childhood seemed to have worked an odd alchemy. It was not a happy time, though neither was it particularly unhappy. In some ways, it was very privileged. Fear played a large part – fear of being bullied, fear of not passing exams, fear of being hopeless, fear of being turned down – and this, together with the need for love and the seeking of approval, now seem significant. Acting became a way of renewing the sense that, 'Yes, I can do it,' coupled with show-ing off. 'I can do it. See. Watch me. Look. Watch me again. See. *And* I can do it really well.'

Why did I become an actor? Is there anything in my child-hood which made it inevitable? It's something I've thought about, though only recently, and I do think that the two things have much to do with one another. Fear and the subsequent need to prove myself ('Prove it!'), both traits inherited from my young years, are certainly in the mix. Acting, drama, is some-thing that one does all the time. There's a gaping hole in the middle of us all, though in some it's arguably bigger than in others, so that everything becomes a bit of a performance, a reaction to the sense of lack. Life itself is a kind of performance. People working themselves up into some kind of activity, putting on a show of being something or other, because in the end it's less painful than doing nothing, being nothing. And perhaps my gaping hole is an especially large one, if only because I perceive it to be so. Thus, the argument goes, I need the acting more literally than most.

I also have a native intelligence and am good at seeming bright in a second-hand sort of way. I suppose these are useful qualities if you want to be an actor. You have to understand a little of what you're doing in order to give it shape, but too much intelligent curiosity may well be the end of you.

If I wasn't an actor, what would I be doing? Acting the part of a dental assistant, or performing the role of a council administrator? Pretending to be a teacher or masquerading as a plumber? It's hard to say. All I do understand is that everyone has that gaping hole in the middle of them, and that what it means – perhaps a fear that there's nothing there, a lack, that you are nothing – is something I carry round with me on a daily basis.

On the other hand, as we shall see, it has also served me pretty well.

2

RADA AND NATIONAL SERVICE

My time at Rada was twice interrupted. In effect, I was at college for four years, from 1949 to 1953, though not necessarily embracing the kind of bohemian existence that might usually be associated with the life of a drama student.

I stayed with my father's sister Aunt Evelyn and her husband Bill, who was a Cockney garage mechanic. They lived in Bromley, so far out of London that though it is known as a suburb, the postcode actually places it in Kent. They lived in a modest but perfectly comfortable two-up-two-down semi-detached house in a road that was full of the same. Although I spent a week or so in a more central YMCA prior to moving there, my accommodation during the time at Rada offered nothing more adventurous than cosy, secure surroundings which seemed oddly and absolutely divorced from the days I was spending at college. The sense of living a sheltered existence punctuated by daily forays into the centre of London was confirmed by my father paying fees. Although I was not, therefore, on a scholarship, I would never experience financial hardship or have to worry about 'getting by'.

Not that I was inclined to test the limits of my father's generosity. As soon as the college day concluded, I would catch the train and scuttle back to Bromley to be home in time for tea. I can't remember, for example, going to see a single play while I was in London. Of course, I was aware of things going on, but I never actually saw them. Aunt Evelyn and Uncle Bill unwittingly abetted this strange separation of habits. Though fussily concerned about my comfort and whether or not I might require another cup of tea, they showed virtually no interest in my daytime activities.

At that time, as it probably still is, Bromley was a quiet, uneventful town, a predominantly middle- or lower-middle-class place. It was drab and prim in the way that English towns are, offering the respectability of shops, churches, a library, an amateur-dramatic group, and an odd, indeterminate sense of being neither in nor out of London. There was talk of post-war austerity, though in Bromley that sort of thing didn't have much impact. People trudged about with a sort of befuddled, drab sameness (the Welfare State had not transformed lives in the hoped-for manner), and there were still plenty of de-mob suits around, though no one actually looked poor or threadbare. Self-contained and pickled in aspic, it steered politely clear of much that was alarming, exciting or ugly.

This uneventful existence quite suited me, because it allowed me to develop at my own pace, taking things in a short, measured stride, never being reckless or taking chances. When, after barely a year, I was drafted to Austria to begin my National Service, I travelled without regret or rancour, not in the least put out that my training as an actor had been interrupted, and even mildly relieved that I would no longer have to endure those classes and exercises at which I was clearly no use, fencing being the most obvious example. This was organized by M. Froeschlin, a ferocious Frenchman who wasted no time in exposing my limitations and in demonstrations cruelly exposing my hopeless lack of reach.

Towards the end of 1949, I arrived at the lakeside town of Klagenfurt in southern Austria. I was a lance corporal in a small group which belonged to something called a 'Branch'. In effect, I was a clerk dealing for the most part with officers' confidential reports, which gave me a gratifying sense of voyeuristic power. There were, however, other reasons for liking the army.

Overseen by someone called Mad Mike West, our splinter group was left more or less to itself. Though I had told the Selection Officer that I wanted to stay in England and be a driver, the Klagenfurt posting suited me very well. The desire for painless invisibility – which had lain behind my original request – was more than satisfied. I liked being told what to do and I liked the satisfaction that followed from the successful completion of fairly limited tasks. I even enjoyed guard duty and being drilled by a barbarous RSM called, I think, Puddiphat, though naturally I hated those times when I had to *take* drill.

This aversion to taking responsibility would be characteristic throughout my acting life. I would work from scripts and took direction well. In addition, I preferred working in a group environment, being part of a greater whole, and not having to be too conspicuous. There were opportunities for acting in the army, though I never put myself forward and it was only when a Colonel Lovender did some research and unearthed my Rada connection that I was persuaded to perform in a revue. Though in a different company, Ned Sherrin also appeared, and I think we acted together in a farce. This lack of recall suggests to me that even though I was a drama student, the fact of being or becoming an actor had not yet established itself in my consciousness. I had drifted towards the theatre but was by no means bound to it. In fact, by the end of my two years' National

Service, I was so content that I didn't much want to come home and even contemplated signing up.

Despite the menial nature of my job, Austria seemed to me in many ways an exotic, even daring place. Because we were stationed at the southern tip of the country, we were close to the borders with East Europe and were told that if the Russians came, it was every man for himself. This at a time when the Cold War was taken very seriously indeed; I was inwardly quite thrilled at the prospect of being at the 'sharp end' of things. The colourful fascination of the posting was embellished by the fact that the local headquarters was run by Austrian Nazis, sympathizers who had been left high and dry by the end of the war but who were allowed to continue in their posts because they made such an efficient fist of things. They were mostly unrepentant Nazis, too, talking freely of the wonderful times they had enjoyed under Hitler.

However, chief among the reasons for liking the place was Camilla Vidonig, a tall, pretty, blond-haired, strappingly Austrian woman who was four years older than me and with whom I had my first proper love affair. I say 'proper', though when I eventually did return to England my virginity was still firmly intact.

I can remember being slightly in awe of Camilla and her family (her father was a cheerful, enthusiastic Nazi), and at one point just being grateful that she tolerated my company. Day by day, inch by inch, I pushed our relationship closer to actual intimacy. It was the first time I had experienced the thrill of the chase, no matter that my sort of chase was being conducted in excruciating, mostly eventless slow motion.

Once, while sitting on a bench amongst some allotments, and gazing at the mountains, I ventured to kiss her, immediately wondering whether I'd risked too much and jeopardized several months of stealthy preparation. Much to my surprise, she kissed me back. Thus emboldened, we went back to her house, which contained not only her parents but also two large and occasionally prickly Alsatian dogs. We arrived. We went to her room. We undressed. We lay together in bed. We kissed. We became close. But nothing actually happened. I felt I had achieved quite enough for one day, and was probably too mindful of the task force still lurking downstairs. So, like a schoolboy easily pleased by a quick trip to the sweet shop, I walked the three miles back to barracks, buoyed up with winged heels.

When I did arrive back in England, Camilla came over to visit me. I was still young and romantically very naive, vaguely persuading myself that I was in love with her and that our chastity was mutually precious, a quaint souvenir of our extended, idealized courtship. There was no need to hurry such things (I told myself) – we had a whole lifetime together to consummate our love. Pretty soon I found that she had contracted TB, and that she had been having an affair with her doctor. I assumed he would not have been as physically bashful as me, and my relationship with Camilla withered, quite organically, on the vine. I waved goodbye to her at Victoria station, by which time I think we were both relieved that things had been brought to a halt before any foolish commitments could be made. At least, a foolish commitment by me. Like almost all first loves, we were inseparable for many months. And then, naturally, we separated.

Resuming my studies at Rada, I continued not making a mark with women. Once, though I don't quite understand how, I managed to get Nanette Newman back to my parents' house, and even introduce her to them. Again, nothing happened. Years later, she was married to the film director Bryan Forbes, whom I bumped into at a party. Obviously he had heard about his wife's visit – I was pleased at the notion that it might have passed into Forbes Family Lore – and he gestured towards her, nudged me blokeishly and said, 'You've been there before, haven't you, dirty bugger?' Feeling oddly gratified, I couldn't quite manage to contradict his version of events, though I more or less salved my conscience by not formally *agreeing* with it either, limiting myself to a series of insinuating nods and suggestive, pimpish hand movements.

My time at college continued in the same undemonstrative, slightly detached manner as before. Acting was still not yet a part of me, though I reckoned I was doing well enough to persuade my teachers that I might at some point be able to make a living out of it. Still, I rarely felt committed to it with the kind of passion or urgency I supposed I ought to be feeling. I enjoyed appearing in productions and was rather bored by such things as breathing and voice exercises. I understood that these were necessary skills, but considered ultimately that acting was something which could not be taught. Because of my peculiar tutelage under Henry Baynton, I arrived at Rada with the sense of performance quite well formed.

Perhaps unkindly, and without doubt unreasonably, I formed the opinion that if my tutors had been good at acting, then they would have been playing rather than teaching. There were exceptions. The formidable Mary Duff, for example, whose star pupil was Dorothy Tutin. Her straight-talking, blunt criticisms were often laced with such wit and perception that in the end you wanted to improve for the sole purpose of impressing her. She could, however, be outrageously awful to students, shouting at one, as he slouched on stage to deliver a monologue, 'For God's sake stand up straight! You look as though you've been gang-banged by a tribe of large Polynesians.'

Then I did something so out of character that I still do not understand how or why it happened. With less than a year to complete at Rada, a lady by the name of Mrs Claretree-Major let it be known that she wanted volunteers for an acting tour of the

United States. Apparently the invitation was issued on a fairly regular basis, the catch being that actors would have to pay their own fares and wouldn't be well rewarded for their efforts once they were over there. It would be hard work in exchange for around thirty-five dollars a week. Though we didn't know it then, we would also have to pay for our own petrol. In addition, Equity would wash its hands of the rogue tour, thereby leaving actors more or less at the mercy of Mrs Claretree-Major, who, it was generally assumed, would be making a tidy profit from the whole enterprise.

I still don't understand what compelled me to sign up. I rarely put myself forward for anything. Though young and naive (this was 1952; I would have my twenty-first birthday in America), my youth was distinguished less by the seeking of adventure than by the quest for anonymity and a life of undemanding, comfortable discretion.

Although it was an impulsive act which was absolutely out of character, I now think that it was an impulsive act which through its very singularity actually confirmed the kind of person I had become. Just as the most audacious people are not harebrained at all times, so the most timid are permitted their few moments of impetuosity. One of mine was about to occur. Such aberrations are rarely defining. They merely add a little light and shade to the general shape of things. In electing to follow the old lady to America, I had become neither reckless nor devil-may-care. Instinct told me that I should go, and soon afterwards a small number of us were aboard the S.S. *Mauritania*, nervously heading to a place that had assumed fantastical dimensions in post-war, austere England. My father paid the fare, and we were met by Mrs Claretree-Major, who was driving a large, pink Chrysler.

The 'tour' took nine months, and during that time we travelled over forty thousand miles. We were billeted in various places (during the rehearsal period, I was placed with a Mrs Hudson in Chappaqua, upstate New York), and when we weren't performing, I earned my keep through gardening, working for 75 cents per hour. A short while after we set off – dragging around with us pretty ad hoc productions of *Henry VIII* and *Peter Pan* – it became clear how arduous things were going to be, and pretty soon several members of our troupe had given up; before long we were down to only six or seven regular actors.

We not only played at some strange locations, such as bars, strip clubs, small churches and, most importantly, schools, but also at strange times. It was not unusual, for example, to perform *Henry VIII* at eight-thirty in the morning in the cafeteria that served an oil well, to a small group of twenty roustabouts. Audiences were curious and watched politely. Once, I was asked where we were from. 'England,' I replied. 'Where's that?' came the response. 'Anywhere near Sweden?'

For a naive and generally unadventurous middle-class boy from the English suburbs, America seemed vast and unreal, each day throwing up new images and experiences which had to be absorbed and accommodated. Going for a stroll in Texas with Mary Grant, a member of the company, entailed being surrounded by gun-brandishing policemen who promptly arrested us for walking – something, evidently, which Americans did not do much of, even then, and which was viewed with deep suspicion. Because we were 'strangers in town' and therefore automatically implicated in a local bank raid, we were detained, then finally released, and eventually driven back to the theatre in a police car.

Though it was all intoxicating and eye-opening, my virginity remained stubbornly unviolated. If this was the unconscious reason why I had travelled to America in the first place – it was, after all, the land of opportunity, so why should it not be the land of sexual opportunity? – it became a frustrated reason.

Perhaps if I had thrown off my sexual inhibitions there and then, and got them out of my system, I would not have trailed them around with me for the rest of my life. Recalling Austria, I may have associated 'abroad' with 'sex', perceiving that such things occurred far away from home and family. I had the chance – I *think* I had the chance – with a Canadian actress called Pat Leith, with whom I flirted, and once, at Lake Michigan, detected clear signs that she might have been willing to go a little further. But too timid to risk it, and frightened of failure, I did nothing, and the Promised Land remained unexplored.

The nearest I came to a carnal experience was meeting Larry from Texas, a big, blockheaded man, who offered me some ointment.

'What's it for?' I asked.

'Your dick.'

'My dick?'

'Your dick.'

'My *dick*?'

'Your feller. Your penis,' he confirmed, with medical precision.

'You're offering me ointment for my penis?' It seemed unlikely.

'Yeah. Rub this on your dick and it will stand up for four hours!'

'Stand up?'

'You know – a boner. A four-hour boner. How does that sound?'

'Fine. It sounds fine.'

'You want some?'

He offered me the container, a small, nondescript metal lozenge, half full of a waxy, greenish substance. I didn't want to know where the other half had gone.

'No thanks . . . but I appreciate the offer.'

Four hours! What would I have done with four hours – he who would have settled for four minutes?

Though I began the tour as one of the pirates in *Peter Pan*, due to the drop-out rate I was soon promoted to play Peter Pan himself. Years later I would play Peter's creator J. M. Barrie, in strange circumstances I could not then have foreseen. Also in the troupe were two other Rada students with whom I became quite close. John Braban, a very handsome and good man but not a great actor, who would eventually become best man at my wedding. (What would I have thought then about the prospect of being married so soon afterwards?) And John Wicks, who later became the projectionist at Leamington Cinema.

We all worked hard, and returned to Rada after nine months to complete our course. I suppose the American tour must have reassured me that I could be an actor, though as my time as a student drew to a close, I was still not certain of taking the plunge. I did win the Kendal Award, though was informed quite sniffily that this would put an end to any aspirations I might have of becoming a professional actor. 'Nobody who wins prizes here does any good,' I was told.

What had Rada given to me? Though I enjoyed my time well enough, and valued the lessons given by Mary Duff and the voice coach Clifford Turner, I doubted whether the overall quality of the tuition was particularly high. We spent much time learning how to dance, learning how to fence, learning how to talk, learning how to walk, even learning how to sit in a chair. Plays came later. So far as I was concerned, the college's main benefit was to make me impatient to get on stage; it seemed we'd only be allowed there once we had mastered the sitting and walking. I couldn't wait to get started. On the other hand, I do believe that some kind of grounding is important, and going to stage school – as opposed to starting at the bottom, for example by sweeping floors in a local repertory company – was as good a foundation as any other. It focused me and brought acting and theatre emphatically into my consciousness.

I'd like to say I also gained some benefit from rubbing shoulders with so many good actors from that time. Though it might well have been true, it didn't feel that way. My main recollection is of doing things because I was told to, merely 'getting on with it', rather than savouring the moment.

Apart from the Kendal and going to America, I had kept a pretty low profile. I had discovered that I could act. The main parts I played were Antonio in *Much Ado About Nothing*, Consul Bernick in *Pillars of Society*, and Ronnie Winslow in *The Winslow Boy*. At least my father would be pleased. Or, more accurately, satisfied. I had proved to him that I could, after all, do *something*. But as I thought about my next step, much of England's familiar way of life seemed to be on the point of unravelling. The empire was in trouble. 'Rock Around the Clock' was only two years away and John Osborne's *Look Back in Anger* little more than that. The 1950s was a decade of confusion: social, cultural, musical and political. And if I had known what would happen in the next few years, maybe I'd have thought differently about becoming an actor. The coronation of 1953 was just round the corner and was the first major event to attract a mass television audience. It has often been said that millions sat down to watch and never regained the use of their legs. More theatres closed in coronation year than in any year before or since.

3

STRATFORD (I)

When I arrived at Stratford in 1954 – reasonably callow, very unworldly, unarguably naive, quite aimless, emphatically virginal – I still wasn't convinced that I wanted to be an actor. I was like a snail emerging from its shell and looking around after a storm. I moved straight into B&B lodgings with Mrs Arrowsmith. Had I known more, I'd probably have been petrified. Waiting for me at Stratford were Anthony Quayle, Glen Byam Shaw and, a little later, Laurence Olivier, though I was so far down the pecking order that I doubt they knew much about the waiting, or anything at all about me.

I did, of course, know something about Olivier, though apparently not enough. Several years earlier, during the Rada interview, I was asked by the Principal, Kenneth Barnes, who were my heroes in theatre. I replied that I did not know, that probably I did not have one. This evidently was not an appropriate answer. If you were an actor at that time, your hero was Olivier. Later, when I'd completed my audition piece, the examiner superimposed this intelligence over my performance and told me to stop impersonating Olivier.

'And don't try to sound like our greatest actor,' he harrumphed.

At that time, I wasn't even sure how *I* was supposed to sound, let alone anyone else. I suppose that 'Sir' and I might have shared a reedy, nasal twang at certain specific moments in our delivery (and I think they would have had to be *very* specific), but the point was that Olivier was the actor we should all aspire to be: he bestrode the profession like a colossus.

So when I arrived off the train at Stratford ('You change at Leamington Spa,' the porter had announced, giving the journey a transformingly spiritual air), carrying a small leatherette suitcase filled with almost all my worldly possessions, I should have been quaking. I was only there, I thought, out of fortune, though I hadn't yet calculated whether it was of the good or bad sort.

When my time at Rada had finished, I was asked by Kate Flanagan (Head of Casting at the RSC) whether I wanted to come to Stratford to 'carry a spear'. Well, yes, I did want to, or rather I didn't not want to. Besides, it would have been impolite to refuse. I went not because I felt the irresistible tug of fame or opportunity or professional betterment or even money (six pounds a week – actually a very serviceable sum in those days), but mostly because someone asked me nicely and I had nothing better to do. As usual, the shape of my life was determined through passive rather than dynamic means. I was nothing if not obedient.

If this sounds a little circumstantial, then I suppose that is a reflection of the way things were done. Casting agents were invited to view hopeful young actors at certain showcase pieces, and took their pick from what they saw. If you weren't snapped up during this process, then there was always repertory theatre. At that time, almost all towns had their own rep. company which provided a solid apprenticeship for aspiring actors.

Nowadays, of course, the theatres have mostly gone or closed down. Instead, television offers an opportunity to make money straight from drama school. The issue of making a living needs to be set against gaining a grounding in the craft of acting. Nowadays, actors enter a business – a business which embraces television, theatre and cinema – rather than becoming part of a tradition. This is perhaps a nostalgic view to take, though I take it without, I hope, too much sentimentality. However, there is a subsequent difference in the way that actors view their profession. Though Kate Flanagan's phone call now seems a casual, even precarious way of gaining entry to the profession, it was not unusual, and was buttressed by an established network of informal contacts and informed gossip – an apparently loose but proven, effective procedure. Anyone who was any good found a niche. The process was comparatively unbusinesslike, but it was for the most part efficient and flexible. Also, because those involved were more interested in theatre than money, it managed to be at once compassionate *and* realistic.

The play in which I was to carry the spear was a production of *Othello*, with Anthony Quayle playing the Moor, and literally that was all I did, along Venetian streets and on the island of Cyprus. I wasn't exactly sure how a soldier carrying a spear should come across – urgently threatening? ready for trouble but unobtrusively so? – so I did just enough to feel that I was doing a 'good job', though never anything that would overly distinguish me or cause me to stand out.

Meanwhile, Quayle was striding around being moody and magnificent, the role exactly suited to his martial manner. He ran the Memorial Theatre (as it was then known) with Glen Byam Shaw, a lovely, kind, avuncular man with a real passion for theatre. They made a good team. Quayle's soldierly power was effectively complemented by Shaw's more delicate touch, though of course Quayle was more sentimental than his manner suggested, and Shaw tougher than his. At fireworks parties, I recall Quayle lining up the children and handing out the sparklers, the significant thing not being his brisk organizational manner but the fact that he thought about the children at all. And this complicated leathery tenderness is what came over on stage, and what made his Othello so compellingly vulnerable.

The other thing I recall about that production was the dreadful notices that Ray Westwell received for his portrayal of Iago. They were quite the worst I have ever seen, even to this day. It was then, I suppose, that I began to realize that if I was going to make a career out of acting – and I wasn't yet sure about this, or even about the rather daunting and grown-up idea of having a career – then I had better be good at it. Or good enough to dodge the notices which Ray Westwell attracted.

After *Othello*, Byam Shaw told me I ought to go off and learn my trade, which I took to mean learning how to apply what Rada had already taught me in the world of professional theatre. He was right. There is a world of difference between having a bag of actorly tricks at your disposal and being able to use those effects persuasively in front of a paying audience on a more or less daily basis. Still, at this point I had no game plan. I was compliant. I was biddable. And so I went to Worthing Repertory Theatre, during which time I was offered a spot on BBC Radio Drama for twenty pounds a week (a fortune, it seemed to me) and hurriedly signed a contract. When, however, I was offered a chance to return to Stratford for Olivier's *Titus Andronicus*, something told me this was an opportunity I should not pass over, although it meant negotiating my way out of the BBC agreement, which Val Gielgud (John's brother, and then in charge of BBC Drama) allowed me to do. He even gave me his blessing in a way which suggested that well-mannered kindness was something of a family trait.

I arrived back at Stratford in 1957, and prepared to play the part of Mutius, Titus's son, who is killed very early on in the piece. It was during this time (three years after leaving Rada) that I eventually began to understand what being an actor meant, how I should go about it, and how I might become any good.

Inevitably, Olivier was a catalyst for much of this. The production of *Titus Andronicus* – directed by Peter Brook – was a huge success. It was a daring choice of play. Perceived as a piece of Grand Guignol and (wrongly, I think) a violent, chaotic, theatrical mess, it was rarely produced. Brook was important in restaging it as an austere and grim Roman tragedy and giving it a kind of barbaric dignity. He made cuts and rearranged the text, designed his own settings of vast columns, racks, cages and naked torches to heighten the sense of impending, ominous doom. To be on his stage was to be in one of Hell's circles. He directed for speed in performance and wrung gripping contrasts from the interplay between abrupt, fleet movement and striking, set-piece tableaux. Any horror was suggested rather than being portrayed realistically, so that Lavinia's mutilated hands were represented by carelessly flowing scarlet ribbons, a grotesque parody of girlish prettiness. And if re-writing and designing weren't enough, Brook also provided the music, all plucked strings, single drum beats and eerie throbbing sounds. Just being on stage, even for a few minutes, was a strange, almost frightening experience, during which my senses were shockingly assaulted.

It took Brook eight months to prepare, devising methods whereby he could play almost sadistically with the nerve endings of the audience. In one performance, twenty people fainted. (The average was three or four.) Drinks sales broke all records. The production received enormous critical and public acclaim.

But for me the most important thing was being able to observe Olivier at such close quarters. He gave a performance of full-blown greatness, somehow achieving an extreme, culminating synthesis of technique and emotion. The verse was spoken with idiosyncratic, masterful perfection, and when he wasn't actually speaking, he created out of his silences a sense of hushed expectation and sculpted beauty. It was spell-binding acting on a grand scale.

The moment that has since stayed with me, and that I felt compelled to watch from the wings every night, more often than not with tears in my eyes, was when Marcus asks his brother why he is laughing after a mountain of misfortune had been heaped upon him (loss of all but two sons in battle, mutilation and rape of his daughter). Olivier's Titus seemed to take an age to reply. He found a place on the stage directly beneath the most powerful spotlight and looked up straight into it. His harshly illuminated and magnified features betrayed resignation and extreme suffering, and he blinked several times into the intensity of the light as if about to weep. Once he had the audience expectant and thrilled, he began to speak, almost whispering the lines, but whispering them in a defiantly hoarse manner, each syllable of every word accorded its fullest expression and weight. He trusted the text and he trusted the production, but most of all he believed that he had the authority to deliver the electrifying response which Marcus's question demanded of him.

> *'Why? I have not another tear to shed.*
> *Besides, this sorrow is an enemy,*
> *And would usurp upon my watery eyes*
> *And make them blind with tributary tears.'*

As the speech went on, Olivier wrung out of it every ounce of emotion, sounding every hard consonant, end-stopping every word. ('Why? I. Have. NoT. Another. Tear. To. SheD.') He had the audience, the rest of the cast and the crew hanging on every wretched syllable. 'That,' I thought, 'is acting. And that's what I want to do.'

Olivier therefore showed something new to me and embodied what acting could achieve. People sometimes talked about him being all technique, but no, there was emotion and feeling there, too. Though I'm a very different actor from him, I'd have been a fool not to find myself watching and learning, taking in bits and pieces, wondering how (if I was ever given the opportunity) I might use them.

Apart from standing and admiring, I didn't have much to do with Olivier. Nobody did. He wasn't the sort of person to whom one could get close. One night, he gashed my finger quite badly with some overzealous sword play. He came into the dressing room as soon as he could get off stage and apologized profusely, offering me whisky and making it seem that my finger was the most important thing in the world to him. He did have this quality, or maybe ability would be nearer the mark, of allowing people to feel that they were the sole object of his attention. If it wasn't quite an act, that doesn't mean to say that it wasn't entirely untrue. It was a habit that was plausible because you felt that while Olivier also knew it was a charade of sorts, he also believed absolutely in that charade. Presently, Anthony Quayle arrived, voicing similar sympathetic concerns and also insisting that we drink whisky together. He was playing Aaron, again blacked up and again being thin-skinned and soldierly, though this time, I felt, the part needed him to be less ambiguous about his warlike nature. It was fortunate that I did not have to go back on stage. By the time they had both finished with me, I was unable to stand, let alone speak Shakespeare. Since then, I have learnt that the ability to make others feel privileged to be the focus of your attention is quite often found among successful politicians, effective headteachers and well-intentioned social workers, as well as actors.

At any rate, it was curious to observe Olivier moving fluently and seamlessly between the consummate, possessed authority of his stage performance and the refocused energies in my dressing room. His portrayal of Titus was something he carried within him, and the stage acted as a kind of trigger. When circumstances demanded, he might well have been able to push it to the back of his mind, but I don't think he would ever have been able to abandon it. Titus was burnt into him, and the summoning of the character became a function of his nervy restlessness while waiting to go on stage, a kind of anxiety that he wouldn't be able to locate the old Roman general, that he had hidden him too well or that the effort to recall him would be exhaustingly beyond him.

And Olivier was jittery. Just before he went on stage, I often had the feeling that it was the last thing in the world he wanted to do. It was as though he wanted to be alone. He hated people looking at him and ticked them off quite sharply if he thought they were staring – and they *were* staring, of course, because he was the most famous actor in the world, delivering the kind of performance that simply emphasized his greatness.

I was too far down the line to be aware of personal tensions in his performance, though the fact that Olivier's wife Vivien Leigh played Lavinia must have added flavour to the proceedings. After all, she was having a well-publicized affair with Peter Finch at the time (though, naturally, I knew nothing of this), and all that ripping out of her tongue and cutting off of her hands, her helplessness and pain, must have played with him on some level.

Too caught up with Olivier the Actor, the only oddness I noticed in the behaviour of this fabulous couple was that almost every night during the European tour, Vivien Leigh would be driven away for the night – for the whole night, wherever she wanted to go, and always without Olivier – by her chauffeur, a discreet, straightforward man called Bernie who was an ex-para. Most people in the company felt pretty sorry for the great man and thought that his wife was leading him a bit of a dance. Except for Irene Worth, I remember, who grew tired of Olivier's burdened soul. 'Larry? Don't talk to me about Larry. I'm so sick of his self-pity,' she told me, though I was never aware of the magnitude of the bad feeling between them.

However, I did know that Vivien was very much the brains of the outfit. She was shrewd, quite calculating, and somewhat ruthless. She generally knew what she wanted and was extremely good at getting it. Olivier was certainly a stage genius, but I never felt I was in the presence of a great mind. However, he did have this friend, a man called Terence Greenidge, who was once in possession of such a mind, though by the time I met him he had pretty much lost it. Apparently he used to be an Oxford academic, a handsome and talented man who went to pieces after his wife died. Olivier used to employ him in his stage and film productions, usually small parts (he was in the film of *Henry V*, for example), but no more than that. Maybe it was generosity that prompted Olivier's patronage of Terence, though a part of me sometimes – and perhaps unfairly – wondered whether the proximity of defeated academe wasn't in some way soothing to him. Terence himself was charming, if eccentric, and I now remember him chiefly for smoking a pipe, eating many bunches of bananas, and, when *Titus* toured behind the Iron Curtain, calculating the length of a tunnel by counting the clicks on the rails as the train passed over them.

The 1957 tour was the first to play behind the Curtain since it had gone up. The original idea was that Olivier and his wife would lead the company in this wonderful train journey across

Europe, calling at Paris, Venice, Vienna, Belgrade, Zagreb and Warsaw. Though the tour had a serious purpose, it would at the same time be an audacious and possibly rather jolly adventure, embracing a kind of all-for-one-and-one-for-all spirit. Paris was quite far enough for the Oliviers, however, and by the time we'd finished performing there, they had already decided to fly to all the other venues. Perhaps, I recall thinking, it was a birthday present from Vivien, for Olivier turned fifty the night of the Paris performance.

Still, the tour did represent for me – a nice, sheltered, middle-class boy – a rare opportunity to see a bit of the world. I was, of course, shocked by much of what I saw. The obvious things affected me precisely because they were the most conspicuous: the relative poverty, the sense of hardship, of individuals and places still struggling to put themselves together more than ten years after the war had finished.

There was also a camp Australian actor called Frank Thring in the production. He owned newspapers (or said he owned newspapers – I had no reason to disbelieve him) and later became an 'epic hero', for example in *El Cid*, though epic in a rather affected, frilly manner. I remember him chiefly for two things: the first was his wedding ceremony (a marriage of convenience at which Vivien was matron of honour), and the second was him leaning out of the carriage window on the train between two of the tour's more unlikely venues, and shouting, 'The Shakespeare Memorial Theatre! By land, sea, and yak!'

The expedition had the whiff of unreality about it, of a sort of holiday from real life. Elderly, dignified Polish men being overwhelmed at the apparent luxury of a sticky bun, reverberating underground tunnels which had hosted shooting matches and executions only a few years before, and everywhere evidence of the necessary, grinding reconstruction from the dismal wreckage of cities. Olivier used to learn by rote a speech of gratitude for each of the countries we visited, though in Yugoslavia he was given a duff translation and began, 'Ladies and gentlemen. Fuck you all . . .', which the audience took as a kind of bluff-hearted compliment, that is, a bit of joshing familiarity from the great English actor, and he was loudly applauded. Language problems persisted in Poland, where we were mistaken for a delegation of post-office workers, and again when instructions for the lighting engineers were mis-understood with embarrassing consequences.

It was actuality glimpsed through a peculiarly English lens, grim fact eased by the burlesque of our expedition, the flying Oliviers and their performing troupe, Terence Greenidge and his bananas, and of course the certain knowledge that we would soon turn round and return home. We were sedated against the experience of full-blown austerity by circumstance and temperament, moments of starkness being counterbalanced by instants of humour or flashes of the absurd, many of these deliberately sought in a very English way.

Despite all the eye-opening and the affecting scenes of hard-ship, I was keen to travel back to Stratford. Olivier had shown me what could be done, had stirred me, and I felt that I had taken my first tentative steps and was eager to try more ambitious, demanding ones.

It was Olivier who persuaded Charles Laughton to play King Lear and Bottom at Stratford (in 1959), both the great men having recently appeared in the film *Spartacus*. This was the centenary season and the end of Byam Shaw's regime, though for this significant milestone he had assembled an astonishing group of actors: Laughton would appear in *King Lear* and *A Midsummer Night's Dream*, Paul Robeson would play Othello, Edith Evans appeared in *All's Well That Ends Well* and was Volumnia in *Coriolanus*, while Olivier himself was back as

Coriolanus. This was the so-called Star Year at Stratford, though, having paid my dues, I was more interested in my own elevation, and played the Fool and Puck in the two Laughton productions.

Laughton wanted Olivier to direct him in *Lear*, and was politely declined. As actors – indeed as men – they were poles apart, different in almost every conceivable way. I think Olivier knew this; directing Laughton would have been a difficult enough task without having to circumnavigate their obvious differences. The discrepancies were immediately apparent to all of us. Laughton observed Olivier rehearsing Coriolanus, and seemed genuinely startled at the sight of the great man hanging from the Tarpaen Rock by his ankles, and moreover hanging with such brio. For Olivier, this was not merely about making the hanging or the clutching-on or whatever seem merely real or exciting, or even about putting on a show, but about wringing from each suspended moment the maximum amount of bravura. He made a whole performance out of dangling. Laughton couldn't understand it. He sniffed loudly, like a length of calico being torn, and said, 'In the movies, I'd get a million dollars for doing *that*.'

Olivier was innately theatrical. Laughton was not. Maybe Laughton understood this, and that is why he asked Olivier to direct him, hoping some of the magic would rub off. Olivier's mastery of technique allowed him to skim with apparent ease over even the most demanding roles. This is what he said to Laughton about playing Lear: 'Lear is easy, he's just a stupid old fart.' Of course, Lear is not easy, but Olivier's one-upmanship over other actors was frequently gained by appearing to be untroubled by even the most demanding roles – a trait I rapidly assumed myself, though with the principal intent of convincing myself rather than others. It wasn't just Lear that was easy; he seemed to be saying, 'For me, *everything* is easy. Now you try.'

This was the worst-possible news for Laughton, for whom the greatness of great roles resided in an unfathomable complexity, the depths of experience they embodied and explored, and the actor's discomfort and suffering in realizing it through the ache of performance. For him, Lear was not merely 'a stupid old fart', but a tortured, flawed human being who struggles long and hard towards redemption and self-understanding. It has been said before, but bears repetition: if Laughton was a deep-sea diver who had to keep coming up for air, then Olivier was a surfer whose skill took him to unlikely places. They had the sea in common and not much else.

So Laughton did the two plays, achieving a hit and a miss. As Bottom, he was sublime: open to ideas, generous with his time and full of initiative. I think he was probably one of the first actors to play the part without a full face mask, though he was no oil painting and there were those who said cruelly that it might have been better if he had. Instead he went for ass's ears and said it was to do with seeing Bottom's eyes, which is very much a film actor's thing, but worked very well none the less. I also remember him insisting on a beard for Lear, which – since he was unmasked for the *Dream* – could have presented a problem. Laughton solved it by dyeing everything ginger, or at least gingerish. It was the only discernible physical difference between the two performances, though a few members of the cast who played in both productions might also have said it was the only difference full stop.

Not everyone enjoyed his performance, however. Kenneth Tynan wrote that 'I confess I do not know what Mr Laughton is up to, but I am sure I would hate to share a stage with it,' and another critic was sent a letter warning him not to return to Stratford, 'because all you'll see is my bottom'. It was hardly word play or wit at its rapier best, but it did the job and showed how much he cared about the performance, and also how sensitive he was to criticism.

Poor Laughton was having a bad time of it in general. Roy Dotrice persuaded him to join in with 'scrumping', which was the act of stealing apples (from an allotment, in this case) in order to make cider. Everyone was surprised when he attached himself to the expedition, perhaps wanting to feel part of a gang, though less astonished when he became the only one to get caught by the police.

Laughton was coming to terms with his homosexuality at the time, though as far as I am aware there was no byplay with the other actors, several of whom were mildly disappointed at the sense of a missed opportunity. (Later, on his deathbed, he apologized to his wife Elsa Lanchester for the pattern of his life; it was the kind of thing you did in those days.) Although I did not have a great deal to do with him off stage, I was always aware of the consideration he had for me as an actor, and the kindliness he showed towards me. It was because of this, and the fact that I genuinely admired his Bottom, so to speak, that I recall playing Puck far more than The Fool in *Lear*.

In association with Peter Hall, who had recently joined the company but was not yet (not *quite* yet) in charge, Laughton gave me the confidence to try things out and experiment. Because, I suppose, Laughton was unconventionally good in *The Dream*, good in his own way, I was emboldened. I was playing alongside a leading actor, yet I wasn't intimidated in the way I might have been if Laughton had been an Olivier or a Gielgud. Could you, for example, imagine those two galumphing across fields and climbing fences to steal apples? Their acting – and the entire sense of who they were – was constructed around a vividly projected impression of invulnerability, whereas Laughton, no matter how good he was in performance, was unravelling before us.

So I played Puck with a kind of impish glee, pushing out my

tongue and tearing round the stage with affected, manic exaggeration, falling just short (I hoped) of being a ham. Robert Hardy, ever the fogey, who later most famously starred as vet Siegfried Farnon in *All Creatures Great and Small*, accused me of 'mugging', by which I supposed he meant the sort of acting which relied on grimacing rather than any considered sense of character. But my Puck was based on a close reading and understanding of the text, and took the devilish, roguish and literally puckish side of the character to an extreme which was absolutely in keeping with Peter Hall's uncharming, unpicturesque, un-fairy-tale production. These days I expect it would be called a 'deconstruction', though at the time it just seemed the obvious thing to do. Hall was, I think, pretty tired of seeing shimmering fairies prancing around the woodland in gossamer wings in a fanciful manner, and wanted to bring out the sheer mischief and naughtiness in the piece. Out also went Mendelssohn.

I expect this had something to do with Hall's youth, his being an Angry Young Man or whatever, and the influence of coffee bars, rock and roll, and never having had it so good. Still, it didn't feel much like that at the time. The important thing, as far as I was concerned, was that he was the director who taught me to root my performances in an understanding of the text. Nothing else was required, he promised. The one thing in life at which I had always excelled was following instructions, and this (despite the immodest portrayal of Puck) was no different. I saw what Hall was trying to do, understood it, and was pleased to oblige. I more or less did as I was told, and loved it. I wanted to give the impression that I could indeed, as Puck claims, 'put a girdle round the earth', that this was not merely an artful trick but an expression of monkey business, of the freewheeling, joyously irrepressible need to indulge impishness. Of course, this was totally out of character for me, and yet the text released me. And there I was, the pointy-eared, tousle-haired, eyebrow-arching, tongue-rolling son of a suburban doctor. But all this amounted to no more than obeying the director. I felt I was creating a role – I was conscious of something original and innovative happening – and for the first time on stage, began to feel that strange, unworldly surge of power that comes with being able to 'hold' an audience: the overwhelming swell of 'power' and 'connection', where the mind begins to operate almost of its own accord, driven into unlikely places by confidence, the potency of absolute appropriateness, and (perhaps above all) possibility. It's difficult to describe this feeling of intoxication; the sensation of feasibility as the mind unfurls, gradually freeing itself from all the usual obligations of time and place. And I remember thinking, 'Hello. I could get used to this.' It seemed so much better than real life, which had by and large passed me by, but for which I now had a viable alternative.

And there was Hall, quietly pushing me on, hardly ever, it seemed, actually looking up from his text, often smoking a pipe, his brilliant mind unlocking my potential as an actor. There is a story that he was so concerned with the book in front of him that during one rehearsal he failed to notice Judi Dench arriving on stage with no clothes on. He was a brilliant if reserved revolutionary and his approach was, to me at least, a revelation. Here at last was the education I had never received, or had fucked up, and though we were almost the same age, perhaps he was a father figure too.

Hall possibly sensed that, given Laughton's frame of mind in *The Dream*, I would be able to manage a different kind of performance. And it's certainly true that in a professional way, I felt I had to love Laughton. I felt able to respond to him, though in *King Lear*, this was not such a good thing. His erratic but barnstorming Bottom was quickly eclipsed by his embarrassingly inept Lear. He just didn't have the physical energy or the power within himself to make a convincing performance out of it, and literally gave a stage reading. There was no emotional hinterland to what he did, little to suggest the struggles that Lear was enduring. There was no madness, no struggle against the elements, nothing. He was booed on the first night. On numerous other occasions, he just came to a grinding halt and had to be prompted. Olivier watched him with concern, though not the type of concern that suggested he was much concerned for Laughton. He merely observed that Laughton's performance would send him back to the text, which was a bit rich coming from him, though you knew what he meant.

Laughton's struggle with Lear enervated and restrained me, just as his playing of Bottom had helped to release my performance. It was a sad experience. On stage, Laughton gradually became more like himself than Lear, his performance becoming an expression of self, and a self moreover that was in dread of being found out, exposed, as if the performance was something so personal it might perish. My Fool was a bridled, bottled presence, an irritant, a goading madness who attempted to tease the insanity out of Lear. I buzzed round him like a mosquito trying to brew a storm in his head, eventually *becoming* the storm in his head. I was more Ariel than Fool, and while my Puck had been earthy and boisterously 'actual', this was an ethereal, frustrated exhibition. Like Ariel, I was impatient to take wing (particularly so after *The Dream*), but was being heavily defeated.

The so-called star year at Stratford came to an end when Peter Hall was appointed the new managing director of the company in 1959, his elevation having been ratified and announced the previous year. For all the gifts and charm of Byam Shaw, his era was coming to an end. His productions were beginning to look lifeless, partly as a result of excessive administration. Hall had always maintained that eras at Stratford and styles of production lasted about ten years. And now it was his turn.

4

STRATFORD (II)

I had already been at Stratford for almost six years by the time Peter Hall took over (six years! They're lucky to get actors for six weeks these days), and was quite ready to move on. As usual, I had no plan. But by this time, somehow, surprisingly, I was married, with children, and had graduated from spear-carrying to playing good, high-profile roles.

Like me, Lynne Shaw was also contracted to the RSC, though not as an actor. She worked in the wardrobe department. I met her after plucking up courage to ask her flatmate to a drinks party I was giving in my bachelor digs. However, when I knocked on the door, Lynne unexpectedly answered, so I invited her instead. I already knew her by sight – she was very pretty – and felt that our RSC connection at least gave us something in common. Two weeks later, we were engaged. I was shocked when she agreed to marry me, almost as much as I had been with myself for having the front to ask her in the first place. And I suspect she was as surprised as me to find herself so suddenly married. We were both innocents. I can't speak for Lynne, but looking back, I now know that I didn't quite understand the full implications of what I was doing. Which is not to say that I had not fallen in love with Lynne or did not want to marry her. Having spent much time and expended a great deal of fruitless energy travelling across two continents and failing to lose my virginity, I supposed, naively, that a wedding was what happened after you fell in love. So we were married in a London Register Office before heading back to Stratford, where we spent most of our ten years or so of married life.

Quite soon, however, I began to recognize that I needed more than the serene comfort we had so eagerly embraced. Although I appreciated how important this 'safe nest' was for me to function as an actor, once I had ventured from this refuge and tasted forbidden fruit, I knew I would probably spend a lifetime juggling safety with ferment. I needed a domestic haven, but desired romance. Accordingly, there were quite often two people in my life, although the inspiriting 'other' was not always a woman and the relationship did not have to be sexual. Though it often was – and Lynne knew and was patient about this, sensing that I would always return to the nest. But it was actually the need to feel a close attachment which was important to me. Even if I regarded sex as the most obviously delightful sign of affection, it was not a prerequisite.

In the meantime, and quite quickly, Lynne and I had two daughters, Jessica and Sarah-Jane, and it was this swiftly created family life which provided the security that underpinned much of my time at Stratford. Falling in love, getting married, having children; this was, I thought, the right way to do things. And Lynne was good and kind and sensible, both as a wife and a mother. She was also the only one of my 'wives' who met my mother before she died, and I think the two of them got on pretty well.

We settled into a comfortable and rather conventional routine

– working, bringing up two children, and even holidaying with other members of the company. At first nothing much was wrong, though the timing of the marriage, which was impatiently propelled by my glee at finally having got someone to sleep with me, obscured the fact that I was neither ready for nor temperamentally suited to such a state. Without there ever being a particular flashpoint, my relationship with Lynne began to fray from the late 1950s until its eventual demise around 1965.

In addition to being unsettled at home, I was beginning to feel that I should leave Stratford. Fresh horizons, new challenges and so on and so forth – these were some of the well-worn phrases doing the rounds in my head at that time. The end of the Byam Shaw era seemed as good a reason as any to push me on my way. It provided a natural break. Besides, I didn't much like Stratford as a place. Although I did quite like living at Avoncliffe – having progressed from Mrs Arrowsmith's B&B to married quarters in a Georgian house in Tiddington, conveniently riverside (as they say) and about a mile and a half from Stratford – I found the town . . . what? Tacky. Unattractive. Fake. Charmless. Fraudulent. All of these and more. It just didn't seem to be an authentic place to live, with its touristy sheen, creeping, shoddy Shakespeareanization, and Butlinsesque mentality. I was beginning to hate the daily walk from Avoncliffe, dreading the moment when the pretty river and the compact, pleasantly rolling countryside suddenly became this rather smug little market town.

However, Hall made me want to stay. He made it exciting. He called the company together and told us his plans. Immediately, things started to make sense and I knew that I wanted to be a part of this new beginning. He used phrases of a radical, almost political demeanour and intensity. 'The strength of a company lies in its artistic security.' 'Actors need to be liberated through training and experiment.' 'I distrust all methods, and all dogmas.' 'Keep open, keep critical.' And with his wispy beard and his concentrated, drastic manner, he did sometimes resemble a revolutionary figure.

Although Hall was not the first to envisage the ensemble idea (I believe, for example, that Gielgud had tried something similar at the Haymarket in the 1930s and 40s), it seemed odd, and brave, to do it from within an *existing* organization. But Hall made it successful.

The idea was actually very straightforward and logical. He wanted to create conditions whereby actors could develop to the fullest height of their powers, under purely artistic conditions, by removing the commercial pressure and the need for success that necessarily inhabit an actor's mind, and which in Hall's opinion are destructive forces that prevent actors from doing the best possible work.

This was to be a system where, famously, the leading actor could dare to play a butler, and where the star concept was actively discouraged; though as Hall also said, 'The people who had star quality, the public made into stars.' It worked well enough. Brilliantly, in fact, for a time – but I'm not sure that it could have lasted much beyond that particular time, with that particular man and the actors he had at his disposal.

And of course it didn't. Such a system has never since been in place at Stratford or anywhere else, at least not to such a degree. Then, most of us were very young, game for anything, and not stars; so of course we were very keen. But in the end, there are people who play leading parts, people who play middle roles, and people who do walk-ons. That's it. There's a sort of Darwinesque pecking order that eventually asserts itself, and those at the top of the list – the ones who, as Hall said, 'the public made into stars' – pretty soon become disgruntled. It worked well enough for those of us it *turned into* stars – myself,

Roy Dotrice, David Warner, for example – and while it was turning us, but I'm not sure how keen we'd have been if we'd been
more old-fashioned, like, say, Eric Porter, who I think found the
whole thing rather irritating.

Of course, the ensemble method also handed ultimate power
to the director, which suited Hall very nicely thank you, not just
because final-word authority necessarily devolved to him,
but because the control came with a degree of real and imagined
consent. Ultimately, he was a benign dictator, though quite how
benign was rarely put to the test because by and large we all
agreed with him. We had to. By creating an almost collegiate
atmosphere amongst the company (some called it 'monastic' –
there was a company spirit in which youth dominated, 'camp'
was almost taboo, and nobody called each other 'darling') and
always working from the text outward, Hall was effectively
insisting that we played the game according to his own rules.
He was the one with the education, the degree from Cambridge,
and the necessary intellectual equipment to interpret the texts.
We were allowed ideas, but he always had the answers. We
played student to his teacher. I remember Glenda Jackson
saying something to the effect that Peter was very complicated
and ambitious though he always at least tried to be 'nice', but I
don't think we were really ever in much doubt about the way
things were being done. Diana Rigg was blunter ('Peter uses
you,' she said), though I didn't care about that side of it. I was a
very willing student. I liked being told what to do. I felt that in
some way I was finally receiving the academic education which
had eluded me during my school days. And I was getting some
very good parts.

I've since thought about this – which is unusual, because I
rarely reflect back or plan ahead, so I suppose it must be
important to me – and now reckon that Hall was shrewd
enough to spot my ability or talent or whatever, but also an

inclination to go along with him, a potential to acquiesce. Instinctively, he knew I *liked* being instructed, and that having confidence in me would tap the best of what I had to offer. After all, I wasn't an obvious leading man – short of stature, and no swashbuckler – and yet he had seen something in me almost from the moment he arrived at Stratford. Seen it, in fact, before I had.

Although Hall had arrived as a kind of 'wonderkid', he was actually less intact than his youthful, unsullied reputation might have suggested. Without knowing the details (I never quite knew the details), I understood that he was going through a tough time with his wife, Leslie Caron. And I recall him being very upset by the death of his great friend, the playwright John Whiting, who had died quite horribly of testicular cancer. This had an effect on Hall, who once came to rehearsals on a stretcher, claiming that he was enduring terrible pains in his own testicles. He directed affairs from the stretcher, though he discarded the prop very soon afterwards.

What does this tell you about Peter Hall? That he was suffering from a psychosomatic illness? Obviously. But I think he *believed* in his pain – he was no prima donna – so it also follows that he was absolutely committed to the art of directing plays. Nothing would deter him (Judi Dench's nakedness, a throbbing bollock, his messy private life, whatever), and in this he embodied the ideals he spoke about so eloquently.

Hall was an immensely intelligent man and very sensitive in the way he handled me. I appeared in a number of productions during the first year or so of his reign, playing parts like Sebastian in *Twelfth Night* (1960), the First Judge in *Ondine*, the surgeon Mannoury in *The Devils* (both 1961), Gremio in *The Taming of the Shrew* (1962). These middling roles, and my reprisal of Puck in 1962, meant I maintained some sort of momentum, that I felt I was still making progress, gradual as it was. And I sensed that Hall was perhaps lining me up for something, waiting for the appropriate project. In this, as far as I was concerned, he was very astute. I was not the sort of actor who could be rushed into a leading role (an *impact* actor; think of the height. Then think of the desire to please, to be commanded. I had to be led gently to the front of the queue). A certain amount of massaging, of toning up, needed to happen before I would be ready.

Then Hall made an important decision. He was under a certain amount of pressure to produce something significant for the quatercentenary, and the story goes that he was walking around the theatre gardens one night when the idea for The Wars of the Roses suddenly came to him. This was to be a monumental undertaking – a trilogy of plays adapted from the three parts of *Henry VI*, and *Richard III*, in which John Barton (an academic who had been teaching literature at Cambridge; Hall prised him away to Stratford) cut, rewrote and rearranged over one thousand words of the eventual seven and a half thousand that made up the finished work. Thus the three Henry plays became *Henry VI* and *Edward IV* (the first two parts of the trilogy), while *Richard III* completed the cycle.

It was an enterprise that could only have been undertaken – only *conceived* – if the principles of ensemble playing held firm. The Wars of the Roses needed the continuity and commitment of a large troupe of talented actors, willing to see the thing through. Characters who were common to more than one of the plays were required to juggle consistency of character with narrative flexibility. It was unusual for a stage actor to be granted the opportunity to develop a role across a series of linked chronicles, but this is what Hall asked several of us to do.

When he called me into his office, I already had a sense that he had been lining me up for something, had been lining me up since Puck, almost four years earlier. Still: Richard – as the Duke of Gloucester and then as Richard III. 'You bet!' I thought, 'Thank you very much, sir.' I remember feeling like a schoolboy who was being rewarded for his behaviour (patience, solid work, effort, good attitude, example to us all – you know the kind of thing) and was now being elevated to the prefectorial body. And like the expectant pupil in front of his headmaster, I also knew not to get too close to Hall. He relished the sensation of being in charge, and I suspect that part of my attraction for him lay in his belief that, in my self-effacing, unthreatening way, I would never rock the boat. Similarly, his interest in politics is reflected in the choice of plays, which are concerned with the mechanisms of power – and this fascinated him.

Although the walk-round-the-garden story of the cycle's genesis is a romantic one, and is the one I heard and swallowed, another version has been brought to my attention. According to this one, Hall had discussed with Peter Brook as early as 1960 the possibility of a series of history plays, but Brook had told him such an enterprise would take at least three years of preparation. So maybe the project had been exercising his mind for a long while, at least a longer while than I presumed. It doesn't much matter. What did was the boldness of the decision and the fact that the finished product was so good, and acknowledged as such.

Hall's habitual method was to call the cast together and explain his interpretation of the text. This was no different. There was the usual stuff about mutual give and take (with himself as final arbiter), about not being afraid to experiment in the early rehearsals ('every door must be opened!' he said), and about breaking down our defence barriers. Then, amongst a little foot shuffling and discreet grinning from the cast, he announced that the themes which bound the plays together were the evils of ambition and the inability of good men to prevent the disorder that ambition brings.

He was part analyst, part guide, part father, part school-master. Given my own history, such things were significant in him being able to get the best out of me. Like Peter Wood before him (who became a great friend and mentor – though he could often be campishly vicious), Hall represented or seemed to represent many of the things which my life lacked. And crucially, despite his multi-roled approach, he was never part actor.

It doesn't particularly haunt me, but sometimes I do wonder why he cast me as Richard. I would not, I think, have been an obvious choice to many people. The *Daily Telegraph*, I recall, judged that my performance was one of 'deadpán politeness rather than sardonic snarls' and that this made me a 'winning' Richard. There is something in this. My natural manner is one of complaisant civility, and if my performance could blend with this a sense of restrained but cumulative desire and striving, the result would be intriguingly fresh, and the sense of Richard's evil unusually enhanced by its being played against an obliging mental backdrop. There was also the question of my height and the usual thing of a small man feeling a most urgent need to succeed. Hall talked of the immediate, contemporary relevance of Shakespeare, and perhaps understood better than anybody that contemporary sin lay in the hands of bureaucrats, administrators and politicians as much as anyone else; perhaps he thought I brought something vaguely secretarial to the stage. He wanted me to be chilling, an embodiment of evil rather than an illustrator of it, and I suppose he reasoned that if he could find it through the outer layers of my disposition, then he would have something deeply realized, authentic and innovative.

'A Richard for the age,' you might say, and certainly we were all keen to escape from Olivier's shadow and the way he had done it several years earlier – brilliantly, but in a very theatrical manner. We worked hard to get away from the old idea of a

Machiavellian villain by making Richard more human, or at any rate more recognizable as a person. Olivier actually sent me a letter, quite a long letter, sort of wishing me luck but also telling me not to take any notice of the newspapers, who were beginning to draw comparisons with his performance – 'you might have seen some comparisons in the press of your old friend . . .' was the way he put it. Essentially, he was restaking his claim as the definitive Richard and, monstrously jealous, was making sure that I understood who was boss. It was the same tactic that Fred Trueman used when walking into the opposition's dressing room before the start of play and chatting amicably to their young opening batsman. Despite or more likely because of all the kind words, by the time Fred left the batsman would be a quivering wreck. It was merely a way of undermining a potential threat or, more charitably, of clarifying the situation.

Playing Richard became a part of my life, as the trilogy did for all of us. Despite the demands it placed on the cast and the directors (there were five: Hall, with John Barton, Peter Wood, Clifford Williams and Frank Evans), the period was so invigorating and exciting that there was no time to feel exhausted. We were intoxicated by the sense that we were involved in an epoch-making production, and sustained by our youth. Being young and unafraid, we plunged headlong into the work. Exhilaration excluded tiredness. Apparently I'm in or was in *The Guinness Book of Records* for speaking the most lines of Shakespeare in a day (the sequence ran fourteen times). The local doctor, Dr Coigley, used to come round and give flagging actors a shot of Vitamin B12 in their bums, though I'm not certain we needed it. There was an extraordinary feeling of collective stamina, drive and energy as the unity of approach that ensemble playing required began to take hold and ripple through our ranks.

I played Richard with all the gear: club foot, withered arm, huge deformed hump, ugly mace on a chain, and phallic dagger. In the fight with Richmond (played by Derek Waring) at the very end of *Richard III*, this is augmented by heavy black armour, a large broadsword, and something which looked like a small landmine attached to the end of a truncheon. Armed with mace and landmine, I clanked around the stage effectively sporting two enormous metal testicles which dangled somewhere close to my ankles. John Barton had the very good idea of Richard being a bit like a bottle-backed spider (something which Antony Sher hit upon when he did Richard in the 1980s), and Hall had me play him not as an individual but as a cog in a historical wheel, accentuating the 'chilling bureaucrat' angle and also ensuring that the progressive momentum of the linked plays wasn't jeopardized by a single distracting exhibition. He drew poison from me, bringing to the surface all the cruelty and aggression in my character, which was expressed through sudden changes of pitch and volume. Because of this, my performance was jarring, dynamic and, I think, very frightening.

I did get bronchitis at one point and for the first time in my professional life had to miss one performance. Charlie Kay understudied me and managed very well, though there had been no time to rehearse the Richmond fight, which was made up pretty much as it happened. Charlie was also involved in the only other moment of hesitation I can recall, when, at the start of the second half of *Edward IV*, he (playing George, Duke of Clarence, Richard's brother) and I came on stage expecting to find Roy Dotrice, our 'father', Edward. He wasn't there, and not having any business to distract the audience, we quietly swapped jokes with one another and filled the silence with giggling. When Dotrice eventually hurried on to the stage, he appeared in a cloud of tobacco smoke, apparently swatting at flies in a frenzied attempt to get rid of the evidence.

And Hall held the whole thing together with a charming but steely brilliance. In conjunction with playing Prince Hal and Henry V the next year, I regard The Wars of the Roses as possibly one of the best things I have done, a kind of zenith. I think the manic vigour of that time also suited him better than almost anything else he might have done, though I suppose he might dispute this. He could never settle for a moment on a single task – too restless, too changeable, too fidgety; though never irresolute – and the trilogy kept him as occupied as a juggling octopus. He was in his element and he knew what he was doing. Now I wonder how he looks back at those productions. His professionalism was admirable. I had this idea of him going home, doing the kitchen, spring-cleaning the house, writing the introduction to a Chinese translation of The Tempest, planning the next day's rehearsals, making phone calls about an opera he was planning to direct in (say) Holland, sorting out his tangled private life, knocking off a column for a Sunday newspaper, reading one or more of the four or five books and/or learned journals he had on the go – and then settling down to some really serious work. The Hall Engine at work.

Despite all this energy, he wasn't a fussy or flamboyant director, and could be fierce to the point of heartlessness if he felt the play needed it. While John Barton was in charge of The Taming of the Shrew, a number of the actors went to Hall and complained about his friend's direction. I wouldn't say that Hall had no hesitation in removing Barton from his position, but as there was only a week to go before the production opened, he certainly had to move decisively. And he did. Hall took over the direction and informed the actors that he was now in charge and there was no time left to discuss things like 'motivation'; the important thing was to get the play on the stage in as coherent a manner as possible. You won't be surprised to learn that Barton was rather put out by all this. Although it had a bad effect on their relationship (since patched up, but more recently dissolved again), Hall made it clear where his loyalties lay. Barton didn't really take charge of a production again, and found or was found a more suitable niche teaching verse-speaking and fencing, both of which he did with an intense, expert brilliance.

Hall's effect was significant not only because he was, for me, the right man at the right time, but also because we were young or youngish, and because he offered something innovative and extraordinary after the 'old guard' days of Byam Shaw and Quayle. And his insistence that everything sprang directly from the text has remained with me and is the one single principle I take into every project, whether on stage, television or film.

It's strange that Peter Brook never had the same influence on me. He was just as youthful and offered similarly novel departures from the conventional way of doing things. However, there was no gentleness about him. He was a *puppet-meister* in a different way from Hall, who had a way of disguising or at least softening the means whereby he achieved his ends. Brook, I felt, bored into specific productions in such a concentrated, preconceived way that the additional and unpremeditated input of the actors was not needed. I liked being told what to do well enough, but I liked being told what to do in the context of having a choice in the matter. I rarely felt that Brook offered that choice and consequently I wasn't swept along by the magic that others saw, although he undoubtedly did wonderful work in individual productions.

In the 1963 production of *The Tempest*, in which I played Ariel, Brook was directing while also working on another project. Being used to (and working best with) absolute, single-minded concentration on one thing at a time, he was probably feeling rather stretched. Compare this with Hall, who gave the impression that his restlessness enjoyed challenges on several fronts at the same time; Hall's juggler against Brook's unicyclist.

Brook's attention was not wholly on *The Tempest*, and in order to get what he wanted from the cast he was having to compensate by being more pushy than usual. It was one of his productions which looked a bit like a Henry Moore sculpture, Ariel's servants being a collection of bandages and shaped wire. Eventually, and after being particularly foul to Philippa Urquhart (who was playing Miranda), he was attacked in public by Tom Fleming, who had been cast as Prospero.

'You can't treat people like that,' said Tom.

'Like what?' Brook replied, apparently oblivious to the offence he had caused.

He told Brook *like what* and told him quite loudly.

'Direct the fucking thing yourself!' Brook snapped, and walked out, never to return and possibly even quite glad to have had the argument which at least left him with only one thing to worry about. Now history tells us that *The Tempest* was directed by 'Clifford Williams in collaboration with Peter Brook,' which apparently grants it the pretty undeserved accolade of an intellectual alliance.

I also recall being directed by John Gielgud and Michel Saint-Denis in *The Cherry Orchard* (1961). Gielgud had once, much earlier, cast me as a black drummer boy (!) in *Twelfth Night*. The old guard still had a place in Hall's revolution – Quayle, for example, played Othello in the same year – though it was a shrinking place, and their achievements seemed strangely out of time, though never disagreeable or unsuccessful. And Gielgud was a delightful man: affable, polite, charming. He also had an odd directorial style which could be best described as 'camp but informed'. In *Twelfth Night*, for example, he watched Willie Devlin, who played the sea captain and had an odd, extraordinary crab-like walk, inching more or less sideways across the stage during rehearsal. Gielgud watched his performance with amusement and then said with campish and barely disapproving innuendo, 'Ooh, Billy! You can't walk across the stage like that.'

He did things with a bewitching humour, and in his own way generally knew what he was up to. Years later, when I was doing *King Lear* at the National Theatre, and he was very frail, he came to one performance. Afterwards he stayed behind, too fragile to come backstage and waiting for us while we came into the auditorium to see him. Though physically weak, his mind and his eyes were still alert and sharp. 'Oooh, dear boy,' he said, his voice like honey running over rocks, 'dear boy. Everything they say is true. It's wonderful.'

Just as Hall holds the most profound directorial influence over me, Olivier, as actor, exerts the most authority. As I've explained, Hall is perhaps the more understandable mentor. On the face of it, and beyond the immediacy of my naive crushes on him, my acting style seems far removed from Olivier's. He now seems dated to me, but there's still a reverence and an affinity which I never felt for Gielgud, or Quayle, or Richardson; maybe a little for Alec Guinness, but perhaps only in the sense that I saw we were actors cast in the same anonymous, expunging mould.

With Olivier, I think it must have something to do with the unknowability of the man. He expressed himself more or less completely through his work, so that his character or personality or whatever was obscured by theatrical flourishes and subterfuge. Though I might be doing a similar thing in a different manner (the contrasting style perhaps being a result of history and circumstance as much as anything else), I feel that I too am to be found for the most part in my work. Despite all the external posturing, Olivier effectively wore a mask of inscrutability. He would have made a good spy, where fabrication has to be second nature and cock-and-bull *is* your profession. Self-erasure. That's what we had in common, what I saw in him and recognized. Someone like Gielgud possessed too much obvious character and humanity for me to feel much closeness to him as an actor.

The poet and critic Leo Abse once said that, 'The spy is a man of identities and each day he must act many parts,' and I some-times think that, like Olivier, I too would have made a good spy. The lack or denial of memory, the instant discarding of one's history, one's baggage, to the point where one is not even conscious of having a history, and the regular re-inflating of self through theatrical identity rather than character – all these, I have learnt, suit me very nicely. I don't recall or reflect upon events, I put things behind me quite effortlessly (wives, children, projects, houses), and I live for and through my work. Other than that, it is difficult for me to know precisely who I am.

The private lives of many artists do not bear much looking at, and mine is probably no different. The personality of the actor is important only as revealed in his work, not his private life. It's a difficult idea to express, but has something to do with the ability of an actor to use *himself* as a means of converting talent and an understanding of Stanislavsky and Lee Strasberg (or whoever) into something greater than mere mastery of tech-niques and mechanisms. In the end there has to be something which amounts to more than these considerations, and trans-forms an actor from a genuine fake into a genuine original. By itself, doing everything right is not enough. Your private, interior self has somehow to be exposed, made vulnerable and available to the playing of a part. Salieri does everything right, but in the end he is still Salieri and not Mozart. Olivier's genius was enigmatic, some unreadable part of himself transfiguring and inspiring his performances. As a creative artist he eradicated self-consciousness and gave himself up to a part in a way I'd never before seen. It was his example I carried with me during the later years at Stratford, when I started to do more than carry a spear. Even if I couldn't emulate him, I knew that I wanted to try.

5

HOMECOMING (I)

The build-up to The Wars of the Roses and then acting in its various productions was a consuming yet exhilarating experience. This I have already said. Yet now there was also time for a private life. I had been married to Lynne for ten years and we had two daughters, Jessica and Sarah-Jane. Then, in 1963, while playing Richard III, I met Bee Gilbert, a seventeen-year-old wardrobe assistant whose job it was to make and fit my club-footed boot. And so I left my wife. This was neither a pleasant thing to do nor a pleasant experience, but I did it and I lived through it. There were any number of beautiful young women in Stratford at that time, many of them actresses (including Judi Dench, Diana Rigg, Dorothy Tutin, Geraldine McEwan and even Margaret Drabble, whose intelligence ensured that she opted for writing rather than acting), and it would be fair to say that such people 'made use of their time'. Though others misbehaved, I tended to marry, or at least embark on a long relationship, though neither necessarily excluded bad behaviour. Bee and I were together for the next fourteen years. We had two children, Melissa (known as Lissy) and Barnaby.

I am not especially good at understanding or analysing why I habitually move from one substantial affair to the next. Someone once called me a 'serial monogamist', which is pretty close to the mark. Still, I also had affairs, though why these should have been underpinned by the almost methodical exchanging of partners rather than, say, sustained bachelorhood or just one (or two!) relationships, I do not know.

Somewhere, of course, as any analyst will tell you – and as they have certainly told me (for eighty pounds an hour) – my childhood was to blame. Pumped out to boarding school aged five and with a well-intentioned but distant set of parents, I needed stability. Or a mother figure. And maybe I didn't want my own life to turn into the benign but dull marathon which I'd observed in my own parents' marriage. But I don't think this explains how or why I have spent much of my life moving from people or putting myself in a position where people moved from me. Possibly a fear of prolonged commitment together with the apparently incompatible need for security has created this peristaltic existence.

I enjoy what I suppose is in a rather old-fashioned way called 'the chase'. And I enjoy the relationship which follows, though once this becomes compromised by the opportunity for another chase, I am lost. In many ways, of course, it is an all-too-familiar story. Though in my case I move forward by not having a pronounced sense of regret for what's gone. There's no end-of-empire atmosphere about me. No pining for a way of life that has slipped into the past and become history. I might be upset at the time, but I get over it quickly.

When I understudied Michael Redgrave – ludicrously under-studied him: he was a strapping six-footer – as Hamlet on the 1958 trip to Russia, I remember meeting the disgraced spy Guy Burgess during the Moscow production. This was, I have to say, only a fleeting assignation. Those who have seen Alan Bennett's play *An Englishman Abroad* might just – *just* – remember Burgess wandering backstage, staggering into a dressing room, making an appreciatively saucy remark about one of the male actors, and then puking into Coral Browne's sink. I was that male actor ('Darling, you've got an admirer,' she informed me), though it was Coral Browne who subsequently visited Burgess and sent to him various items of clothing from his London tailors. The point I am making is that Burgess, in permanent exile, listening to his single Jack Buchanan record and hankering for Jermyn Street, pined for a way of life that had all gone into the past. He needed the sense (the music, the dress) of another era, whereas I, for whatever reason, was just able to get on with it. As I said before, I was intrigued by the idea of being a spy, though not one like Guy Burgess, who was not an especially good one.

So. Bee fitted my club foot and we started an affair, after which we fell in love and I left Lynne and the children.

There is a scene in *Richard III* quite early on where Richard woos the Lady Anne over her dead father's coffin. Richard has killed her father. He has also, for good measure, been responsible for her husband's death. It is the most unlikely romantic encounter, and yet Richard has his way, even telling the audience that though he may have won Anne, he doesn't intend to keep her for long. There are parallels here with my own life at that time – the doubtful wooing of Bee, who was only seventeen, and the sheer challenge of it. No doubt something could be made of that, as could my playing of Prince Hal and Henry V the next year (1964), when I have been told that I became 'impish' off stage as well as on it.

If this is true, it is purely coincidental. I have never knowingly used my own life as the template for a role. In fact, I would go further and say I categorically deny that for me any such link exists. I have known a few British and quite a few American actors who 'want to find a way into a part' and therefore seek a parallel experience. Not me, however – though the opportunity to do so was certainly there when Peter Hall asked me to create the role of Lenny in Harold Pinter's *The Homecoming*. After all, Lenny was in competition with his patriarchal father Max, played by Paul Rogers, and the persuading of his brother Teddy's wife to leave him was in effect an intense, highly charged 'chase'. Pinter's writing does tap into the subconscious in acute, unnerving ways, and he understands exactly how much of life is like a game and how much of it is about winning, no matter how apparently civilized the tussle might seem. So there's a fair chance that something in the actor's life will mesh with the script. And I suppose as far as my personal circumstances were concerned, it's all there in *The Homecoming*, if you can be bothered to look for it: anger at my own reticent father fuelling Lenny's battles with Max; the pursuit of Teddy's wife, Ruth; the chance to emulate a brother; my own shadowy mother reflected by Pinter's 'no mother'; the fear of *outside*, beyond the walls of the house.

Well, it's one argument, but not one to which I subscribe. For a start, the tension between Lenny and Max is caused by over-familiarity as much as anything else, and I didn't really know my father. Or my brother, come to that. The mocking and the baiting is very focused, and based on a complete understanding of how the other one works. I wouldn't have known how to start an argument with my own father, let alone needle him in such an accustomed way.

Later, Bee told me that while I was playing Lenny I apparently became rather suave and sexy. There is, I believe, a photograph of us taken in Danny La Rue's London club during that time, which might corroborate a little of what she says. It is a decadent image of two people in love and enjoying life. I think I am smoking a cigarette. Now, it hardly seems credible that I could ever have behaved in that way, be the carefree and haughty person I recall staring back at me from the photograph.

By the time *The Homecoming* reached New York, we had become a very confident cast, so convinced were we of the play's qualities. I remember Paul Rogers observing that rarely could a more 'arrogant bunch of players' have taken the stage. Such was our disdain and self-belief that we were even able to jeer (mildly) at the tremor-inducing comments made by the New York critics. Walter Kerr of the *New York Times*, for example, announced that 'Pinter has dragged us all, aching, through a half-drugged dream.' Another critic admitted that he felt 'spoiled and diminished' by the experience of watching the play. And Alex Cohen told Hall, 'You'll be off in a fortnight.' To which Hall had cheerily and infuriatingly replied, 'That's marvellous news. I need my actors for something else back in London.'

The production was actually at its best in America. Before going there, we had been given a six-week rehearsal period followed by a short tour. It was tried and tested, and honed to an absolute cutting edge. Frank Rich, the influential drama critic of the *New York Times*, gave it a bad review, and for a short while it did indeed seem as if we would be packing our bags and heading back to England. But then it caught on. Audiences got the hang of it and puzzlement gave way quite quickly to approval and then, in a very American way, to adulation. *The Homecoming* went through the roof. The critics began to rave about the play, Pinter, the cast, Hall, and everything about it.

I don't want to labour the rather cute point about a smallish suburban man from Essex being surprised by thunderous applause when walking on stage (and *just* walking on stage), but that is what happened. By that time, in my mid-thirties, I felt I was a good actor making my way in a hard profession, some- one who had lately and by chance landed a series of wonderful roles, though I never considered myself 'a star'. I wouldn't even have known exactly what one was. But to be treated as one (as we all were) was invigorating, so when I think back to that photograph in Danny La Rue's club, maybe it is not just Lenny I see leering back at me, but an oddly intoxicated, transformed Ian Holm.

We really did feel that the play was so good that New York could take it or leave it. If they didn't like it, well fuck them!, we'd just pack up and go home. Before *The Homecoming*, Pinter had just written a wonderful screenplay for Penelope Mortimer's *The Pumpkin Eater*, and as a writer he was therefore in very good order at that time. I think he still regards it as being amongst his best writing, and I remember him telling me then (and on several subsequent occasions) that structurally it was absolutely his best work.

Hall and Pinter had important things in common, and as director and writer worked very well together. Both, for example, worked closely from the text, focusing on it with fierce and absolute concentration. This suited me very well. Over the previous eight years or so I had got very used to Hall's approach, then and now believing it the only honest way to approach a play.

As an actor himself, Pinter was also instinctively interested in the relationship between the actor, the writer and the audience, not wanting to give too much away, or pin ideas and nuances down in case they came between any kind of 'reaction'. He understood better than most how an actor worked and knew that really good performances came from some indefinable place within. You couldn't direct the actor to that place or explain where to find it; it was simply discovered during the course of acting out a role.

Again, this sat very comfortably with me. I thought about text and character and then, without any sense of being programmed or of delivering a role, walked on to the stage and performed. I read later that Pinter had said about me, 'He puts on my shoe and it fits! It's really very gratifying.' I took this to mean that he expected actors to concentrate on his language – 'the stress and rhythms will tell you what you mean, Ian,' he emphasized – and by and large I was able to do this.

Some actors are disconcerted by 'just' performing and need some kind of interpretation to help them understand a character. Pinter, however, never gives anything away. He believed that once you started to explain the text, it put the lid on things and made them stale. In a moment of weakness I once asked him about the iron mangle business in *The Homecoming*. All he did was shake his formidable, bear-like head (his you-should-know-better-than-that shake) and say, 'How do we know it ever happened?'

Critics and actors tried to find all manner of stuff in the play. Pinter rebuffed each inquiry with a polite but very, very firm jerk of the head, often answering a question with another question.

'Is Teddy really *you*?'

'How do you mean?' would come the gruff reply.

'Well, you've been away from the stage for six years.'

'So what?'

'And Teddy's been away from home for about the same time.'

'Has he?'

'It says so, in the text.'

'Does it? How do we know it's true?'

'And what about Teddy's wife, Ruth? Isn't she like your work?'

'Eh?'

'He's brought her back, to the family, to your public.'

'He only *says* that she's his wife.'

During early rehearsals, Pinter was usually around (with gold pencil and notepad), and I remember someone asking him about Sam's sexuality, thinking that he'd detected a whiff of femininity in the character and, what's more, backing his idea with some quite detailed observations about the text. He was fixed with a beady stare before having his little theory quashed. 'What's all that about, then?'

None of this is particularly surprising if you know anything about his other plays. In *The Lovers*, for example, a man leaves his wife at home when he goes off to work and visits her at lunchtime as her lover. There's an ambiguous fluency about Pinter. It's all rather like one of Beckett's stage directions which instructs that a door is 'imperceptibly ajar'. Pinter loved Beckett, especially his obliqueness and cheery unwillingness to explain things or ascribe to them a particular meaning, and was hewn from the same raw material. In fact, both men did literally have a sort of sculpted quality about them. Beckett's angular chiselled features and carved hair-do against Pinter's moulded bearishness, the simultaneous sensation of hard and soft material coexisting in the same body; the hint of Billy Whizz in the hair and his Henry Moore roundness that was still impenetrable and solidly resistant to the touch. And these physical contradictions were reflected in Pinter's demeanour, which was simultaneously gruff and sensitive. He could be boorish and amusing, kind and bullying, dismissive and attentive, fierce and affectionate. His capricious behaviour kept people on their toes and defied easy categorization, very much like the determined open-endedness of his plays.

He was also, of course, the East End boy made good, who was equally at home amongst gangsters and royalty, and seemed to enjoy both in equal measure. There were stories of him socializing with the Krays in London, and while in New York he mixed with all kinds of odd people. At the time, he was married to Vivien Merchant, and I recall visiting them in a lavish apartment just off Regent's Park. It was lavish in a showy kind of way – I think of gold taps when I think of that apartment, though there was a lot else to think about, most of it expensive, or at least designed to seem expensive. Deep carpets, heavy Sumo-like coffee tables, and the entire flat luxuriantly accessorized (the cunning bottle-opener, the special but quite tricky curtains which required some kind of knack to open them, the lights which didn't look much like lights – you know the sort of thing). And in this setting, the diamond: Vivien sprawled on the sofa reading *Titbits*. Much of it went over her head – Pinter was beyond her – though she did play Ruth in *The Homecoming* (and played her as an ice maiden), which naturally led to even more speculation about the meaning of the play, speculation which of course Pinter straight-batted right back to every frustrated questioner.

Actually, I suspect playing a straight bat was something of an effort for Pinter. He loved cricket; once, in Paris, he spent a whole night discussing the game with Beckett (another fan, and the only Nobel Prize winner to be included in *Wisden*). As a batsman, I always imagined Pinter would be a fierce but artful milker of bowling, subtly aggressive, but always on the offensive. Not quite the yokel bludgeoner Ted Burgess he wrote about in his screenplay of *The Go-Between*, but not the passive tapper-back of questions either.

Cricket was exactly his kind of game. At one level, it has a deeply authoritative veneer of respectability and romantic, old-world charm, both of which I suppose were attractive to his working-class, very twentieth-century urbanity. But it also allowed for demonic and brutish transgression (Burgess again, belting the ball and putting two fingers up to the local aristocracy), so you could be both an insider and an outsider. It is also a very competitive game, though not necessarily reliant on physical intimidation as a way of competing, and Pinter loved a game. After all, that's what his characters did on stage:

they played out some kind of contest, and what is *The Homecoming* about if not gaining supremacy over other people, where dominance guarantees a measure of knowledge and identity? With its complex layering of laws and rituals, and its intensely psychological nature, it is easy to understand why Pinter liked cricket so much. It appealed to his need for mental warfare, and the essentially restrained manner of the conflicts (all undertaken within a strictly adhered-to code of behaviour) precisely mirrors the exacting language and controlled atmosphere of his own plays.

Pinter was often hurrying off to listen to the latest Test Match score and wasn't above including references to his favourite game in his plays ('Who watered the wicket at Melbourne?'); his passion for cricket was more consuming than for others who professed an interest. During The Wars of the Roses, for example, I can recall Peggy Ashcroft's love of the game, and her organizing a charity match in which I strode to the wicket in Richard's full armour, including club foot, which meant that I needed a runner. I don't think Pinter would have liked that kind of fluffiness, but he would have admired Ron Haddrick, a South Australian member of the cast who had played cricket to a high level. We used to play the town of Stratford, at the time a very good club side. In particular, they had the Pargitter brothers (both bakers, I think), who used to open the batting and flay our weak bowling to all parts of the Avon. Haddrick got tired of being beaten and weary of the town side's jibes, so one year he called in two friends, George Tribe and Frank Tyson, both of whom had played international cricket.

I do think Pinter would have liked that. He could be explosive, though I always felt he rather preferred to do something else to get his way, as if the mere suggestion of violence should have been enough. Really, he wanted you to think, 'I am a very civilized sort of chap.' But brute force and cruelty were certainly in his armoury, and he liked you to be aware of them even when they were not deployed. This accounts, I suspect, for the undercurrents of destructiveness that bubble through much of his writing.

On one occasion in New York, during a party, some furniture was thrown from Pinter's penthouse apartment. The next day a company meeting was called and one of the cast came under suspicion for what I suppose would have been vandalism or destruction of property, or whatever. I think a police inquiry was mentioned. The incident caused a black hole of distrust and wariness to open up between us all, and for two weeks we lived in chary discomfort. Then Pinter called another meeting, and the whole thing was resolved, or at least brushed under the carpet. Nothing explicit was said and the matter, though concluded, was left curiously unexplained.

But the man is undoubtedly a genius. I sometimes wonder why it is that I find his work so appropriate to my own ways of working (we worked together several times after *The Homecoming*, the last as recently as a 2001 revival of the play, when I played Max), and am drawn to the idea that in some way we are both unknowable. The difference, of course, is that Pinter's inscrutability is loud and mythic, whereas mine merely announces a kind of suburban blandness.

Still, I think we understood one another. And playing Lenny after Richard *and* Prince Hal *and* Henry V meant that I was having the time of my life. Which actor would not think that?

When the part of Lenny was originally offered to me, I met Pinter in a pub. At that point I had not given the work much consideration, and wasn't overwhelmed by it.

'I have to tell you that I don't much like the play,' I started to say, 'but I like the part.'

'It doesn't much matter about you *liking* the play,' Pinter replied, 'so long as you do it.'

Of course, over the next few months I would change my mind absolutely about the quality of the drama, though I felt that here – immediately – there was some kind of understanding between the writer and the actor.

As he usually did at the start of a production, Peter Hall called us together to explain quite broadly how he would be approaching the play. He talked about it in terms of battles and conflicts and said a fair amount about weaponry and 'the law of the jungle'. 'The way Pinter's characters operate,' he announced, 'is to behave as if they were all stalking round a jungle.' He said it was an abrasive and uncomfortable play and that we should be prepared for a tough time. Pinter, he said, made even more demands on the actor than Shakespeare.

I doubted Hall was right when he said this, but I soon learnt that he was completely right. The discipline of playing Pinter is exhausting. There is nothing out of place in his scripts – not a sentence, a word, a full stop, or even a comma. Especially the comma. It's all there and it's all essential – and as an actor you've got to concentrate very hard indeed on the text. It's hard enough at the best of times, but I was coming from the Henry plays, where I had been given licence to show off (especially as the impishly miscreant Hal), and to have the brakes applied so completely was very difficult. It wasn't just the discipline that was hard, because of course there's much of that in Shakespeare, but the stillness, the sense of almost claustrophobic inertia. This, I remember, drove Cyril Cusack to distraction when we came to do the film version five or six years later. It was not a particularly good film, and Cusack, who had not been in the original stage production, took the part of Sam. Now Cusack is a brilliant actor, but he is at his most effective when allowed to build up his own original sense of character, twitching, humming and haa-ing to establish a kind of Cusack music. He wasn't allowed to do that for Pinter (though he did . . . a bit), and as a consequence had a pretty torrid time, feeling the pinch of stillness more than the rest of us, who were by then getting used to it.

Broadly, I played Lenny as a younger version of Max (and later, in 2001, Max as an older version of Lenny), binding (*entrusting*) myself to the rhythms of the text and allowing the character to emerge. I discovered how much charm he had, and how difficult it was to be charming – it actually takes balls and concentration. This was odd, because I had naively assumed that charm or allure or whatever was instinctive and that therefore I didn't have it. I may have been a lot of things but I never thought I could be magnetic. But Lenny was, and this is something I discovered during the short provincial run, developed at the Aldwych, and then brought to a head in New York. And possibly that is what Bee meant when she talked of my attractiveness at the time, though I hasten to add that her observations were expressed with as much surprise as admiration.

Perhaps Pinter's writing does allow an actor to inhabit a character more than is usual, so that you don't act out a role so much as become that person. As I've explained, I'm sceptical about this sort of thing, but with Pinter maybe some kind of exception could be made. Though if it did happen, it happened inside-out; that is, the text led me to an unfamiliar place rather than me interpreting Lenny in a particular way and imposing that specific reading on the performance.

Actors are never puppets in Pinter's plays, and don't travel down the usual dramatic channels. There's something more raw and real about his characters, which means that you're always doing more than just playing a part. That's why he is so difficult, I think, and why many actors can't do him properly. Instinctively, they want to animate a preconceived character study, and the writing just won't allow it. Paul Rogers and I discussed this. He said a bit about Lenny's beautiful mohair shirts and then announced that he (as Max) would like to walk into Lenny's bedroom.

'Why's that?' I asked, aware that I was beginning to sound a little like Pinter.

He considered. 'Because I think Lenny would have wall-to-wall carpeting and the most marvellous furniture. To walk into Lenny's place would be like walking into another world.'

I disagreed, saying that Lenny's room was more likely to be completely bare, but that in any case it was important *not* to know how he would furnish his room or dress or whatever. The most important characters in a Pinter play are often absent (Jessie and MacGregor, for instance), and it was important that we shouldn't know much about them beyond what the script tells us. Likewise Lenny's room. To fantasize beyond Pinter's words would be to introduce something made up which would unbalance the play's delicate mechanisms.

I still tend to believe that it's just 'me' reading the script, taking direction, and doing it. I know it would be more interesting if I was able to say where 'it' comes from, but I don't. Or rather, I don't think about that side of things. Lenny is merely a text and how I imagine that character would behave. I put Lenny on for that production and then discarded him. I do much the same when walking down the street, tending to mimic people (their walks, their looks, their mannerisms) who pass by me on the pavement. Finally, you might say I do something similar with family. To be with Bee, I cast aside Lynne, a ten-year marriage and two children, and became (I suppose) a different person. Hmmm.

One day, while we were rehearsing the play, Peter Hall drew me to one side and said, 'Teddy is the biggest bastard of the lot, you know.'

I said, 'I think I know that. At least, I know it now. When

we started, I thought I was the bastard. Or Max. Or even MacGregor.'

'It's Teddy,' he concluded.

To those who are familiar with the play, this may seem odd. After all, Teddy is the cuckolded husband, and the man who eventually loses his wife to his brothers and his father. But Hall was right, and Pinter confirmed it to me: 'If ever there was a villain in the play, Teddy is it.'

The point I think they were both making is that Teddy opts out of the game, opts out of life; he turns out to be a coward and a spoilsport. Ruth recognizes that and estimates that he will be a bad bet for the future. It's not merely the 'logical incoherence' of Christian theism which he decides is not his 'province', but life itself. Having left the family once, he does it again, feebly and without a struggle. For Pinter, withdrawing from a contest is worse than the least admirable behaviour within it. It's an odd thing to say, but I felt at the time that I – like Lenny and the squabbling Max, or Pinter and his abrasively complicated social life, or Hall and his domestic/professional juggling – was also involved and playing the game. I may not have been doing so blamelessly or even decently, but *The Homecoming*, I now see, was the culmination of my years of developing into a good actor and becoming a properly engaged person, more Lenny than Teddy.

I talked earlier about not looking back or having regrets, though one of the parts I would still like to do is that of Archie Rice in John Osborne's *The Entertainer*, another (though older) degenerate whose attractiveness comes from his refusal not to turn his back on life, to keep milking applause from the ever-thinning audiences. I don't think Osborne will last in the way that Pinter will. *Look Back in Anger* is fine for its time, but it doesn't have the same kind of subconscious sweep and power as Pinter.

Lenny was a pivotal role for me. Of that I have no doubt. That time and the years leading up to it, Stratford in general, they all created me as an actor and, to a point, as a person. They were happy days, though not in the Beckettian sense. And how long ago it all now seems. Schoolboys wearing caps, messing around in boats on the Avon, cricket matches in armour, actors stubbing out cigarettes prior to making an entrance, the Mayor of Stratford and his lady wife attending first nights. I felt cut off from the rest of the world. The Age of Aquarius, *Oh! Calcutta!*, London's bohemia, Sandie Shaw, *Darling*, James Bond, Christine Keeler, Mary Quant (and the mini skirt!), The Stones, The Who, even The Beatles. All this more or less passed me by. I wasn't aware of it because I felt it had nothing to do with me. Bee had LPs by The Beatles, but then, as now, I actually possessed very little. Acting was what I did and nothing else much bothered me. I was content in my little nest at Stratford playing Richard, Duke of Gloucester, Richard III, Prince Hal, Henry V, and creating the role of Lenny. Who could not be happy in such an environment, especially given the roles I was playing, the success I was having?

6

ALL CHANGE

Just as the entire Age of Aquarius passed me by, so did the 1967 Summer of Love. We were told to 'tune in, turn on, drop out', whereas all I felt ready for in the lead up to this flowery era was tuning out, turning off and dropping in. The Summer of Love affected different people in different ways, and although Mick Jagger was doing things with Marianne Faithfull and The Beatles were singing that 'All You Need Is Love', my own life was much less psychedelically charged.

When I look back now, I even wonder if all that stuff really did happen and, if so, what I must have missed, though I am slightly reassured to recall that *The Sound of Music* soundtrack was one of the bestselling albums of the year. And the song which hung around the charts longest was not by The Beatles or The Tremeloes or even Dave Dee, Dozy, Beaky, Mick and Titch. It was Engelbert Humperdinck with 'The Last Waltz'.

Maybe I was in the wrong place at the wrong time. There may well have been a part of me which was hairy and druggy (what was I? Thirty-five? Thirty-six?), but there was another part which was pure Von Trapp.

The irony is that I had discovered how much I liked being in love, so it should have been absolutely My Time. In fact, I liked being in love so much that I embarked on an existence which required regular fixes of it. My drug was not LSD or marijuana or whatever, but romance. Falling in love was a comfort to me. The affection of a woman acted as reassurance. And sex was tangible proof of being loved, proof that I was worth something.

In 1967 I did the New York run of *The Homecoming* and then my final play at Stratford, appropriately a rather aged Romeo in *Romeo and Juliet*. By that time, I had left Lynne and my two daughters Jessica and Sarah-Jane, and was with Bee.

In many ways, I had been very happy with Lynne. We lived, as I've said, at the large, rambling Avoncliffe complex in Tiddington, one of several company families who were quartered there. Now, of course, like so much else, it has been destroyed. It was a large house with extensive gardens which led down to the river. Leslie Caron, Peter Hall's wife at that time, seemed to do much of the gardening and during their stay she grew a fine display of azaleas at the entrance. The house was reached via a grand drive which gave the building a sense of imposing remoteness, though in truth it was a friendly, even welcoming place, with airy, comfortable rooms. In a sense, it was the place where I grew up and learnt how to make and then break a relationship. It was the place where I witnessed the early years of my first two children – of Jessica, for instance, becoming distressed at birds being caught on the poles dotted around the garden, and taking a wounded robin down to the boiler room in the hope of saving it.

I quite liked being part of a community, tenuous though it was, though on the whole I think I preferred fewer people and more intense contact. Be that as it may, married life was fine; but it is revealing to recount the reasons why I felt the need to rupture apparently contented situations, a habit which has stayed with me throughout my life.

The chase, the romance of falling in love and the state of excited passion it leads to make me feel alive to the fingertips – in the same way, I suppose, that acting does. For me, both are heady and stimulating, the most spectacular sources of encouragement imaginable. In addition, both involve a certain amount of showing off, even of showiness, and demand some tangible form of appreciation. Once I had experienced the highs of romance, I knew that I could never be satisfied with mere contentment. After a while – and perhaps even quite a long while – the sense of heightened reassurance runs dry and I need to fall in love all over again.

Lynne had been very good to me; she was kind and smart and looked after me in a demonstrative sort of way. My split from her was illustrative of the emotional tensions in me, of the unreasonable and maybe impossible need for both security and adventure.

Although I liked to walk between Tiddington and Stratford, I also sometimes drove, by that time having done well enough to afford a car. Several times I had given a lift to Bee, a young dresser whom I had first met during *Richard III*. We had flirted and discovered a bit about each other. Sometimes I would see her walking back to her digs on the Tiddington road and I would give her a lift. She came from an unconventional, bohemian family in Cornwall, and I found myself intrigued by the kind of (to my resolutely suburban mind, at least) freakish life she had led. Her mother Molly was a regular on peace marches, electricity was a fairly recent inclusion to the household, and their lives seemed to be completely free of the middle-class, middle-English expectations with which I had been brought up.

I knew that I wanted to have an affair with her, so during one of the lifts I drove her past her digs to some quite secluded spot and asked her straight out whether or not we were going to have one. She replied that it wasn't really up to her. I asked her what she meant.

'I'm not the one with a wife and family,' she said rather wisely.

This was quite obviously true. Bee was barely old enough to be out of school, let alone have a family.

Anyway, we did have an affair, and it turned out that she had been rather shocked when I asked her. Apparently, I was regarded at that time as a 'good family man', which I suppose in some ways I was and in other ways I would always be. But it was never as simple as that.

Bee then moved to London to live with her sister in Hampstead. She turned down a job as stage manager in Barrow-on-Furness because of the possibility that our relationship could develop. This would have been directly after the filming of The Wars of the Roses, and just before *Henry V* and *The Homecoming*.

By that time, I was also in London with Lynne and the girls, staying at Observatory Gardens near to Kensington High Street. We went on a family holiday to Switzerland – in January, I think – which was not a great success. This may have been a self-fulfilling prophecy. I came home early and told Bee that I intended to leave Lynne. So when everyone else arrived back, I was often rushing out to see Bee, usually on the pretext of walking the dog or buying some bread, or whatever excuse came readily to mind. We escaped to Cornwall together. I was clutching a copy of Pinter's new play and said I needed time to digest it. Having revised my earlier assessment, I had now decided it was a brilliant piece of work and asked Bee what she thought, though without telling her my own opinion. She read it and also judged it a remarkable work. If anything acted as a catalyst to our affair becoming more than just that, *The Homecoming* in 1967 was that thing.

Then, back in London once more, the emotional cramps began. First I was with Bee, then I announced that I couldn't leave Lynne, after all. Bee ran away to Cornwall and I followed, saying that I *would* be leaving Lynne.

Then the thing turned into a kind of slow-motion Feydeau farce. At one point, I thought it would be a good idea if Lynne and Bee met and resolved the situation. So I arranged a meeting and then set off to take a walk, leaving them to it, rather hoping that they could sort out my life for me. It was a scene which, I later learnt, contained some soap-operatic dialogue. Lynne quite reasonably asked Bee, 'What about my children?' and Bee, who was newly pregnant, replied, 'And what about *my* child?'

Of course, I wanted them somehow to square the circle; how could my loving Bee (the agent of romantic reassurance) be achieved without upsetting Lynne and the children (the keepers of the nest)? I needed and wanted both, and thus the first love triangle of my life was formed.

Bee went into Charing Cross hospital when our baby miscarried, and still vacillating, still strung out, still hoping that these two mother figures would provide some kind of resolution, I said I wouldn't be doing anything until *The Homecoming* opened – an opening which Lynne attended, though only after I had been on holiday with Bee to Ibiza. Soon afterwards I was living with Bee in a small flat in Primrose Gardens. And soon after *that* she was pregnant again, this time with Lissy, our first child.

Recalled in such matter-of-fact detail the whole episode – or rather, series of episodes – seems, what? Odd? Callous? Irrational? Bee has since told me that in amongst the mess of it all (the miscarriage, the people being hurt, the apparent indifference of my own hard-boiled self-interest) she thinks that above all else I was innocent. Not innocent of guilt, but *an* innocent. Not able to comprehend the situation properly and believing that somehow it would all work out, and that in particular other people would resolve the chaos.

Mmmm. It's difficult for me to comment on that, but I do know that the shadows cast by the leaving of Lynne became very familiar during the rest of my life. The need for a calm domestic sanctuary at the same time as seeking the reassurance of a dynamic romance was to become a continual dilemma. In addition, the 'innocence' that Bee speaks of – the sense of being uninvolved with life, being empty, being nothing – is an aspect of my character that on the one hand facilitates my acting, and yet also signals a kind of inner void.

Here is a strange thing. I have never voted in my life. The reasons are, I suppose, to do with an instinctive detachment from politics, but also because I am genuinely unable to make up my mind on political matters. I seem to agree (or disagree) with all politicians in a dispassionate and entirely unprejudiced manner. I do not – cannot – hold the necessary convictions which would align me to one party or another. Similarly, though these days I do not think this is so unusual, I do not have a religion. But neither am I particularly *ir*religious. Of course I'm not. I'm not 'particularly' anything. I still say my prayers every night, addressing them to 'God' or 'Gentle Jesus meek and mild', though without knowing who either of them are, or much wanting to know. I generally give thanks to them (for my life, for the people I care for), whilst at the same time silently acknowledging that they probably don't exist.

I remember my father becoming quite religious after my brother died. He and I, though not my mother, would troop off to church every Sunday. Something of the habit has stayed with me, though not the essence of the thing. Afraid of the consequences if I absolutely broke with the practice of godliness, but also fearful of meaningful involvement, I have developed a lukewarm disposition which is neither one thing nor the other. In addition, the reminders of childhood custom must be in some way comforting, though as with women, I have reserved the right to take advantage of that comfort.

I think saying my prayers is no more than a mantra, perhaps like knowing your lines. Most actors have their own routines and are generally grateful for familiar lines to which they can cling. Some mumble them before going on stage, often walking round a bit as they do so, even when the lines are not from the play they are in at that moment.

Quite recently I have undergone therapy, and 'undergone' – with its echoes of surgery, ordeal and deprivation – is probably the right word to describe it. And I went into the thing properly; that is, expensively and in New York. I'm not, however, convinced by it. I have just read something about Terry Gilliam (Monty Python animator and film director, with whom I later worked on *Time Bandits* and *Brazil*) saying that as far as he's concerned, 'Therapy is the worst thing a crazy person can do. Creative madness pays my mortgage.' I do not think I'm crazy (at least, not in the Gilliam manner) and I don't think either that I'm as creative as him, certainly not in the same dynamic manner. But I understand what he's saying; what is unfathomable at the heart of us all is probably best left unfathomable. It's there for a reason.

Conversations with my therapist would go something like this.

'Ian?'

'Yes.'

Pause.

'Who are you when you disappear into all those characters you do?'

'I think if you took them away there wouldn't be a lot left.'

Pause.

'But who *are you* to do the disappearing?'

'I don't know. Nobody.'

Pause.

'That's very interesting.'

'Why?'

Pause.

Silence.

People are. Things happen. And so it now seems quite natural that post-Lynne, post-Stratford, I should have drifted into films. The change was seamless and managed quite without upset or disorder. Just as I'd become an actor, gone to Stratford, married and then divorced, it was more of an elision than a transformation.

And this was the Summer of Love. I had been at Stratford for around thirteen years. During that time I had developed into a leading actor and had, as they say, 'learnt my trade'. The end of Peter Hall's tenure also seemed to mark a natural break, and it seemed like a good time to move on. The possibility of 'doing films' had actually been in the air for a while, and there had been talk of me being in *The Charge of the Light Brigade*, which came to nothing. We sort of knew that American producers were raking England for new talent and unusually had been drawn out of London by the success of the Stratford seasons. And so I had a few drinks in the Dirty Duck with the American director John Frankenheimer, and soon I was offered a part in his new film *The Fixer*.

'Me?' I thought. 'In a film. In a *proper* film? Gosh.'

I agreed straight away. It was to be shot in Budapest later that year.

Bee accompanied me – her mother Molly agreed to look after Lissy and Barnaby (who was born in February of that year), both of whom had been experiencing terrible earache. So much for tuning in and dropping out. I had shattered one nest to create another one almost immediately. But I was excited at the prospect of doing *The Fixer*. Although I had done a couple of other films (versions of Peter Hall's *A Midsummer Night's Dream* and The Wars of the Roses), they were theatrical spin-offs. We didn't really know what we were doing, and though each film had its moments, they were usually quite stagy moments. When I watch them now, all I can see is strange, manufactured black and white artiness with the production values of an industrial training film. Which isn't to say they were bad, but they certainly weren't Cinema.

But Frankenheimer was the real thing. For a start, he was American. I was vaguely familiar with his work, and *The Manchurian Candidate* had received good notices for its modish use of Wellesian deep-focus. He'd worked with Sinatra on that film, which in our eyes already lent him a certain burnished significance. He'd also done *The Birdman of Alcatraz* with Burt Lancaster. And just before *The Fixer*, he'd done *Grand Prix*, a film of impossibly glamorous ambition.

When we met, I saw that he was also good looking in a sensual kind of way. The trouble was, I found it hard to like him. I think he'd reached the point in his career when he felt it was time to do A Really Important Piece of Work. He'd settled on an adaptation of Malamud's novel *The Fixer*, which he believed was a masterpiece.

'Y'know, Ian,' he told me, 'it's a work of fuckin' genius. And we're gonna tell the whole fuckin' world about it.'

I found him both shy and aloof, which gave his speech a sort of reticent aggression, as though he was never quite sure that people would understand him. He was reserved but liked commotion, and although it wasn't immediately obvious, he was sharp enough not to suffer fools gladly.

'Who do you want me to play?' I asked.

'Grubeshov. Yeah. We've inked you in as Grubeshov.'

'Who's he?'

'He's a ruthless bigot.'

'Is it a big part?'

'Not the biggest. That's Yakhov Bok. We've got Alan Bates for that. He's more hero material. But Grubeshov is *pretty* big. Grubeshov is by no means a cameo.'

'In what way am I ruthless and bigoted?'

'You torture Bok. You use every form of mental and physical punishment you can to make him confess.'

'And does he?'

'Does he what?'

'Confess.'

'Nah. Not really.'

'Oh.'

'But Grubeshov is pivotal, Ian. I want you to know that. Pivotal. Without Grubeshov, Bok could never attain heroic status.'

The story is set in Kiev in 1911 and tells of a disenchanted Jew, Bok, who has run away from his village to the big city. He is arrested on suspicion of murder, but decides that dignity is more important than confession and refuses to give his name to a crime he did not commit.

'You know, Ian,' Frankenheimer told me, 'it's a film about potential. Po-tent-ial. It's about the human condition. It's about the fact that we – we as human beings – are capable of a great deal more than we might think.' I nodded. 'And that's why we had to get the finest English actors possible.'

This was a far cry from Stratford and Olivier and Hall and Pinter, where one was generally terrified of making a mistake and not being perfect or outstanding or intelligent. Here I was being told – and told before I'd even started acting – how good I was. And not just good: 'the finest'.

I think it was important for Frankenheimer to believe that he was in possession of the best meat in the market. He was really quite driven and absolutely convinced that *The Fixer* was a film in which he could give hope to people. He often said it was the only film he'd made which didn't involve a compromise of some kind. And he was always trying to make things better, even to the point of going back to Budapest after the filming was supposed to be finished and re-shooting scenes. All this was entirely laudable, of course. Frankenheimer also brought a sense of intense concentration to the set which, in the same way that he could be both hesitant and truculent, was often qualified by shouting and the levels of quarrelsome noise he would tolerate.

One time we were shooting in a cave and I remember him yelling, 'Get that cocksucking extra outa here!'

There was a French cameraman called Henri Domage who lived up to his name and used to give me a conspiratorial look whenever Frankenheimer became truculent. It was the conniving look of someone else who was actually a rather quiet bloke and was beginning to wonder what the fuck he'd got himself into.

Although he had a wife who went by the extraordinary name of Evans Evans, Frankenheimer was having an affair with the screenwriter Dalton Trumbo's daughter. It didn't make for an easy atmosphere. One way and another, the director's attempt to make a masterpiece wasn't working out. Of course, masterpieces rarely do when you're specifically aiming to score one. He also had a red Ferrari brought over to Hungary, which initially was the cause for great interest amongst the locals. But then he roped it off so that they couldn't get too close, and I heard that they put sugar in his petrol to stop it running too far.

Although Frankenheimer seemed to have a great deal going for him, the film just didn't add up. Alan Bates was very kind to Bee and me, but the real friendship we made was with Dirk Bogarde, who was playing the part of Bibikov, Bok's ally and a government lawyer. Obviously he was more used to the strangeness of being on a film set and had no illusions about either the project or the reasons why he was there.

For a start, he hated the subject matter. The novel, he said, was bearable, 'But full of juicy prose about the Jewish problem in Tsarist Russia. I can see *that* filling seats, can't you?' He wanted to know why Frankenheimer had asked for the dialogue to be rewritten. 'I don't like the novel, but at least it's tolerably well written. Whereas this new dialogue –' and here he would hold up a copy of the script, 'it's *frightful*. Do they really *have* to rewrite?'

Bogarde was there with his partner Tony Forwood – or rather he wasn't quite there all the time, sometimes staying at the Hotel Bristol in Vienna, about four and a half hours away. He was chauffeured to Budapest in a Rolls Royce when required on set. Otherwise, he had as little to do with the film as possible. Originally, the company was put up at the comfortable Hotel Gellert, but because our rooms were being commandeered for a conference, we were moved to a miserable, utilitarian block in Pest which was a parody of all that was bad about Communism. Bogarde hated it, and hated it with a passion. Whenever he could, he headed off to Vienna.

Once I asked him why he was doing the job at all. He gave me a rather severe look, his habitual look, the one that eventually teetered on the edge of a smile without ever quite making it. 'I turn it down, they offer more money. I turn it down again, they offer more money, and a car, *and* a chauffeur. And in the end – as Forwood pointed out to me with his customary reasonable-ness – we do need the kitchen to be rebuilt. So here I am.'

Although Bogarde was irritable and quite touchy about certain things – 'fragile' might be the best way to describe him – he was, in his own way, totally at ease on the film set. He was a star and he knew it. He understood exactly what he was worth to the film, and the appropriate manner and scale of his reward. The whole thing was a kind of game which he had mastered. So when some last-minute changes were made to the terms of his contract (I don't know the details, but I suspect they were relatively minor alterations), he absolutely refused to do anything until his rights had been properly restored.

Though relations between Bogarde and the director were rarely more than polite or functional, Frankenheimer brought him a bottle of champagne as a peace offering. They shared an uneasy toast to the success of the film, though afterwards Bogarde often made reference to the fact that Dom Perignon was all very well, 'but *warm* Dom Perignon? I think not.'

Actually he was a very kind man, though not necessarily at ease with himself or his feelings, and often seemed to be on the point of wincing, as if expecting a light slap or anticipating a bad smell. In one scene as the aristocratic lawyer Bibikov he had to drink a glass of champagne, and I remember that expression suddenly decorating his face when he discovered that not only was the glass plastic, but that it also bore the legend 'Pan Am'.

I was new to film and very much liked the pampering that came with it, even to me. Although I understood Bogarde's insistence on being in Vienna well enough from his perspective, I was happy enough being holed up in Pest for the duration, even though it was like Tower Hamlets on a rainy afternoon.

Bogarde was quite saddened by the city and described it as being like a 'kind of terrible Sunday'. It was true that it still bore the scars of war and the 1956 revolution, but there was a shabby grandeur about it and (significant for me, this) it certainly wasn't Tiddington. There were, for example, very few trees lining the streets; they had either been cut down and used in barricades or burnt as firewood. Buildings still bore the marks of war. Many were shell-pocked, some were still gutted. The people, however, were wonderful, making do with comparatively meagre resources and even managing to look chic amongst the general drabness, the air of resignation and the intimidatingly heavy presence of Russian uniforms. The food was unspeakably dull; the 'tourist restaurants' were haunted by Gypsy musicians and there were violins at every table. The food when it came was cold and served on cold plates. But the crew was very good and everyone was charming.

Bogarde liked the people, but was saddened by everything else, blaming Communism and pronouncing it joyless, grey and vindictive. 'Have you ever known an amusing Communist?' he asked me one day. 'Or a witty one? Or – least of all – a *funny* one?'

Although he was hardly a pure-bred Englishman (being Spanish-Scots on his mother's side and Dutch-English on his father's), there was something yearning and nostalgic about Bogarde, something old-fashioned and archetypally, traditionally English, and I sometimes thought that his slightly wounded or affronted air had a bit to do with his sense of a lost (English) world, or of his country and its way of life unravelling before him. I think he saw in Budapest what England might become. 'I wonder if the trade union lot have done this trip,' he once remarked, and he was often fearful of what was happening to the old country – in particular, angry about the Wilson government and what he saw as a slow, determined decline, with the unions eventually strangling incentive. 'Where in God's name will it all end?' he asked me, and because I gave no sign of knowing the answer, he said, 'Like this. Like bloody Budapest. That's where.'

Bee and I became a part of Bogarde and Forwood's entourage, which is a not very nice way of saying that we became friends. I think they particularly liked Bee, whom they referred to as Snowflake – very young, and therefore 'pure as the driven . . .' – and I tended to tag along in my usual un-assuming way. Tony Forwood, who had once been on stage before becoming Bogarde's business and domestic partner (the actual nature of their relationship was enigmatic, but I have no doubt they loved one another), I think quite respected me as an actor, though he was so charming and well-mannered it was difficult not to feel delighted with him.

Bogarde himself was perhaps a little dismayed by my stage work. Although he had worked in the theatre very early in his career, he was not comfortable there and was an infinitely better screen actor. But he was very generous and, in effect, taught me how to act on film. He told me that it was all in the eyes and that less was more. Put like that, it all sounds very straightforward and easy, and for a while I thought as much. Then I watched Bogarde closely and realized he really was a brilliant technician, achieving the most subtle effects with the merest indications of movement or expression. Although this kind of stillness and minimalism does not come easily to a theatrical actor, it some-how suited me and I took to it with very little fuss. So suddenly, even effortlessly, I 'went into films'.

I had the impression that Bogarde liked to be on the periphery of things – although he was an actor, he preferred not to be with actors, even while he was working. The same applied with his Englishness; he admitted to feeling more French than English, even though he embodied a distinct kind of Englishness. A few years later, he and Forwood would leave the country and set up house in the South of France.

Although I liked working with actors and had become some-thing of a 'good company man' while at Stratford, Bogarde had a strange, almost impatient view of them. He told me that while he had plenty of time for the greats – Olivier, Gielgud, Richardson and so on – he was, on the whole, irritated by actors. On a very few occasions he would invite Bee and me back to

Vienna so we could spend time with him and Tony, and some-times he would chat about our mutual profession in the back of the Rolls.

'You know, Ian, there are so many different kinds of actor, and most of them aren't worth a candle.'

I nodded. Uneasily.

'There's the second-echelon lot, for example, those who are new wave, currently fashionable . . .'

I smiled back, thinking that in some way I was being got at.

'Though currently fashionable only because they are violently anti-Establishment. They like the idea of coal mines and railway yards. You know the kind of thing.'

That, at least, got me off the hook. I did more nodding.

'Until they get a taste for high living, that is. Then, of course, they are no longer anti-Establishment. Most of them are, predictably, quite ugly. I wonder when this vogue for ugliness will end?'

Now I wondered whether he was warning me about the pit-falls of success or merely calling me unattractive.

'Well, they won't last – unless they stick to Brecht or Wesker. Then there are those awful social actors, you know – the kind that are very busy with the spastics and so on. All they really want to be is *knighted*. They're social climbers of the worst kind, not at all interested in their craft. Oh – I've been doing appeals on the telly for thalidomide children. I must be careful or I'll be in the queue for an MBE or something.'

All this makes Bogarde sound rather more peevish and sour than he was; he was in truth very generous to me, and often very funny, and so long as certain ground rules were adhered to concerning his comfort and circumstances, then all was well. If at times he came across as fragile and bruised, there was also a sense that this might have been a mask. He was a very reserved man, and I often thought that some of the things he said and did were mannerisms, and mannerisms used to conceal the fear that actually there wasn't much going on beneath the surface, an anxiety that was both modest and unjust.

Perhaps he recognized in me a familiar sense of emptiness, and in Bee its remedial antidote. Certainly there were technical parallels in our screen careers. He had tried to shake off the trappings of being an international star, coming to hate the chirpy Simon Sparrow character he played in the Doctor films. He was convinced, with very good reason, that he was not just handsome but intelligent and talented, and picked increasingly non-assertive, discerning roles to demonstrate the fact. In effect, he reinvented himself as a soft screen presence who relied on control and an air of fragile but enduring gentility. And it was this sense of inventive control that he passed on to me and which remains the best lesson I have ever had. In many ways, we are very different actors, but on film we both developed the habit of playing around the main action, off the beat, as it were, and becoming pivotal rather than leading players. We were both at our best when not expected to carry a film, at least not carry it in the conventional Hollywood manner. That perceived similarity, deriving perhaps from a dread of emptiness (more founded in my case than his), may have been one of the reasons why we developed a friendship and why he gave me his time.

What he told me about actors in the back of the Rolls was not, I now understand, bitchy or undermining, but the acknowledgement of one non-assertive actor to another. He knew that I wasn't a film star either by temperament or technique or physical attribute.

Although I can't deny that I felt more comfortable with Tote (which was how Tony Forwood referred to himself) than Bogarde, all four of us became friends during filming of *The Fixer*. Over the years, we would stay in contact, visit one another, correspond, and recall those strange days in Hungary.

The last time Bogarde and Tote ferried us back to Budapest after a weekend in Vienna, they packed a bundle of *Playboy* magazines into the boot and left one on the dashboard, open at its revealing centrefold.

'What are those for?' I asked. 'Are you going to give them to the crew?'

'They,' said Bogarde, 'are for the guards at the border.'

'They'll find her,' said Tote, brandishing Miss December or whoever, 'then search for the others, and confiscate the *lot*!'

They both looked like triumphant schoolboys, but could see that I didn't understand. 'Then they'll leave us alone,' Bogarde explained.

'And they won't spend hours taking the car apart.'

It was true that a few weeks before, the guards had taken up the entire floor of the Rolls to search for stowaways and smuggled goods. Bogarde thought it was something about being British they didn't care for, and he quite liked the fact that he was driving around a Communist country in this expensive symbol of national pride.

'Those guards can't read,' he said, 'but they sure as hell know a pair of tits when they see them.'

7

INTO THE WILDERNESS

Bee and I kept in regular contact with Bogarde and Tote, sometimes going to spend weekends with them at Adam's Farm, then when they moved to France visiting them every summer at Le Haut Clermont. For the next dozen or so years, they were very good friends – or 'super chums', as Bogarde would call us. I did more and more film work, punctuated with television roles (a few good, a few bad, a few downright awful) and a handful of plays. The cosiness of film work appealed to my lazier side. Bee thought it was because I liked the money, enjoyed operating from a safe nest and not having to deal with the grinding routine of repertory theatre, and sallying forth to make a few bob.

I talked about this with Bogarde, being vaguely aware that in some way I was beginning to sell myself a little short, that the work was not doing me justice. I suppose this was an inevitable feeling after the ambitious highs of Stratford and Pinter. Bogarde had been through the same kind of thing, and offered useful advice. He told me the profession was necessarily about balancing 'the bread bit with one's pride', and though there were moments when things got out of kilter, you just had to accept it and get on. He said I was lucky because all the work I had done early on had allowed me to earn 'self pride for no bread', whereas he had done things the other way round, so that when he did *Accident*, for example, for not much money, he felt 'poorer but richer', but then when he needed money for taxes or a new kitchen, he did things like *The Fixer*.

Frankenheimer's name came up quite often in conversation; Bogarde referred to him as 'Frankenstein' or 'the dreaded Frankenstein', and the film as 'The Misery'.

'The thing is, Ian,' he told me, 'too much work like *The Fixer* will make you physically ill. I don't think that in the long run it really works. Once one is out of the wood, so to speak, and can steady oneself financially – even a little – "Back to Quality" is the motto. Self-respect for a man after a certain age is terribly important in actors. Does one want to be a Burton? An O'Toole? Or a *Leslie Phillips*? Besides, I find the parts that don't pay well are usually the most interesting. I got pennies for *Death in Venice* . . . we had to pay our own expenses, even . . . but what a chance to act for the cinema! It was worth *paying* to be in it. So, Ian, if your hunch is to piss off out of the inhuman, spiritless work, then play it. It does no good to one's soul . . . unless one happens to be Kenneth More, and therefore soulless.'

And I think that Bogarde was right. During the years following *The Fixer* I did try to keep the 'bread' balanced by the 'pride', but it was difficult, and landed me some horrible work. At first, I found this hard to bear. I had become used to playing material which gained me respect as well as a living. For the obvious reasons, film and television roles were more difficult to predict. Thus, for example, I made *A Severed Head* in 1971, which had showed all the right signs – a novel by an acclaimed writer (Iris Murdoch), which was adapted by a good screenwriter (Frederic Raphael). Though the director Dick Clement was known mostly for his comedy work, he also seemed to offer some guarantee of quality. The result, however, was a muddle; it was worthy but unspectacular. Bee thought that the British film industry's obsession with turning everyone into a star (it had worked a bit with Alan Bates and Albert Finney, for example) was foolish.

Although *A Severed Head* offered me my first nominal film lead, I now know that I was miscast. Realistically, my physical size and technical range made me a perfect character actor, though it was some time before casting agents and producers understood this, and I suspect I didn't appreciate it then either. I recall meeting Dame Iris some years after the film had been made. She was walking through Hampstead and I went over and introduced myself. She looked at me in a sort of benign, rather glazed manner, then her face broke into a beatific smile and she said, 'Why, of course. You're my Martin.'

The truth is that, so far as films went, Bee had hit on something. I rather enjoyed them. Not all stage actors did – Alan Howard disliked them, Michael Bryant hated them, Michael Gambon learnt over time to feel at home, and even Judi Dench found them awkward, only hitting the straps later on in her career – but I took to the medium almost immediately. As much as anything else, the method of work and the ambience appealed to me. I liked, for example, the fact that every single person on set was working towards a single specified moment, something you never quite got in the theatre. There's more money at stake in films, of course, and I suspect this concentrates the mind wonderfully. Whether I'm any good is for other people to judge, but years later, while filming *Lord of the Rings*, Ian McKellen said, 'It all seems so easy for you, Ian. You seem so relaxed, as if you understand film intuitively.' Now McKellen is a brilliant actor and can do film work very well indeed (in *Gods and Monsters*, for instance), but he is essentially a dramatic actor, and though that kind of staginess suited his playing of Gandalf, generally I think it is a strain for him to pare down a performance for the camera.

The ease I felt on set was reflected in my domestic life. In 1972, Bee and I had bought Wassall House in Kent, a largish, three-hundred-year-old place in the country with sloping floors, which, initially at least, came to resemble a youth hostel. It was spacious but not grand. We – or, I should say, Bee – kept chickens, dogs roamed around, and the house always seemed to be full of children. Lissy and Barnaby would walk down the lane and help to milk the cows. Jessica and Sarah-Jane came to visit. And I would go running along the small roads, surprised at how much I liked it.

I got into the habit of inviting people with whom I was work-ing down to Wassall for the weekend, and Bee was a wonderfully welcoming, casual hostess. Alice Lee Boatwright – known as Boatie – was a frequent visitor. She had been intro-duced to us by Bogarde and Tony Forwood, and had once been a casting director (on *To Kill a Mockingbird*, for example). She was also at one time married to Terence Baker, a crazy, often drunk Irishman, who would later earn notoriety as Jeffrey Archer's agent, famously providing him with a false alibi and then dying prior to Archer's court case. Once Boatie stayed at Wassall with Gig Young, an actor who had really made his name in *They Shoot Horses, Don't They?*, for which he won the supporting-actor Oscar. At the time, he was supposed to be on the wagon, though Bee and I watched as our vodka kept disappearing. He also arrived with an assortment of suits and tuxedos, evidently assuming that 'a weekend at Wassall House' meant cocktails on the verandah at six and formal dinners, rather than sitting cross-legged on the floor and eating stew. A little shamed, Bee and I gave Boatie and Gig our own bedroom, though they were woken early by Fido, our friendly mongrel, who hadn't worked out any change in the sleeping arrangements. Gig was very put out by this intrusion, and in any case his relationship with Boatie soon withered, something for which she was always grateful. Two or three years later, in 1978, Gig and his fifth wife were found shot dead in a New York apartment. It was assumed that Gig had done the shooting. Boatie joked, 'If Fido hadn't arrived when he did, Gig and I could still have been together. That dog saved my life!'

A couple of years after moving in to Wassall, we built a swimming pool, though only after reluctantly uprooting an old quince tree. By the time the pool actually had water in it, the summer had gone and the autumn rains were just beginning. I had never learnt to swim, being wary of water ever since my brother Eric had frightened me in the sea, and being short with heavy shoulders, I was the wrong shape to find the simple act of floating very straightforward. Bee taught me to swim. I learnt by staying close to the side and moving very slowly, my head disappearing beneath the water often and for quite long periods of time, like a kind of defective prototype submarine.

So here I was, safe inside my nest, nipping off to make a bit of 'bread' whenever I had a job. And as Bee pointed out, I was a nice, quite well-off middle-class boy from the suburbs who had never not had money – or not *not* had it in the way that her bohemian family had gone without – so it was only natural that I should take some primordial comfort from its presence.

Projects came and went in something of a blur during those years. For television I did the disastrous *Napoleon and Love*, from which I emerged more or less unscathed. I seem to remember the original project was to follow the whole of Napoleon's life, though lack of money only allowed it to focus on his romantic exploits. It was rather like a series on Churchill concentrating on his contribution to oil painting. There was also a piece called *Lloyd George* for Harlech, which was done at a time when not many people were doing stuff in Wales. We were left more or less to ourselves and, I think, made a good programme. My chief recollection, however, is of going into the pub in George's village home. One of the locals – old, beaten-up, lived-in face, hand tight round a glass of stout – called us over and said, 'You know why there's a huge stone on top of Lloyd George's grave, don't you?'

There was indeed a large monolithic slab of marble laid on top of the great man's resting place, though I didn't know precisely why it was there and accordingly shook my head.

'To keep the bugger's cock down,' the old man concluded.

Apart from *A Severed Head*, I did *The Bofors Gun* (1968), *Mary, Queen of Scots* (1971) – which degenerated into a kind of village pageant in which I was Rizzio and learnt to play the lute – *Young Winston* (1972), and in 1974 something called *Juggernaut*, which was directed by Dick Lester. It was also the first time I acted with Barnaby. I played Nicholas Porter, the owner of a cruise liner which was, the script announced, supposed to symbolize England. That is, everything on board went wrong. It was meant to be a sardonic commentary on a fading, troubled country, with the passengers all being stoic and sensible while everything around them fell apart. Omar Sharif played the seedy, demoralized captain whose ship was threatened with a bomb planted by a demolition expert called Jones. I just remember being grateful that as the owner I was not on board the hired Russian cruise liner that was used, and which set sail deliberately to find bad weather. It returned – eventually – with reports of horrible storms off Iceland and everyone getting drunk to deal with it. The story was that the bar closed only between seven and seven-thirty in the morning.

When I told all this to Bogarde and Tote on one of our visits, they thought it quite appropriate that a film made about the awful state of 'the home country' should itself be pretty awful. By then they had moved to France, fed up with England and

Englishness and the lack of culture. 'I read the reviews,' Bogarde said (he always read the reviews), 'and though some were jolly funny, I think your reputation is still intact. After all, everyone knows that sometimes an actor does need the lolly. The only thing which sickens me is the Great Unwashed who care for that more than *The Homecoming* or *Richard III*. It's really chips with everything, isn't it?' This was characteristic; warming to a theme in such a way that he could eventually become cruelly, irresistibly, unreasonably funny. 'I sometimes feel that we shouldn't indulge their silly little brains,' he continued, 'and force them to watch *proper* things *properly* done. However, that's another argument. I do LOATHE their silly faces and their sillier minds. So there!'

But of course *Juggernaut* was not seen by many people, least of all the Great Unwashed. However, all the films were worthy, if uninspiring, and in a strange way, so I was informed, made me something of a household name, though a name in what kinds of household I didn't know. All I did know was that I was more or less gainfully employed and quite enjoying myself.

Sandwiched somewhere in the middle of all this, in 1969, was Richard Attenborough's *Oh! What a Lovely War*. This was a sprawling, stylized musical satire about World War One, set on Brighton Pier and starring just about everybody, including the three knights – Olivier, Gielgud and Richardson – and Bogarde. I hadn't met Attenborough before this, but knew that he had bought a place near to Bogarde and Tote in France, for which, to their delight, he had paid over the odds. Still, I found myself warming to him as the film was shot, and by the end I wouldn't hear a word said against him. He was genuine and kind, and though his reputation for 'luvviness' was in some ways deserved, his manner was entirely genuine rather than affected. Most important, he was a sort of head prefect for the British film industry, and respected as such. Which was just as well with the cast he had assembled, otherwise the project would have skewed out of control.

I played the French president, and was given a bald pate by Stewart Freebourn, one of the best make-up artists in the business, who claimed he was among the pioneer users of bald caps. One of my memories of the film is sitting with such a cap, waiting to go on set, on a bench next to Ralph Richardson, who was staring intently at the sea. He sat quite still, charming and abstracted, locked into his own world, looking as though he belonged on an entirely different planet from the one he actually inhabited. It was sometimes difficult to work out whether he was rather simple – though simple with good-mannered grace – or somehow very wise and above merely mortal considerations. He never quite seemed to know where or even who he was, and this gave him an air of dreamy mysteriousness. It was exaggerated, I thought, by the way he was scrutinizing the English Channel, as though on the point of some significant but unsayable discovery about human existence.

We had been sitting there for some time when I wondered whether I ought to say something.

'Look. There's a cormorant,' I finally announced, pointing up at a largish bird which was swooping low over the set.

Richardson didn't move a muscle. He continued to stare at the breakers, apparently oblivious to all around him. I felt foolish and didn't say anything else, grateful after a short while to be called on to the set.

Two hours later I was back on the bench again, and after a short while so was Richardson.

'It was a tern,' he said, looking implacable and straight ahead.

Richardson was also present when Olivier invited me along for lunch at his house, which was in Brighton. Gielgud completed the set of theatrical knights, while at the other end of the table I sat in awkward reverence with two other commoners,

Paul Damon and Joe Melia. It was an extraordinary spectacle. I seem to remember there were a lot of stories about Edith Evans. The three great men held forth to a captive audience, telling and re-telling anecdotes, all intent on having the best or the last word and doing it 'in character'. Olivier was all rhetorical flourish and nervous energy with frequent slaps of the table, Gielgud giggling frivolously but still managing to be rather reserved and stiff-backed, and Richardson always on the point of leaving before turning back at the door and saying, 'Oh yes, I've just remembered . . .'

However, despite the odd highlights and the increased sense of financial security, I was still vaguely uneasy about the quality of the work I was doing. 'I think your reputation is still intact,' Bogarde had suggested ominously. But how long, I wondered, could it withstand the mild, persistent slapping of mediocrity?

I was reminded of such misgivings several years later, in 1975, during work on the film *Robin and Marian*. I played King John, and the only thing I can remember about it was waiting at the bottom of a steep hill for the mounted Kenneth Haigh to gallop towards me. The shot was a tricky one and I was required to hang around for several hours, dolled up in kingly robes, uncomfortable and bored. Suddenly I saw Kenneth thundering towards me. I had not heard the director Richard Lester call 'Action!', but as the horse drew up in front of me and Haigh said his lines, I shot out a reply.

'Cut!' shouted Lester. He strolled over and put his arm round me. 'Really nice, Ian. *Really* nice.'

'Is that it?' I asked.

'Thanks very much, Ian. Really nice. I do hope next time we have a bit longer with you.'

And then he walked away.

Around the same time I also did *Shout at the Devil*, an

action-adventure film set in Africa and directed by Peter Hunt. If *Robin and Marian* reminded me to ask why I did films at all, *Shout at the Devil* supplied a few of the answers. My relationship with Bee had come under strain, mostly because of an affair I was having. I took the job as much to get away from things as anything else, and going to Africa was a fair distance to run. Perhaps appropriately, my fear of deep water almost got me drowned, as I became entangled in a kaftan while shooting a scene in a river.

Roger Moore and Lee Marvin were also in the film, and though I became quite friendly with Marvin, Moore was never less than charming and delightful, calling me 'Shakespeare' and – in contrast to the very tough, masculine roles he often played (remember he was then James Bond; admittedly a rather camp one, but still Bond) – not afraid to show himself as completely faint-hearted.

One scene required Moore, Marvin, myself and, I think, a make-up artist to go quite far into the jungle, and we duly took off from Johannesburg to fly into the Kruger National Park. We hit bad weather and had to fly through cloud for forty minutes or so, during which time the small plane bucked and reared alarmingly. Most of us were quiet and pensive, contemplating the worst though willing it not to happen, but Moore squirmed and whimpered for most of the journey. Eventually, he lay down on his back and started to undo his trousers. Then his hand disappeared down the front of them.

'What the fuck are you doing, Roger?' snarled Marvin, who was accustomed to Roger's clowning around.

'If I'm going to Heaven,' Moore replied, ever the actor, 'I want to go with a smile on my face.'

But humour and geography couldn't keep my domestic circumstances from catching up with me.

One day Bee telephoned and said, 'Your little ivory tower has collapsed. I know all about your affairs . . . and by the way, I'm having one as well.'

I began to cry and eventually collapsed, sobbing and helpless, into Lee Marvin's arms. Now Marvin was a genuinely hard man. He knew from his war experiences the depths of cruelty and evil to which men could sink. He had probably committed such deeds himself, and had made a career in films from playing persuasive incarnations of evil. He was a man of violence who looked capable of raw brutality and made even someone like John Wayne look artificial and glossy. So what was this type of man going to do with a smallish British actor carrying on like a child about the relatively unimportant news that his partner was having an affair?

As I blubbed, Marvin gazed at me with a kind of blank, chilling hostility that was somehow softened by understanding and an inexpressible desire to be kind. He stroked my hair. 'Ian, let me tell you one thing. We all go through an awful lot of fucking in this life.'

He was very kind and the rest of the film was fine, though the dilemma remained. I was using films to escape from the mess of my life, some of which (the temptations, the nagging sense of mediocrity) was caused by film itself.

Though I had not abandoned theatre altogether, even these attempts to balance the books (as it were) were hardly great successes. In 1970, for example, I did two plays, *The Friends* by Arnold Wesker and *A Bequest to the Nation* by Terence Rattigan. Amongst the cast of the first was Victor Henry, probably one of the finest actors I've ever met. *The Friends* was to be performed at the Roundhouse, and as part of the company bonding process, Wesker invited us all back to his house for food and drinks. What started as an evening of warm conviviality somehow descended into one of sour madness. Afterwards, nobody talked to Wesker and everyone decided they disliked him intensely. This was somehow linked to the discovery that Wesker's even temper and apparent amiability were dependent on people's good opinions of him. When it became clear that he wouldn't respect anyone who didn't think he was marvellous, things began to unravel.

As a consequence, the production was an eerie, nightmarish one, with the author having to write notes to the cast on a board as there was no other way of communicating. This lack of correspondence was also apparent in the actual playing, and I seem to remember that the in-fighting and general hostility surrounding the production even became the subject for a feature in one of the Sunday papers.

A Bequest to the Nation was better, though it was neither a happy nor a fulfilling experience. It opened in September at the Theatre Royal in Haymarket, and I played the part of Nelson, with Leueen McGrath as Lady Nelson and Zoe Caldwell as Lady Hamilton. It had been over a decade since Rattigan's last hit, and as a playwright he had not only become quite reviled (often by Ken Tynan, his *bête noire*), but worse, ignored. He was quite ill and living in semi-retirement in Bermuda, apparently playing endless rounds of golf with himself. I suspect to Rattigan's surprise, the play actually did pretty well, running for three months and 124 performances. In addition, it prompted a revival of *The Winslow Boy*.

However, I couldn't help feeling that I was participating in a relic, that the play was somehow out of its time and the goodish notices were inspired by nostalgic generosity as much as any-thing else. It wasn't a bad piece of work and it wasn't a bad production, but a story set almost two hundred years ago about a great patriot who maintains his dignity even amid the struggles of an irregular private life was hardly at the cutting edge. Rattigan was a refugee from a time when writers were forced to hide ideas behind a story their audiences would accept, and increasingly I felt awkward in the role. It did pay well (I don't recall the figure, but Bogarde wrote to Bee and me as 'Darling Snowflake and Millionaire'; this must have been around the time we bought Wassall House), but somehow it wasn't the meaningful, soul-saving work for which I had been searching. Still, there were good moments. Brian Glover, for example, was also a member of the cast, playing Hardy. He used to be a wrestler and was fond of getting me in an arm lock and shouting, 'How's that for a half-Nelson?'

I had dinner with John Gielgud, I think at some time during the run, and he remarked how happy I must be to be back on stage. 'Back where you belong,' he announced silkily. He always thought that films were slightly odd, even vulgar, regarding them with amused tolerance as one does energetic puppies. I replied that it was good to be back, though the experience wasn't quite as satisfying as I'd hoped. There was a rumour that he too had been asked to play Nelson and so I asked him about it. He looked at me and giggled. 'My dear boy,' he said, 'I'm too old, too tall, I'd have lost Trafalgar, and I certainly couldn't fuck Emma.'

It is difficult to discern patterns in one's life while that life is being lived (difficult, that is, to see what would nowadays be called karma), but looking back it is clear to me now that pressures were building within me – pressures of mildly but persistently thwarted expectation, of a slight falling off, per- haps, and a sense that things were getting away from me. The period of eight years or so after Stratford and *The Homecoming* was a crucible of simmering frustration, occasionally expressed, never absolutely remedied, and soothed by regular work and the comforts of money. Though I never did anything truly awful or received such scathing personal notices that I was jerked into some kind of response, I did feel as if I was drowning, though drowning gently and pleasantly.

One episode in particular seems to encapsulate all this. In 1969 I had several meetings with Stanley Kubrick about playing the part of Napoleon in an ambitious film he was planning. I allowed myself to believe that this was 'it' – the lead in a big movie (a *Stanley Kubrick* movie) that would be guaranteed critical respectability. Double top.

My agent Julian Belfrage told me that the great man wanted to see me and that the whole thing was 'VERY SECRET'. First, we spoke with each other on the phone.

'Ian.'

'Yes.'

'It's Stanley.'

'Yes.'

'Stanley Kubrick.'

'Oh, yes. Hello.'

'I thought it would be a good idea to speak before we met.'

'Absolutely.'

'Ian, do you ride?'

'How do you mean?'

'Do you ride horses?'

'No. Why?'

'Doesn't matter. We'll deal with that when we get to it. OK?'

'Yes. I mean, I suppose I could learn,' I said with blank eagerness.

Remember that at this point I had no idea about the Napoleon project. Kubrick had this way of being able to focus very intensely and with disarming casualness on fragments of conversation. You never quite knew where he was headed or whether he was much interested in your answers. So he changed the subject, abruptly and entirely.

'I liked what you did in *Richard III*.'

'Thank you. Did you see it?'

'Very fine work indeed, Ian.'

'Thank you.'

'We should talk about it sometime.'

Though we never did, at least not in detail. For the next six months or so I was a regular visitor to Kubrick's home in Hertfordshire, and was drawn into his strange, not-quite-whole world, always with the carrot of Napoleon dangling just out of reach.

Sometimes I drove to his house, sometimes a taxi picked me up from the railway station at St Albans. There was never any realistic chance of Kubrick venturing into the outside world. Getting to his house at all seemed a way of imprinting his fundamental mysteriousness on you. From St Albans I drove along country roads, through ornate metal gates, past a Gothic-looking lodge, down a private road, past a 'Private Property' sign, then through two more sets of gates, and finally to a huge house, which was, it seemed, deliberately and even boastfully set apart from the rest of the world. Kubrick's Kingdom. Though even this cryptic statement was qualified. Although the house was enormous, it was somehow not grand, being low and wide rather than high and imposing. It was homeliness gone wrong. There were several cars on the gravel drive, though none of them looked much cared for. Or even as if they were for driving. They just sort of littered the place, as if the thought had occurred that driveways ought to have cars.

I walked up to what was a relatively modest front door. Kubrick opened it himself (I had expected Gormenghast-type servants), looking a bit like the man who'd come to fix the boiler. He was smallish and shy. For a split second, it seemed as if he was the one waiting to come in and I was expected to invite him inside.

He stuck out a hand and said, 'Hello. I'm Stanley.'

Inside was strangely like outside, the house full of disordered belongings incidentally scattered around the vast interior in the same unintentional way that the cars had been left on the drive. There were some paintings by his wife Christiane on the walls, mostly bright landscapes or colourful floral pictures that were out of keeping with the vague sense of abandonment.

For several months I kept returning, to eat meals and talk with Kubrick, always talking about Napoleon, though never in any concrete way, and sometimes about other things besides. He gave me books to read on the subject of Napoleon and suggested other things I might like to look over. He was absolutely immersed in cinema and found it difficult to talk about much beyond this or his own projects. But he had a tentative, mildly beguiling manner that made you feel very intimate with him, as if you were getting on.

This impression would often be reinforced during our talks by him saying something like, 'Have we done anything useful today?' as if you had somehow attained a position of some authority. He was nice, smart and 'thick' with me without ever being personal. It was intimacy without commitment.

I think he was interested in me for his Napoleon because I was the right size (i.e., small) and because, in his mind, Richard III was a similar kind of man, able to combine cruelty and aloofness with an engaging allure.

'Have you thought of anything yet, Ian?' he'd ask at the start of our sessions.

'After what we talked about last time?'

'Yes.'

'A bit. I'm not sure Napoleon should be entirely without humour,' I might say.

'Really? Interesting.'

'He seems to appeal to so many different kinds of people.'

'Go on.'

'Well, I'm wondering if humour might be a sign of flexibility. You know, that he can see things from more than one angle.'

'That's good.'

'Thank you, Stanley.'

'Think you can play him like that, Ian?'

'If that's what you want.'

'I don't know what I want, *exactly*.'

As the months went by, I began to sense that he was more interested in me (or what I could offer) than I in him. Without him giving himself away, I felt dimly as if I was being subtly mugged of ideas. Being with Kubrick was exhausting, not because I was trying to keep pace with him, but because he was taking something from me without offering much in return.

Encouraged by Kubrick and with the role of Napoleon more or less (so I thought) in the bag, I started to take riding lessons, falling off quite often but gradually getting the hang of it. Once, while shooting something for television in Wales, I went over the top of a horse's head when it suddenly and unaccountably changed direction. I remember a woman standing just outside the field watching the whole thing. She came over to me and said in a plummy voice, 'Why didn't you hold on to the *reins*?' I merely got up, dusted myself down, and remounted.

And on it went. I read Kubrick's books. I ate with Kubrick. I talked with Kubrick. But still there was no firm offer. Everything but.

I knew that Kubrick was a ranking chess player, and that he was therefore used to playing this kind of game. But I could never quite believe that I would not be playing his Napoleon at some time in the not very distant future. I began to think irrationally: maybe he's taking his time because he'll never do anything until he's absolutely sure it will work. After all, I reasoned, he's a Jew, and possibly sensitive to being rebuffed. I had also heard, for example, that many years ago, when Kubrick was a writer, Gregory Peck had hurt him over some work. All this, I convinced myself, had made him afraid of giving too much away, of acting impulsively, of committing himself.

Then I read in a newspaper that he was considering David Hemmings (and later, I think, Jack Nicholson) for the part of Napoleon, that David Hemmings would be his choice of actor when the project got made. No mention of me. I tried calling Kubrick on the phone and was – in the politest, gentlest, mildest way – given the brush-off. I never saw him again. The film never got made. There were so many other Napoleon projects in development that Kubrick turned his attention instead to *A Clockwork Orange*.

At the time, I was very disappointed and probably very angry. Now it seems like part of some oddly inevitable design, the distress and gentle, impatient disenchantment an irresistible culmination of events that had gradually been squeezing me since *The Homecoming*.

The project which brought all this most sharply to a head was the shooting of Zeffirelli's *Jesus of Nazareth* a few years later in 1975/6. By that time, the string of modestly acceptable but ultimately harmful roles I had accepted were taking their toll, and my relationship with Bee – stretched to breaking point by my inability to resist the thrill of the romantic chase – was in a fragile state.

When it was agreed that I would be working with Zeffirelli, Bee and I decided I should take a tax year out of the country. We rented a farmhouse in the South of France, not merely for financial reasons, of course, but also to sort out our own relationship. The farm had its own vineyard and the idyllic setting, I am sure, helped the healing process. We spent the time reading, walking on the nearby beach, swimming and generally relaxing. Bee's sister Jannie came out to teach Lissy and Barnaby. We returned to England briefly, to see friends and organize ourselves, and then we went off to Africa as a happy family. Joel Grey saw us off from Wassall. I remember him waving at our departing car and singing, 'You're off on the road to Morocco . . .' It seemed like a good omen.

Jesus was shot in Tunisia and Morocco, and was made over a period of almost two years. Lew Grade produced it, and Zeffirelli was invited to show the full humanity of Christ in a kind of extended, sequential epic of His story for television – from miraculous birth to Crucifixion to Resurrection. Although my part was relatively slight (all roles were relatively slight, save that of Jesus, who was played by Robert Powell) – I was Zerah, of the Sanhedrin – I was on call for almost the whole of the four months I was out there. I didn't have much to do with great chunks of the film and I therefore didn't really feel part of the project. It was, I suppose, a harsh illustration that in film you are really only a small cog in a very big wheel. And as I liked (and needed) to feel part of the whole deal, I became increasingly irritated by the peripheral part I was playing.

It was the worst side of making movies. I disliked intensely the idea of 'slotting in' for a few days, and here I was, on a seemingly infinite loop of slot and re-slot. I was never entirely 'in' or 'out' of the picture, and this caused me, I think, to become gradually unhinged. The gruelling physical locations only made matters worse. These days, of course, Tunisia and Morocco are good holiday destinations, but thirty years ago the hotels were basic, the food was inedibly cold (even when sent back to be reheated it returned in much the same dreadful state), there was very little to do, there was too much dust, and the baking-hot weather sapped whatever was left of your energy.

In addition, Zeffirelli seemed to have chosen his locations with authenticity as the only criterion. Often, they were so authentic that they had no electricity or power. He was under the mistaken impression that the actors and crew were as gripped by the story as he was, and set about making the film with a kind of blinkered, well-intentioned mania. He wanted the best casting for each role, which meant that the cast list read like a *Who's Who* of famous actors: Olivier, Steiger, Mason, Quinn *et al* were all lined up for their piece of this biblical epic.

The project, however, was dogged by difficulties and fall-outs. Initially, Zeffirelli had been very enthusiastic about his casting of Powell as Jesus, seeing something magical and charismatic in the young actor's eyes. Powell, however, struggled under the real and imagined scrutiny of so many great actors, and the director soon tired of him, at one point even telling him, 'Darling, just go and watch Larry [Olivier] and ask him to give you some acting lessons.'

There was an increasing sense that we were pawns in Zeffirelli's great operatic project. He produced rather beautiful, very detailed drawings of how he wanted each scene, each shot to appear, cramming them with architectural detail and crowds of people. Even Lew Grade, who generally loved the idea of films being so much window dressing, felt compelled to point out the difference between film and television.

'Everything's too big,' I heard him say to Zeffirelli at one point.

'Is big subject,' he replied.

'Yes. But remember, this is for television. The screen is smaller.'

'I know that. So what you suggest, eh?'

Grade considered.

'This next scene, for example,' he eventually said, fingering a script and pointing to the one set in the Garden of Gethsemane.

'Yes. What about it?'

'It's got the Apostles in it.'

'Yes. They were all there. That's the point.'

'But twelve of them. Twelve Apostles! Can't we have a few less?'

Above: My mother and father – sober, undemonstrative, well-meaning people.

Left: Me on a blanket with my brother Eric, in the jacket, looking down at me. The woman looking after us all is not my mother, but a family friend called Ina. Had I been a girl, I too would have taken this name – an anagram of 'Ian'. **Below, left:** And the first photograph of me.

Below, right: My father is at the back, on the left. Next to him is Mrs Mayberry. I suspect he had a soft spot for her. Her husband, Dr Mayberry, is in front, wearing the bow-tie. I am in an uncharacteristically rakish position, school cap set at a jaunty angle. My mother is directly behind me.

Right: As a schoolboy. I knew the precise whereabouts of the camera's lens.

Top: Henry Baynton, provincial actor of some distinction. He took a keen hand in my early development.

Top, right: Watching and admiring Olivier in *Titus Andronicus* (1957). Maxine Audley is Tamora.

Centre: Curtain call for *A Midsummer Night's Dream*. I played Puck and Charles Laughton (ginger hair) was an acclaimed Bottom . . .

. . . but a less successful Lear (**above**). Here I am, clinging to the wreckage.

Right: *Twelfth Night* in 1958: I played Sebastian and Dorothy Tutin is Viola. Between us, Geraldine McEwan is Olivia.

Top: My off-stage role as husband and father. With Lynne, friends and family at Jessica's christening. She was my first child – and as the middle picture suggests, I was delighted by this sudden change of luck with relationships. Soon after came Sarah-Jane, pictured here in a mobile shopping basket in the garden at Avoncliffe.

Above left: As Richard of Gloucester/King Richard III in Wars of the Roses (1963–4). A major breakthrough for me.

Above: With Eric Porter in *Henry IV, Part 2* (1964). I am Prince Hal . . . soon to become Henry V (**above right**).

Below left: RSC discussion group for Pinter's *The Homecoming*, 1965. Peter Hall is on the left (facing) and I am in the centre. Pinter himself is on the far left sofa with his back to the camera.

Below: As Lenny in *The Homecoming*, with Paul Rogers as Max.

Bee is Hiawatha. Our children, Barnaby and Lissy.

Top left: With Richard Attenborough and Lee Remick in *The Severed Head* (1970). The year before, Attenborough had directed me in *Oh! What A Lovely War* (**right**).

Left: As Zerah of the Sanhedrin in *Jesus of Nazareth*. A gruelling shoot which eventually took its toll.

Above: As Hickey in *The Iceman Cometh*, playing opposite Patrick Stewart. The play had an unexpectedly profound and unpleasant effect on my career, the significance of which is only hinted at in the programme's apology.

THE ICEMAN COMETH

HARRY HOPE	NORMAN RODWAY
ED MOSHER	HARRY TOWB
PAT McGLOIN	ALAN TILVERN
ROCKY	BOB HOSKINS
CHUCK	DAVID DAKER
PIET WETJOEN	HAL GALILI
CECIL LEWIS	RICHARD SIMPSON
JIMMY TOMORROW	JOHN WARNER
JOE MOTT	CY GRANT
LARRY SLADE	PATRICK STEWART
HUGO KALMAR	PATRICK GODFREY
WILLIE OBAN	GARY BOND
DON PARRITT	KENNETH CRANHAM
PEARL	PATTI LOVE
MARGIE	PAOLA DIONISOTTI
CORA	LYNDA MARCHAL
HICKEY	IAN HOLM
MORAN	LARRY HOODEKOFF
LIEB	KARL HELD
DIRECTED BY	HOWARD DAVIES
DESIGNED BY	CHRIS DYER
LIGHTING BY	DAVID HERSEY
STAGE MANAGER	PHILIP HOARE
DEPUTY STAGE MANAGER	ANDREW LORANT
ASSISTANT STAGE MANAGER	PHILLIP SEDDON
SOUND	ANNA COOKE

There are four Acts
There will be an interval of 5 minutes between ACT I and ACT II
and an interval of 20 minutes between ACT II and ACT III
Act I is 1 hour 15 minutes, Act II 50 minutes, Act III 50 minutes
and Act IV 55 minutes approximately.

Aldwych Theatre London WC2 Licensees: Theatre Consolidated
Chairman P. D. Abrahams. Managing Director John Hallett.

Owing to the indisposition of

IAN HOLM

there will be the following
changes of cast for this
performance:

HICKEY played by
ALAN TILVERN

PAT McGLOIN played by
RAYMOND MARLOW

Left: With Lee Marvin and Roger Moore in *Shout at the Devil* (1976). Above: The same film, this time only with Lee Marvin.

Above: On and off set with David Warner in *Holocaust* – for a while, I seemed to play nothing but members of the Nazi High Command.

Left: Filming *The Lost Boys*. A complex situation in the making: with writer Andrew Birkin and Barnaby. Bee is in the background, hovering between us.

Below: As J. M. Barrie in *The Lost Boys*. Barnaby is on my left.

Though I made a stage comeback in Chekhov's *Uncle Vanya* only a few years after my breakdown in *The Iceman Cometh*, it is a production that for one reason or another often slips my mind. Even now, I have very little recollection of it. Here I am with Nigel Hawthorne, who was sensitive and thoughtful about my return to the stage.

I believe that Zeffirelli tried to persuade Grade that the film should be made as if it was going to be shown on the big screen, but the tension between them only contributed to the cast's sense of being ground down by a project which was, if not out of control, never a smooth operation.

Even Olivier grew restless with the apparent timelessness of the thing. David Watkin, the lighting cameraman, complemented his director's zeal by turning each shot into a deep, rich oil painting and trying to re-create the look of an Old Master. Each set took on the look of a brilliant still-life, and it took David an eternity to set up each one. The heat from the sun and the warmth of the lights made for an intolerably unpleasant atmosphere. Olivier felt it was time to say something, though when Zeffirelli pointed out how good each frame looked, Olivier said he should not forget how much the actors had suffered while these dazzling frames were being set up. Especially him. 'Though of course,' he added mischievously, 'it's nothing compared to the suffering of Our Lord.'

In addition, Watkin was a narcoleptic who would simply fall asleep while on set. Sometimes we would be waiting impatiently for what we presumed were the finishing touches of a set-up, only to discover that he had dropped off for a few minutes. He was, however, wonderful at his job, and at his best during the moments in the temple when the Sanhedrin met under the High Priest Caiaphas to interrogate Christ. Although he brilliantly caught the splendour and magnificence of the scene, Grade was once again snapping at Zeffirelli's heels while the rest of us stood around getting hot. This time he was worried about over-running, and suggested cuts in the number of words we should speak. The scene included a number of 'greats', and it was usually impossible to ask actors of such renown to reduce their parts, especially as there wasn't in fact a great deal of money involved in the first place.

Again, Olivier, who I now suspected just wanted to get out of there, acted as a kind of shop steward.

'Darling,' he said to either Grade or Zeffirelli (or both? or neither?), 'I'm going to offer you a little flower. A couple of flowers. Can I cut these lines together?'

He showed them the script. They nodded. The rest of us took our cue.

With characteristic modesty, I said, 'I've very little here, but I can do with even less.'

We all looked at Quinn, who was playing Caiaphas and could probably have made do with a *lot* less. He stalled. Olivier grew impatient. 'Surely, dear boy, if you read it carefully you'll find a few things you can do without quite well.'

But Quinn wouldn't be moved, and when Olivier insisted, Quinn deliberately strung out his remaining lines so that they occupied more or less the same amount of time. Mason and Olivier wrung their hands in exasperation as Quinn spoke. 'Loooorrrrrrrrrrrd, Ourrrrr Gaaaaaahhhhhhhdd,' he warbled, mangling the words with sing-song elasticity.

Such truculence wasn't unusual behaviour for Quinn, who was generally a difficult and moody bugger, keeping more or less to himself and playing chess all day, every day.

'I think you'll find, dear boy,' Olivier said after the second or third take, 'that darling Franco has the scissors when it comes to what will be shown and what will be cut.'

Whenever Zeffirelli got fed up, he would shout, 'I am bored now. Let's call it a day,' and off he'd go to find some Arab boys, arriving back at two or three in the morning, leaving the cast to take off their heavy robes, unstick their parodic beards, troop back to their ghastly hotels, and wait for the whole thing to start again the next day.

The result, of its kind, wasn't bad. Despite everything, I liked and admired Zeffirelli. Though his strength wasn't necessarily in understanding actors, he did, I think, recognize that I was feeling the pinch and tried to indicate to me how important was the role of Zerah.

'You are the scribe of the Sanhedrin,' he told me after a week or so. 'It is your job – a very, very important job – to indicate that Judas never did anything haphazardly.' He had this notion that Judas thought he was helping Jesus, that the 'betrayal' wasn't intended as such, and that Judas only kills himself when he realizes later he has actually harmed Jesus. 'So, Ian, you are Stalin's Yagoda, Hitler's Himmler, Napoleon's Fouché. You are key figure. OK?'

Then again, a few weeks later, when he thought the point needed reinforcing, he put his arm around me and said, 'Ian, in every system there is always a Zerah, the secular arm, the executor. You are that man. You are Zerah. Remember that. OK?'

Despite Zeffirelli's encouragement, I grew increasingly detached and distracted. There was nothing to do and nothing to stop me pondering my circumstances. I became friends with Rod Steiger. Bee, who had been there through all the irritation, had eventually had enough and gone back to England. Things weren't going well between us and there was a great deal of mutual suspicion. Lissy, who was now eleven, stayed on, *wanted* to stay on, even after so many months of hell. I came to rely on her, and she – along with casting director Leo Davis and her partner, actor Tony Vogel – became my mainstay. Still, I flirted with several actresses and then the producer's daughter. I was impatient and agitated, not merely with *Jesus of Nazareth* but by proxy with the paths that my career had taken. In my mind, this film came to epitomize the more general feelings of dissatisfaction and even doubt which had been mixing inside me for a number of years. The physical discomfort and the primitive conditions of Tunisia and Morocco only made things worse. I was eventually dubbed Gnome Noir by Ian McShane, who was also working on the film.

So when I was offered the chance to play Hickey in the RSC production of Eugene O'Neill's play *The Iceman Cometh*, in London and with a good cast which included many of my old Stratford friends, I accepted without hesitation. Here, I reasoned, was my salvation. Honourable, satisfying work among people I knew and trusted. I would get through *Jesus* and everything would be all right. The anticipated comforts of the play and London became something of an obsession. I stroked my increasingly ridiculous beard and counted the days.

8

THE ICEMAN GOETH

In retrospect, and considering the unreasonable amount of expectation I invested in *The Iceman Cometh*, it is not surprising that immediately prior to the very hot summer of 1976, I went mad. Or sort of mad.

After a couple of years' absence from the stage, largely spent doodling in undemanding film work, I was anxious for a return to the kind of roles which would once again stretch me. And the substantial role of Hickey did seem an excellent way to start. This is what Irving Wardle wrote in his review for *The Times*: Hickey, he said, offered 'a definitive portrait of the salesman turned guru'. It was generally accepted that the actor playing Hickey did a very good job. However, the actor he was talking about was not me. Wardle observed, almost *sotto voce*, that this actor, Alan Tilvern, had taken over the role from 'the indisposed Ian Holm'.

The word still rankles. *Indisposed*. What did people think when they read that? It implies a slight ailment, maybe a cold or a touch of the flu, and carries with it the suggestion that I was in some way disinclined to do the part. It hints at malingering, even – a childhood association, this – a problem of the bowels. And actors are peculiar people, prone to all manner of self-indulgent tantrums. On the temperamental side, quite liable to go off the deep end every now and then, and you *do* hear such stories about the likes of Richard Burton and Elizabeth Taylor. Thus 'indisposed' seemed to me a polite, euphemistic way of saying that I wasn't quite up to it. It's an obscuring piece of theatre shorthand which could mean almost anything, but is often taken to mean 'deficient'.

The word, which might have been designed to protect individuals by dampening public curiosity through its unspoken ambiguity, would these days produce precisely the opposite effect. Thus while I was being indisposed in a reasonably anonymous way, other, later indisposees have not been so fortunate. Daniel Day-Lewis's breakdown during a performance of *Hamlet* (of course) was followed by a media interrogation concerning the relationship between Dan and his own deceased father. In what ways, journalists asked, did he draw on personal grief to help define his portrayal of the student prince? Had his father actually come back to haunt him while he was on stage? And, more recently, Stephen Fry's decision to walk out of a Simon Gray play provoked a manhunt of Hannayesque proportions, and even inspired a book by Gray himself on the subject of the cowardly Fry's villainous betrayal.

I'm not certain whether I count as a celebrity (I don't *feel* like a celebrity), but I do know that things *vis-à-vis* fame have changed in the last twenty-five years or so. A few weeks ago, I saw a piece about me in the *Evening Standard* which announced, '*Lord of the Rings* star flies to America in cancer scare'. Now, I *was* in *Lord of the Rings* and I *had* been to New York for treatment of prostate cancer, though by the time the *Standard* got hold of the story (if that's what it was) the news was almost a year out of date. If my *Iceman* breakdown had happened today, it would have made the news, and I would have immediately been dubbed something like 'Unstately Holm' or 'Holm Sick'.

I am glad that my own crisis occurred at a time when the general public seemed less concerned with people like me. Twenty-six years on, however, I don't believe I would have been able to abscond from *The Iceman Cometh* with such shadowy ease.

I came across Wardle's piece only recently and quite by accident. It raised uncomfortable memories. I didn't see Alan Tilvern's performance (though everyone who did speaks highly of it), and it now seems peculiar that I could have spent so many weeks rehearsing something with such intensity, never to make it on to the stage for the start of the official run. When the play began – two weeks late, the postponement a strategic hiatus to see if I could get sane – I was off walking on Dartmoor.

What happened? In what way was I 'indisposed'?

I experienced some kind of breakdown – a cessation of terrifying proportions. Over time, it has been elevated to a soundbite of almost legendary status, being reported factually as a seventeen-year absence from the stage (not quite true), and psychologically as causing a long-term dread of the theatre (again, not strictly true).

Drying, cracking up, having a crisis of confidence, being temporarily insane . . . call it what you will, the condition is something which all actors carry around with them, even if they never experience it directly. It can attack the good, the bad and the moderate. It is both a specific and a generalized condition, seeming to arise out of singular, individual circumstances, yet afflicting those it assaults with an indiscriminate, all-too-familiar carelessness. Though the symptoms and the conditions might be altered, I don't suppose my experience is therefore much different from that of other actors; but it is the only one I know.

The lead up to it probably goes right back to the 1967 production of *The Homecoming* at the Music Box in New York. On stage, I was finding it very difficult to maintain my discipline in terms of stillness and accuracy, something I have always encountered with Pinter, whose plays make severe demands on an actor's concentration. Tiredness and malaise caused me to hold on to objects during the play, and occasionally I would find myself gripping the edge of a chair or leaning against a table in the middle of a scene. I didn't think too much about it at the time, took my prescribed Librium, got on with things, and filed it away at the back of my mind.

And then, as I've already explained, there was *Jesus of Nazareth*, during which I worked only for a total of about ten days, yet I had to be 'ready' at all times. The wild locations, Zeffirelli's idiosyncratic demands, the intolerable climate and the lack of basic comforts – all the things which drove cast and crew to the edge of dementia – now began to extract some kind of price. In my head, O'Neill's play had become the light at the end of the tunnel, the reward for an unpleasant job dutifully performed. I looked forward to it, keeping it in mind, turning over the challenge, thinking about the character Hickey I would be playing, even visualizing with increasing nostalgia the small changing rooms which always smelt of something damp, the cramped conditions, the familiar faces, the palatable food, Wimbledon, daily newspapers, and the cool balm of England in May.

These things helped to keep me going in Morocco and Tunisia. Without realizing it, I was already putting myself under pressure, giving the production a meaning and a symbolism it could not possibly realize. By the time I arrived back in England, *The Iceman Cometh* had assumed in my mind almost psychotic proportions, becoming an emblem of salvation.

As I've said, Bee and I were also going through what can best be described as a sticky patch. Things had not been going well since the filming of *Shout at the Devil* the previous year, a not-very-good film about men behaving badly in Africa, the macho values of which had filtered through to the cast, who spent much of the time carrying on in like fashion. We had spent the next twelve months trying to work things out, and arrived back in London tired, edgy, uncertain of one another and, despite the anticipation of working on stage again, at a pretty low ebb.

We were not even in our own home, and had to rent a house in Fulham owned by Francesca Annis and Patrick Wiseman. Our own place in Kent was too far away for the daily routine of rehearsals, so we settled into yet another temporary home, and made the best of an uncomfortable situation.

Almost from the start, things were not right. I have always been a scrupulous actor, wanting to know a play absolutely, even before rehearsals, this being a necessary position of security before I feel able to take risks. The playing of Hickey would be difficult enough, and as I've already indicated, the secure nest out of which I was used to operating had become, over the previous twelve months, quite unstable. I buried myself in Hickey, becoming even more than usually obsessive about learning lines and 'getting' the character. I developed a grinding routine of going over the play in the bath every morning, then doing the same on my daily walks across Hyde Park, before arriving at the Aldwych and rehearsing the same material during the day, going over it in my head on my homeward walk, and then taking it with me, once more, into my evening bath.

So compulsive was my behaviour that I knew nothing of contemporary news: the end of the Cod Wars, the disgrace of Jeremy Thorpe, the beginning of the rise of Thatcher, Mohammed Ali's fight with the battered Richard Dunn, or a pound of butter going up by four pence, all issues which were making the front pages of the newspapers at that time.

I was literally soaked in Hickey.

And who is Hickey? A big-spending, travelling salesman who attempts to bring happiness and truth to a bunch of derelicts and has-beens in Harry Hope's saloon. He does this through the destruction of illusion, the wrecking of others' dreams. Since his last visit to the bar (he goes there for an annual binge), he has turned into a kind of evangelist, and now wants to change people's lives. Those other people, all types drawn from O'Neill's own life, talk about Hickey for what seems an eternity before he eventually arrives – and when he does, he isn't what they expect. From that point, he hardly draws breath. Waiting, then talking. That's what Hickey's about.

Thus, I had a long time to think about things before I even arrived on stage, and the weight of expectation that had been piling up since *Jesus of Nazareth* began to bear down on me. During rehearsals, I became increasingly tense and edgy. Something deep inside me, perhaps buried since the production of *The Homecoming* nine years earlier, began to assert itself. After one of the previews, Bee and I went out for a meal with Joel Grey and his wife. We had met Joel during *The Homecoming*'s run in New York. He had been playing *Cabaret* at the Imperial Theatre next door. I always thought of it as two little guys getting together. Though it was good to see them again, I hardly spoke all evening, being too preoccupied, compulsively replaying Hickey, even over the dinner table. Much later, Bee told me that Joel – always a competitive actor – thought it the best thing I had ever done. I doubt this news would have done much good, even if she had passed it on. When Patrick called to ask how we were getting on in his house, I barely recognized him. Quite often a remote sort of father, I now became rather isolated from Lissy and Barnaby, despite the special bond that had formed between Lissy and me in Africa. I couldn't find comfort anywhere, even with my children.

In addition, at that time Jessica was merely a peripheral part of my life, and Sarah-Jane, now in her teens and doubtless recalling and reviewing from a new, sensitive perspective the loud arguments Lynne and I had had once we'd moved from Avoncliffe to Observatory Gardens in London, was beginning to apportion blame. She wrote a letter saying, in effect, that she didn't want to see me ever again. Rather than fighting my corner, I allowed her to drift out of my life for several years. Reasoning to myself that I was merely respecting a point of view, I never felt that I was being callous – though I now see how it might have appeared that way.

As I became detached from my families, so I was drawn closer to my work. The play was the thing, and I was trapped deep inside it.

The move from rehearsal to stage to dress rehearsal and then to preview only intensified the knot of dread that was beginning to tie itself tight inside me. I began to feel apprehensive, to seize up on stage, and have what I assumed were panic attacks.

As set, lights, costumes, actors and audience were gradually added to the process, my adrenalin levels jumped dramatically, and I felt that I was headed towards a car accident, a steep drop – anything that involved a terrible shock to the system. But I still thought I could handle it, and was by all accounts still giving a good performance. Joel and Bee were full of praise, yet as first night loomed, I knew that things weren't right.

The preview period is usually dominated by mingled emotions: expectation of acclaim and intimations of doom. Mine, however, were mostly to do with doom. Even so, Bee joked, 'Don't blame your nervous breakdown on me,' perhaps recognizing that there was some kind of danger, and also understanding that at some level it might have been connected with the fragility of our domestic nest.

I kept going, assuming as I had always done that nerves (if that's what the feeling was) were a natural and even necessary part of acting, and that the mastering of them was part of the process. The play was good. The cast was good. I was good. I kept going.

On the night of the final preview, however, I knew – I *knew* – that something was going to happen. I marched out of my changing room, found a phone, and called Bee.

'I want you to come tonight,' I said, probably quite sharply.

'To the play?'

'Yes.'

'But I've already seen it.'

'I know.'

'Twice.'

'I'd still like you to come again tonight.'

A pause, probably of Pinteresque proportions.

'How are you feeling?'

'Not good.'

'The usual "not good" . . . ?'

'No. Another kind of "not good". This is different.'

So Bee made her way to the Aldwych, and took a seat in the Dress Circle, though I didn't see her before the curtain went up.

Somehow, I got through the first part of the play, though I do remember sweating in the wings while I was waiting to go on, suddenly feeling cold and clammy, and people asking me if I was all right. Although I did not realize it, I had started to seize up. I kept forgetting lines, something that I had never done.

We kept going. The cast was very professional, and just about covered the cracks. Norman Rodway, whom I knew from *Romeo and Juliet*, where he had played Mercutio to my Romeo, kept peering at me in a quizzical manner and asking, 'Weren't you just about to say . . .', before feeding me a line. Bob Hoskins played the bartender Harry Hope, and busied himself cleaning the glasses and wiping the counter, not wanting to get caught in the smash that seemed to be heading his way. His character had not set foot outside the bar for twenty years, yet his fiddling performance began to suggest that he couldn't wait to get through the door. Patrick Stewart seemed to slow down his movements, as if he was circling a dangerous animal, his face expressing blank terror every time I looked at him or took a step in his direction. As he closed himself off to me, and his features blanked, he began to look increasingly like a hard-boiled egg. And the rest of the cast (Kenneth Cranham, John Warner, Patrick Godfrey, all playing versions of O'Neill – the busted cop, the timid Trotskyite . . .) began to prowl the stage as if they were burglars who had suddenly heard a police siren and were afraid of being caught red-handed.

Then the moment arrived when I knew I would not be able to continue. I was giving a monologue from a chair at the front of the stage. The rest of the cast was behind me and, despite their previous efforts, now unable directly to intervene or assist me. I kept drying, even at one point addressing the audience with something like, 'Here I am, supposed to be talking to you . . . there are you, expecting me to talk . . .' Getting off the stage was quite complicated and involved a choreographed manoeuvre through and past the other actors, who were frozen in a kind of tableau. Eventually, another member of the cast, Norman Rodway (who had also been at Stratford with me and made his name playing Hotspur in Orson Welles's film *Chimes at Midnight*), responded to my distress and led me off, though at that point no one was sure the audience had noticed anything was wrong.

I had only been off stage for a few moments before I knew some kind of buffer had been reached, that the game was up. I walked briskly past the stage manager, who waved a flimsy arm at me and uttered something quite polite like, 'But you're due back on almost immediately, Mr Holm.'

'I'm off,' I replied, 'and I'm not coming back.'

I knew that I could not continue – knew that it was a case of 'could not', not 'would not'. Personal crises are difficult to describe, at least in words that make much sense. An actor might understand me saying that it felt exactly the opposite of turning in a good performance, where there is brilliant intellectual clarity, a sense of boundless, inexhaustible energy as the chambers of the brain open up, one by one, until you are able to think and act on many levels. Then, you feel invincible, as if you have suddenly tapped into areas of being which, in the normal run of things, are not available to you. Your whole existence is lit up by a dazzling sense of potential as energy forces its way through your system, as mind and body become completely aligned, seemingly in perfect working order and capable of anything.

The opposite of this is a feeling of absolute vulnerability and incoherent hopelessness.

That night, I was good for nothing. The chambers closed down. I was overwhelmed by a feeling of catatonic inertia, and felt like a self-conscious fool thrashing around in a mental fog. And that was only what had happened on stage – the start of it.

By the time I got back to the dressing-room area, I had even lost the ability to walk. The black curtain which slowly cowled my brain had become a complete hood only a few moments after I strolled past the stage manager. I experienced complete meltdown.

Bee, meanwhile, had been waiting for the play to resume, and quickly realized that something was wrong. David Jones, who was running the theatre at that time, ran to her and said, 'There's something wrong with Ian.'

She made her way backstage and found me, by this time lying prone in Norman Rodway's arms while he soothed me and stroked my hair. We were both on the floor, my head in his lap. He was caressing me like a child. I was unable to speak or to focus on anything. My eyes were wild and staring, though staring at what, I do not know. The whole cast was gathered around, concerned, and no doubt wondering what the bloody hell they should do next. Patti Love, who played the prostitute, was weeping.

By that time, I had shut down completely.

This, I think, is a very different proposition from merely losing your confidence or giving a bad performance, though both things come into it. Bad performances make you feel self-conscious, sluggish, and out of focus. Most of all, they make you feel as if you are out of tune with everyone and everything around you, and that this is somehow common knowledge. I, however, was incapable of giving a performance of any kind, though I suppose 'no performance' is a species of 'bad performance', especially if you are in the audience, and during my last few moments on stage and the brief walk back to the dressing-room area, I may well have passed through such feelings of flatness and self-splintering.

I don't know what happened or what people said while I was on the floor with Norman. Presumably, in the English way of things, most of what happened occurred in near silence, with a bit of concerned shuffling and now-what-do-we-do coughing. Maybe someone tried a small joke, by way of breaking the ice, of transforming the instant, injecting momentum back into their suddenly stalled lives. Or maybe, as one told me later, there was a more basic and self-centred feeling of worry, which went something along the lines of, 'Fuck me. That could be me down there.'

What happened next has been pieced together through my

own disjointed memory and the information that people have given me about that night.

At some point, maybe after five minutes or so, I tried to get up, and levered myself clear of Norman's arms.

'I've got to go,' I said.

'Where to?' asked Bee.

'I've got to go. I've got to get up and *go.*'

All I knew was that I could no longer be near a stage, or in a theatre at all. I neither knew what I was doing or what all the people gathered around me were up to. Suddenly, the actors and crew, those people with whom I had been working very closely for several weeks, were nothing more to me than nameless, undifferentiated, meaningless bodies.

I must have looked insane staggering around the backstage area, not really making much progress, not knowing who I was or where I was going, watched by an increasingly curious cast, and gently shepherded by Bee.

After having witnessed this awful burlesque with what must have been mounting dread, the director Howard Davies then announced, with almost comic timing, 'I don't think Ian can continue.'

It was then that people realized there was still a play to finish, and an increasingly restless audience to confront. A copy of the script was found for Alan Tilvern, an announcement was made out front, and the show went on.

By this time, and having been left alone while the play continued, I was sitting childlike on a sofa, shaking, my head in my hands, mumbling quietly to myself that I had to get out, something which (despite my single-minded insistence) I had still not managed to do. Not getting out of the Aldwych was rapidly becoming my very own Dunkirk.

Eventually, I was taken to Dr McClellan, my own doctor, who was usually a stomach specialist, but was tried and trusted by me for all parts of the body. By chance, he was working late and was still in his surgery when Bee phoned. He said that I should go over to him immediately.

I calmed down during the taxi ride to Harley Street, becoming strangely silent, though the physical manifestations of my experience were starting to take effect. Once again, I became clammy and was shivering with cold.

Back at the theatre, people realized my absence would not be a temporary one. Bob Hoskins and Patti Love (I was told much later) were halfway through a comic routine, probably wondering what had become of me and wondering if I would recover, when David Jones marched on to the stage and like an irritated policeman called the performance to a halt.

By this time I had reached Dr McClellan's consulting room. As I entered, he stood up, walked over to me and said quite gently, but with enviable timing and feel, 'Ah. The iceman goeth.'

In truth, he couldn't really do much to help me, but his mere presence and the fact that he was nothing to do with the theatre must have helped to steady me. Although I was still having difficulty working out where I was or what I was doing, I was composed enough to spend the evening back at Francesca and Patrick's house.

The next day, and in consultation with the theatre, I went to see Dr Anthony Flood. In those days, psychiatrists didn't much want to talk to you; that was considered rather American. Instead, Dr Flood told me that I was suffering from a depressive ailment, which was curable with drugs, and that he didn't want to question me about my grandmother or even about my relationship with my mother. Then he gave me some pills.

'Up to you whether you take them or not,' he said. 'And by the way, what are you going to do now?'

Bee answered for me, and said we were thinking of going on holiday to Portugal.

He looked at me doubtfully.

'You might get as far as the airport,' he observed, 'but be careful. It's a short step there, and a very long one back.'

When 'we' said that Dartmoor was an alternative, he said, 'Much better! Plenty of exercise. Do you the world of good. You'll feel great. Of course, when you get back you'll feel terrible. Now, how are you, do you think? Can you go back on stage?'

'I . . . I . . . I . . .' I stammered.

'Thought not.'

Dr Flood picked up the phone, called the Aldwych, and told them that there was no chance of me returning to the play in the foreseeable future. As soon as a decision had been made and responsibility taken away from me, I began to feel better.

Over the next two weeks, I was gradually eased back into the land of the living. While Bee's mother Molly looked after Lissy and Barnaby, we went walking in Dartmoor – long, bracing, talkative walks during which I re-established some kind of equilibrium. As Dr Flood had predicted, the exercise acted as a kind of purgative and the horrors that had been nesting inside me were slowly expelled.

Except, of course, that they weren't. At least, not absolutely.

The opening of *Iceman* had been postponed, and on the way back from Dartmoor, we stopped at Howard Davies's house in Bristol to discuss the possibility of me continuing in the role of Hickey.

Howard's house was a large, happy home. He lived a generous, liberal life and was surrounded by the things he loved – his family, books, music, friends. I suppose he might have been called 'bohemian' – conjuring up as the word does all manner of louche, unruly behaviour. Happily, this was not the case with Howard. He and his wife were charmingly sympathetic, curious about my plans but never pressing, and treating me more or less like a normal person. While we were with him, I felt I would be able to resume in the play, and we parted on the understanding that that was what would happen.

However, within fifteen minutes of leaving Bristol, I had turned completely grey.

'I can't do it,' I croaked, 'I'm *not* doing it. It's either me or the play.'

Bee looked at me. 'Fine. But you've got to tell Howard,' she said.

I was too scared to go back, so Bee called Howard from a phone box. On hearing the news, he was as congenial as he had been half an hour earlier when he must have thought he'd rescued his Hickey. Maybe he had known what the reality was.

Over the next few months, while I was away from the theatre or anything to do with acting, I seemed to be functioning more or less as normal. There were, however, some odd physical manifestations of my malaise. My sense of balance became erratic. Occasionally, I found myself unable to walk down streets without holding on to lamp-posts or, Marcel Marceau-like, pressing against shop windows to keep myself upright. Sometimes I leapt back at the sight of my own reflection. My sense of taste and smell disappeared for a short time. And I found extreme behaviour, such as people shouting or laughing too loudly, very threatening.

Throughout all this, and in his reassuringly old-fashioned way, Dr Flood was a Titan of support, a Cordelia among psychiatrists, giving it to me straight and kindly. It helped that Bee and I liked him immensely. He said that my mind was like a box that had been shaken up, and things hadn't been put back in the right way. It must have been more complicated than that, but his persuasive demystification of what had seemed such a terrifying experience was exactly what I needed. So was his unceremonious manner. After all, I reasoned, if he is being so blunt, then there can't be anything *too* wrong with me. Remembering my own father and the inmates of the asylum, I knew that sympathy was often doled out in inverse proportion to the extent of a patient's illness. It was a quirk of the profession that those for whom compassion did the least practical good often received it in the largest quantities. Based on this crude calculation, I guessed that my breakdown must have been at the lower end of the scale. *Not* a permanent affliction.

But this was not the way it seemed during the early days, when I couldn't get out of bed without falling over and the very thought of acting made me dizzy. At the time, I was terrified. I had no idea what was happening to me and there was a lingering fear that I would never work again.

Not working would have been the end for me, because acting was – is – all I could do. It's the reason I exist. Actors don't *like* to work. They *need* to work. And that's because the instrument they use for acting is themselves, so that 'work' and 'self' are, in the end, indivisible. Without acting, actors don't exist. And I was no different.

As it was, I took a rest, and then Mary Selway (one of the most respected casting directors in the country, sadly recently passed away) offered me a part in Mike Newell's *The Man in the Iron Mask*. The film was made in France, and although I was put up in a hotel, there was room for Bee and the children (their presence was a condition of my accepting the part), and everyone was very supportive. It was a small part in a not very important film. Unlike Zeffirelli, Mike Newell was very mindful of his cast; there was a good atmosphere, and I found myself being cushioned back into work. I had a dreadful fear that I should also be unable to perform in front of a camera, but I quickly discovered that this was unfounded, chiefly because I knew that mistakes could be rectified merely by doing another take.

So I could still act. At least, I could still act in films. Theatre remained a problem for me, though I think this has been exaggerated. I actually went back on stage as early as 1979, for a production of *Uncle Vanya* at Hampstead Theatre, and although it wasn't a particularly happy experience, I don't believe this was entirely due to my state of mind. It was difficult, but no more than that. The fourteen-year gap between *Vanya* and Harold Pinter's *Moonlight* (at the Almeida in 1993) opened up because I was offered good film and television parts. *The Iceman Cometh* left its scars, and although going on to a stage has always been an issue since 1976, I don't consider that the damage is crippling. My stage fright is a good line which contains a grain of truth. It's one which newspapers are fond of trying out, but essentially it isn't accurate. As with so much in life, the truth is more mundane.

Having said that, and excepting the Hampstead production, I did steer clear of theatres for several years. The first time I went back into one was much later, to see Lena Horne in concert – this was probably in the early 1980s – and I was in complete awe.

'How does she *do* that?' I asked Sophie Baker, who by that time had become my wife, and with whom I'd gone to the concert.

'What? How does she do *what*?'

'That! Perform. Stand up in front of people and do things.'

'Well, you do it.'

'Not much. Not now. Not on stage. Not like that.'

I wagged a finger at Lena, marvelling at her ability to move around and sing at the same time.

'Don't be daft,' Sophie said, 'of course *like that*.'

I was like a child, startled by the apparent miracle that was unfolding on stage. It seemed impossible that anyone could do such a thing, and I am still in awe of actors who perform the same piece night after night. Recently, for example, I asked Alan

Rickman how he coped with the repetition in *Private Lives*, which ran for a long time on Broadway, and he knew exactly what I meant. 'Sometimes we have to *crawl* through it,' he said.

I don't think that the *Iceman* experience changed me very much, though I suppose you would have to ask others about that. I need a solid base from which to work, and reverted to type as quickly as I could – a fussy, controlled Virgo, rather strange and detached, but comfortable with it. And although I consider myself to be a reasonably brave actor, I have to do it from a secure position, unlike people such as Nicol Williamson and Victor Henry. In that respect, my private and professional lives are entirely dissimilar.

What I do know is that all actors fear 'meltdown'. Though few have experienced its full force, many have had close shaves, and no one is unaffected by its possibility. Even Laurence Olivier was vulnerable – I can recall standing in the wings as a young man in *Titus Andronicus*, staring at my hero with woozy amazement as he was preparing to go on. He noticed me gazing up at him, and snapped, 'Don't look me in the eye. Don't ever do that again!' Nicol Williamson had a method all of his own for dealing with nerves, rarely allowing them to get the better of him, and sometimes just saying to the audience, 'I'm sorry, ladies and gentlemen. I'm not very good tonight.' Another actor I knew once went on and said, 'Ladies and gentlemen, I used to be rather a good actor, but alas, not tonight. I'm going home, and will, of course, refund all your money.'

Although these people broke the barrier between actor and audience, they probably had good reasons for doing so, and thereby managed to deflate the build-up of nervous pressure within them. I did something similar in the 2001 production of *The Homecoming* at the Gate Theatre in Dublin, sensing a crisis, walking off stage, pulling myself together, and then going back again. This, however, is not quite the same thing as Charles

Laughton, who used to give readings rather than performances, and would at some point turn to audiences and apologize for all the 'plot' he was giving them.

Just as all actors probably have their own particular kinds of breakdown, so they also have different strategies for dealing with them. And acting is a profession in which 'going mad' is a kind of occupational possibility. Dr Flood told me that some Victorians believed specific experiences drove people crazy, though to his knowledge acting was not on the list. These included such things as disappointed love, blows on the head, low self-esteem, the horrors of a storm at sea, the excessive desire to have children, and onanism.

Well – yes, yes, yes, yes, yes, and no.

9

THE LOST BOYS

Without rationalizing the situation or even having to think much about it, I knew that I could not go back on stage after *The Iceman*. I stopped going to see live performances of anything (plays, obviously, but even concerts – even *recitals*). The whole business of being in an auditorium and being a part of the two-way transaction between performer and audience now gave me the terrors.

For a time, I worried that I would not be able to act again. And acting was the only thing I knew; it was the only thing I had ever done. I took some pride in the fact that I had never had another job, though now I wondered whether I might have to think again. How did one become, say, an accountant or a dentist or a carpenter? Because I was essentially unassuming, and ambitious only in the kind of acting work I wanted to do, there was no Plan B. Doing films suddenly became very important as they represented the only immediate realistic chance for me to continue as an actor.

So after my short holiday in Devon with Bee, I went to work on *The Man in the Iron Mask*, which was being directed by Mike

Newell in France. He was very generous to me, and because he was so solidly professional, well able to appreciate what I needed. On set, he handled me with resourceful flexibility. He came from a generation that had learnt its trade on British television and always treated writers, actors and crew with genuine respect. Which was just as well, because when I arrived I was obviously in a state. Patrick McGoohan was also in the film, and though he was a fine one to talk, he did say, as I edged with Eeyore-ish caution on to the set for the first time, 'Oh no, not another fucking manic depressive.' And only a short while later, the cameraman Freddie Young complained to Newell about McGoohan and me, asking in the sort of way that was meant to be heard, 'Who cast these two idiots?' Though he may have also said it because we were very different heights, and this would have caused certain technical problems, I was certainly sensitive, probably over-sensitive, to any kind of objection to my presence.

What had been intolerably irritating heat in London now seemed ideal holiday weather. The film was shot at a chateau about fifty kilometres outside Paris, which had been put up as a kind of dry run for Versailles. It had been built by a man who had paid for it (and been arrested) by ripping off the Exchequer. That was McGoohan's part. Otherwise, there was a colossal portmanteau cast. Bee arrived with the children and we stayed in a friendly hotel, so the shoot took on the look – and partly the feel – of a family holiday. We (or perhaps Bee) re-created the nest which had been slowly unravelling itself during the previous two or three years, after ten years of great laughter and happiness, and which I needed firmly in place for me to function properly. After some initial nervousness, I decided to enjoy myself on set and play the relatively small part I had with as much swashbuckling energy as I could muster. Although I got through the film without too much obvious difficulty, I was aware that in some way I had been changed. The *Iceman* experience had scarred me. For the first time in my career, I had been made aware that I couldn't do something.

I think the most significant impact it had was to make me feel insecure as an actor, though not necessarily as a person. That has always, to a degree, been the case. It was awful to realize that maybe I could no longer manage the only thing I had ever felt equipped to do. I think this is different from stage fright, which is more a momentary paralysis or fear, which often manifests itself in the forgetting of lines or the garbling of a performance. Stage fright might often be more immediately spectacular, but the eruptions of a crack-up happen deeper down in the bunkers of the soul. And they never quite cease.

No. What happened to me is, I think, more fundamental than mere stage fright. It is something which reaches into the core of your being and disallows even the possibility of going on stage, let alone having nerves or anxiety attacks once you're there. I've seen it in other actors, and although it can last for either a minute or a lifetime, once it has happened it is forever present, a time bomb of frailness, vulnerability and unconfidence, waiting to detonate. I remember it happening to Olivier at the Old Vic when he gave a particularly brilliant performance of Othello, so good that he was applauded off stage by the rest of the cast. He simply brushed them aside and headed back to his dressing room, refusing all visitors. Eventually someone felt bold enough to go in and congratulate him. 'The eyes don't lie,' as Bogarde told me, and Olivier's were full of a primitive fear and alarm.

'But you were so good,' the visitor said, taken aback at his show of consternation.

'Yes, yes,' Olivier answered, 'but how did I do it?'

Olivier knew he was good – knew he was often brilliant – but rarely was he *so* good that his lack of control (his *say*) in the matter was exposed. And if he didn't have control, how could he be certain that one day he wouldn't be as bad as that night his Othello had been good?

Derek Jacobi also suffered, and his response was to get back on the stage at Stratford and do a whole series of make-it-or-break-it parts. It worked. He blasted his way out of difficulty by creating momentum.

My problem was that I had neither Olivier's iconic energy nor Jacobi's terrified drive. One was spurred on by the need to be a public figure and his religious devotion to acting, the other by the kind of dread that is only found in a hunted, pursued figure. I, however, was less motivated. Or at least I was motivated by different things. But I was badly marked by the experience.

I suppose one way out of it would have been to drink. Drinking is associated with actors because . . . well, because it represents a way of unwinding after the intensity of being on stage. It's difficult to be Hamlet and then go home and kiss the children goodnight. Acting is also a very companionable profession which often requires that you spend time socially around the people with whom you are working. But perhaps most of all, drink allows you to become someone else, another version of yourself, which is in a sense the condition to which most actors aspire.

Bee often told me that I was rather a good drunk – 'good', I think, in the way I became convivial, irreverent and apparently very funny. I don't mind being any of these things, though I don't much enjoy pubs. There's a difference between liking a drink and being a drinker. I like to drink and am aware of not knowing when to stop.

Recently, my therapist in New York told me that I was an alcoholic, though I argued that she only said so because of cultural differences.

'You should see some of my friends,' I said rather sourly. 'Now *they're* alcoholics.'

'And how does that make you feel?' she asked after a suitably thoughtful pause.

'How's it meant to make me feel?'

'You tell me.'

'I don't know. I've never thought about it before.'

'Maybe you have an allergy.'

'To drink?'

'Is that what you think?'

'You suggested it.'

'Did I? That's very interesting.'

But of course it wasn't. It turned out that she wondered whether my memory loss might be linked to drink, though I pointed out that I'd always had a terrible memory, at least a terrible memory so far as my own life went – indistinct at best, wildly and microscopically selective at worst.

Alcohol can mean many things to many people, and one of them is oblivion, though there are more innocent gradations of this along the way. After the breakdown, I suppose oblivion might have been useful, but then what would I have become oblivious *to*? I neither liked nor disliked myself enough for such complete disregard to be an attractive alternative. It implied, rather, a kind of obsessive narcissism, and I (at five foot something and unassumingly suburban) was certainly never consumed with myself. Quite the opposite, in fact, which is probably one of the reasons I went into acting in the first place.

So oblivion was no good to me. And I was never one of those people who treat drink as a kind of hobby, heating the wine glass and chilling the cream on the back of the spoon or whatever. And I was never compulsive or addictive. To my work, always. To women, yes. To adultery, sometimes. But never to drink. Though now, as I look back from the vantage point of being seventy-two years old, I worry that I am suddenly drinking too much. I still don't much care for being drunk, but *getting* drunk is occasionally irresistible. I've found a good Polish restaurant that serves very good vodka. I have a friend who stays in my flat, cooks for me, and we drink together. It's possibly to do with age. Or, like Roger Moore, maybe I want to be happy when I go to Heaven.

But however you categorize my relationship to alcohol, I know I am not and never have been a Roaring Boy in the Burton or O'Toole mould, and that drink, though it might have supported me through the crack-up in a temporary sort of way, was pragmatically, efficiently rebuffed.

Around the time that I was talking to Kubrick, I did a play for television called *Omri's Burning*. It was about a drunk in Wales, and I remember it partly as being very good, and partly as the one and only time that I became a method actor. For six weeks I lived the part of a drunk bum, sleeping in my clothes, not washing, walking round the streets and drinking excessively. But afterwards, I was able to stop – quietly, quickly, efficiently, and without ever looking back.

I think this habit of moving on is to do with the kind of actor I am, which is in turn linked to the kind of man I am. At Stratford, I was terrified of O'Toole, probably because he was so melodramatically different, so alien to me. Whereas I was busy serving a several-year apprenticeship, O'Toole seemed to explode from nowhere. I now know this wasn't quite the case (after graduating from Rada in 1955 he had done over fifty stage roles and displayed great versatility – he just *seemed* to explode from nowhere), but his independent manner, his confidence, his star quality, his air of ruined glory . . . all of these had nothing to do with me. Peter Hall once told me that O'Toole had 'the sparks of genius', and I sometimes wonder whether, if he had stayed at Stratford (unlikely!), people would now be talking of

'O'Toole's Henry V', 'O'Toole's Richard III', and even – though it does seem preposterous – 'O'Toole's Lenny'. Not that I saw him as being in direct competition with me. It would have been like comparing chalk with a bicycle, but there was something unconsciously gladiatorial and threatening about him. I developed into a company man and chipped in, whereas he never seemed as if he could take direction, just telling the director how he was going to do a scene and then doing it.

He was an enigma wrapped in charisma and sprinkled with booze. And the drink was certainly a part of it, encouraging his gift, oiling though also dissolving his talent, and helping to create the louche, genially insolent shaman that he became. In many ways he is an actor from the nineteenth century. I am, I suppose, a modern actor – professional, dedicated, business-like, and self-effacing – but O'Toole is strangely ridiculous, often riveting, and unpredictably raw.

I mention him here not only because he strikes me as the kind of actor I am not, but also as an apologia for my not having taken to the bottle. For someone like O'Toole it is a part of his being, though not of mine.

And too many drops of the hard stuff can actually spoil an actor. Nicol Williamson, for example, had a great talent which was adversely affected, I think, by drink and a self-conscious desire to dazzle. A natural eccentric, he was a great jazz fan; I recall him phoning jazz clubs in New York and staying on the line for thirty minutes or so while the band played requests for him. This was the only time I can recall him using the telephone with any degree of enthusiasm. Mostly he regarded it as a sign of weakness to answer a ringing phone, and quite often he would even refuse to identify himself when calling people, who would then have to guess to whom they were talking.

We had worked together on *The Bofors Gun*, in which Williamson played an Irish private serving with the British army in post-war Germany, and at one time we were quite close. Still, there was always a dangerous edge to him, and his savage, often cruel powers of observation were acutely sharpened by drink. He, Bee and I used to eat together so often that it became a sort of weekly ritual. Then one night, during a meal out, he got terribly drunk, and after an hour or so of noisy philosophizing from him, I went to fetch the car. When I arrived back at the restaurant there was no sign of him or Bee.

Bee said later that she had also been very drunk and couldn't recall much, except that quite early on in the evening Williamson had declared his love for her and promised to make 'an honest woman' of her. He had been prickly with me all evening – and he could be *very* prickly – and though I had put it down to the drink, maybe it was also connected with his amorous designs. He must have bundled Bee into a taxi while I collected the car. I knew that he had what I shall call a 'soft spot' for her, and guessed that he had gone back to his flat. We were all the worse for wear, the lines between serious intent and tomfoolery blurred by drink.

What followed was a kind of gruesome though comic burlesque. Having located them, I played the part of the jealous lover by shouldering open the door, shouting something Edwardian and melodramatic like, 'Think of the children!' and then marching her out into the night air. When I saw the look on his face (those poached-egg eyes staring balefully at me), I thought he was going to kill me.

And thinking of the children was more or less what we did for the years following my crack-up. We stayed together, making do and behaving like a family. It was probably more than I deserved. Films came and went. I did something quite dreadful called *March or Die* in which I played an Arab and learnt to ride a camel. This was directed by Dick Richards, who became known not unkindly as 'the man with two Christian names'.

And then I played one of the Nazi hierarchy in something called *Holocaust* which was directed by Marvin Chomsky, whom I rather liked. It featured an American actor called Michael Moriarty who was deeply into 'The Method' and would constantly be telling Chomsky, 'I'm going to have to go really deep for this bit. Can we talk about it?' At which point, the rest of us knew we might as well give up for the next couple of hours or so as the indulgent actor and his furious director went into a huddle somewhere. And then there was something good for television called *Mirage*, in which I played a man who sold the secret of the design for the Mirage jet.

In other words, Bee and I got on with it. Apart from not being able to go back on stage, I found I was still able to function as an actor. In that respect, I had not changed a great deal. Nor had I turned to drink or embraced religion or become addicted to psychotherapy. We ticked by with more or less consensual normality. And then, in 1977, *The Lost Boys* was offered to me, an ambitious three-part film about the writer J. M. Barrie, written by Andrew Birkin. I recognized it immediately as something which I wanted to do. The writing was committed and powerful, the character of Barrie exerted a strong pull, and the BBC was obviously dedicated to producing a project of real worth. A few years earlier, one script had been submitted in outline. Then production had been put back because it was considered too packed for a one-off BBC play. It also coincided with my bout of chickenpox, a further reason for delay. Birkin had been given unprecedented access to Barrie's archives, and there was simply too much material to shoehorn into the conventional drama slot. Here was a chance to produce a definitive work, and to its credit, the BBC abandoned its original schedules and backed Birkin to write a longer, more involved script.

This, I thought, was the piece I had been waiting for. I met Birkin, who had a thin Easter Island face and legs like stilts, and liked him straight away. We also had things in common: he had worked with Kubrick on *2001* and, strangely, had a passion for Napoleon. He was very much the compulsive schoolboy, obsessive and easily immersed in projects (like Barrie, like Napoleon), much as a young boy would treasure conkers or cigarette cards. It seemed entirely appropriate that such a person should be the author of a play about a man who raged against the damaging dullness of having to grow up.

I reported all this back to Bee and said, 'He's right up your street,' meaning no more than that he was an oddball, the sort of nonconformist she might have come across during her own bohemian upbringing. In fact, Birkin had gone to Harrow. Though his mother was the actress Judy Campbell and his sister Jane had become something of a public figure (married to John Barry and then becoming Serge Gainsburg's partner, with whom she notoriously dueted on 'Je T'Aime'), he was in some ways quite middle class – though admittedly aristo-bohemian-upper-middle class. Apart from anything else, Peter Pan is a hero of the empire, the perfect Edwardian boy, so maybe *that* was what attracted Birkin to him. Still, all that mattered for the moment was that I had been offered an excellent script and the BBC was squarely behind it.

Soon after, when I heard Barrie's voice on an ancient recording, I slipped almost straight into his character. It sounds glib to say that 'something clicked', but it was almost that straight-forward. As soon as I got the sound of the voice, everything else just seemed to fall into place. There's a scene right at the beginning of the film when the six-year-old Barrie climbs on to a chair to get a better view of his brother's coffin, though this was later cut. I suppose it could be argued that because both Barrie and I had experienced the loss of an elder brother, I was immediately able to sense his tone of – what? Terminal sorrow? Grief qualified by innocence? But acting a part is never, of course, quite so straightforward as merely seeking out similarities between you and the subject, even one so apparently significant as the loss of a sibling. With Barrie, as with all the other roles I have taken, it's really about instinct and about losing yourself in the character. That may be why I find it a relatively uncomplicated process: there isn't much of me to lose. Any resistance to a new character is therefore quite slight.

Having said that, *The Lost Boys* then became a drama within a drama. While Birkin was doing research for a book on Barrie, something which must have overlapped with the filming, he used Bee as a kind of photographic researcher. They spent a lot of time in Dover with Nico, the last surviving Llewelyn Davies brother, going through old photographs and documents. They brought back material which had never before seen the light of day, and spent time processing original undeveloped photographs, many taken by Barrie himself. And so they fell in love in the dark room.

What was an awkward situation while we were filming became critical for me when, a few months later, Bee took our son Barnaby to New York. At this point, Bee and I were still together, though there was obvious tension. Birkin was in Los Angeles and asked them to join him, and I think that was when she made the decision to leave me, which she communicated immediately on landing at Gatwick.

In a sense, I was hiding inside the character of Barrie during much of that time. I allowed myself to be taken over by him, although I don't wish to make the process sound too mystical. I used Barrie to hide from myself. He became a way of siphoning off anxiety, the usual exhilaration and excitement that is generated by such a renewal being counterbalanced, and desperately intensified, by the loss of Bee.

However, when I referred to *The Lost Boys* as being 'a drama within a drama', Bee's romance and eventual decamping with

Birkin only proved to be the half of it. I have already talked of the peculiar symmetry between Barrie's circumstances and my own, but the loss of an elder brother is followed in the play by Barrie's wife Mary leaving him for the writer Gilbert Canaan.

I hope I acted with the same resigned dignity that Barrie did, though I suspect I had my moments. Bee did say it was inevitable that something like this would happen. We had been treading on eggshells for a few years, and during that time she had become a different person. 'I grew up with you, and was very happy,' she told me, 'but now I'm a woman.' No doubt I threw myself about a bit and probably shed tears, but when we went to see the psychiatrist Dr Flood, he told Bee, 'Do what you have to. Ian will survive. He's a survivor.'

The only thing I got angry with Bee about was what I considered to be her improper use of Barnaby, who was playing the young George Llewelyn Davies. Birkin had fallen for Barnaby in the same sort of idealized, nostalgic way that Barrie fell for the Llewelyn Davies brothers, in particular George and Michael, and I felt that Bee had used him as a Trojan Horse. It may have been an unfair assumption on my part, but in so many ways it made sense. Birkin's obsession with youth and the cynical corruption of adulthood was probably what drew him to the subject of Barrie and Peter Pan in the first place, and Barnaby was a beautiful naïf.

The Lost Boys therefore drew us all into a complicated web, with art imitating life and then life imitating art. If I had some material circumstances in common with Barrie, then Birkin was more emotionally in tune with him. And Bee was flitting between us, Bogarde's innocent now more Tinkerbell than Snowflake.

But even then Barrie wasn't finished with us. In *The Lost Boys*, Barrie's initial favourite, George, is killed at the front during the First World War. Later, his younger brother Michael (who had taken over from his brother in the writer's affections) is drowned in a tragic accident a few weeks before his twenty-first birthday. This is unbearably ironic, as Barrie has for some time refused to buy Michael a motorcycle lest he be killed en route to Paris, where he wanted to become an artist. Recently, at a memorial concert, I read a poem written by Anno Birkin, Bee and Andrew's oldest son. He had been killed in a motor accident in Italy, having arrived there from Paris two months earlier; he was exactly the same age as Michael Llewelyn Davies.

10

ALIEN

I had more or less assumed that my life – that all life – was pretty shapeless. When I look back on my 'career', I tend to view it as a series of fortuitous though random events. I suppose I had some sort of talent and knew what I wanted to do (or rather, knew what I didn't want to do – i.e., just about anything else), but apart from this relatively flaccid hint of resolve, nothing. The idea that one could shape a life in any kind of definitive way had never occurred to me. People who dash around offices, meeting deadlines and building careers, are no more in control of their lives than I am. Although I might feel that by shaping a character or developing a role I am somehow exerting an influence, bossing the moment, it never amounts to much more than a satisfying distraction. Life doesn't really have much balance or form.

It's only when things fall apart that one begins to realize how shapeless and indeterminate the whole thing is. The only real shape that lives have is tragedy, with hope and embryonic youth gradually giving themselves up to forbearance. And forbearance without the dignity of fatal flaws, catharsis and redeeming speeches. Perhaps Olivier was right about Lear after all: he is fucking easy. All we have to do is examine ourselves. *The Lost Boys* was a reminder of all this. Its triptych of a drama within a drama within a drama (Barrie–me–Birkin) reinforced the point with an almost elegant wretchedness. And I lost Bee – had been losing Bee – in sections. The writing had been on the wall for a while, most vividly since *Jesus of Nazareth*, but for a number of reasons we had held things together for several years beyond that. 'Think of the children,' I had exhorted while I was extracting her from Nicol Williamson, and now I know there was some truth in it. Although I think our relationship had been doomed for a few years, you cling to habits and attempt to preserve the things worth preserving.

Bee and I did not separate during the making of *The Lost Boys* or immediately afterwards, or even soon afterwards. True to the timetable of our disintegration, it happened over time and with messy but courteous imprecision, as if by taking our time we could get more used to the idea. I recall doing a film called *S.O.S. Titanic* around that time, actually after *Alien*, and Bee being encouraging about an affair I had with the actress Kate Howard, knowing that I needed romance and the comfort of love to get me through dark times. The film, appropriately, sank without trace. Kate was tall and very beautiful, I think she was also a model, and Bee still has a letter from our daughter Lissy, who would have been eleven or so at the time, saying that Kate was staying at Wassall House and looking after me and helping me to adjust to things.

This seems a very grown-up thing for an eleven-year-old to be saying, but Bee had brought Lissy and Barnaby up in an environment of emotional transparency. This was completely at odds with the closed, emotionally secretive upbringing I had experienced, and they were probably the better for it.

Bogarde wrote this to Bee:

I am sad that you and Ian have, what they call, split . . . and I know, I think, how distressed it must have made you feel . . . I think you have done it quite marvellously, with tact, patience, and care. When two people, whom one loves on quite separate levels, have to break up it usually means that sides have to be taken, for some obscure and quite tiresome reason. A bit of 'Love Him can't stand Her' goes on. But with you and Ian that is out of the question.

And Tote wrote a few days later:

But how marvellous that it does seem to have all worked out well for you both, and that at least you are both close to each other at the end of it all. God! When one thinks of what some people do with their relationships when it all goes wrong . . . It's lovely for you both, not to mention the children, that you have both been clever and grown-up about it all . . . it seems so mad, when two people have got along together for ages and then suddenly have to become enemies, but that's what an awful lot seem to do, wrapping themselves up in their shrouds of injured pride and boring everyone witless. Anyway, do give my love to the old boy and tell him to find a nice quiet mature lady who doesn't chatter all day!

It now seems strange that in the midst of such protracted hurt – the end of a relationship which had lasted for around fifteen years – we should have been sending signals of such soothing wisdom. Bee must take much of the credit for this. Though I had a few undignified moments, I think that probably by the time it happened I had lost all appetite for apportioning blame in matters of the heart. The marriage or the union fails, and that's that.

And what about the effect on the children? Lissy and Barnaby were coping. And what of Jessica and Sarah-Jane? I think they liked Bee, even though she had no obligations towards them. Although she represented tangible evidence of their father's earlier transgression, she had done her best to make some kind of connection with them, once looking after them when Lynne went to Greece for a holiday. Though a symbol of my previous wretchedness, in their eyes Bee was not to blame, so the demise of our relationship offered my daughters scant consolation. I suspect it simply showed further evidence of my own inability to conduct long-term relationships.

Despite the letter she had sent to me three or four years earlier, Sarah-Jane and I were now on reasonably good terms. She was training to be an actress and we had met, by accident, at Lynne's house. I knew she was about to appear in a play at college and asked if I could come and watch her. 'I haven't seen you for three years!' she retorted. 'But I would still like to come and offer some advice,' I replied. Somehow, we patched things up.

In the meantime, however, Jessica and I had drifted apart. It seemed that I could never quite be on good terms with my first two daughters at the same time. Confused and enraged, they dipped in and out of my life, almost taking turns at being estranged and reconciled, wary of commitment and afraid of being disappointed.

Bee's withdrawal was gradual and, as Bogarde said, executed with 'tact'. She had the gift of including everyone in her life, of ensuring that no one should feel passed over or ignored. It was as Bogarde said in his letter, and so I think that Lissy and Barnaby felt as if their family had somehow grown bigger rather than being split asunder.

Eventually, Bee and the children left to live with Birkin at Iverna Court (the large, rambling flat just off High Street Kensington, where I was the sitting tenant), while for the time being at least I kept Wassall House, somewhere familiar for the children to stay and be with their father and so on and so forth. But when the house was empty – and I was relieved that this was not too often – I can remember sitting motionless in the kitchen, seemingly positioned at the centre of a great vacancy. Without an audience, without a gallery of onlookers, I became habitually anxious about my own lack, my constant fear of being *a nothing*. The world seemed to have moved on, though apparently by leaving me behind. Lissy's letter about Kate Howard reminded me of the person she had become – somehow no longer a child, though maybe not quite an adult, either; responsible, kind, trustworthy – a displacing mass which left me reeling. And separation too had created a space in which I could stumble and sway, isolating me, cutting me off.

At times like this you resort to cliché, or rather you find yourself vulnerable to cliché. And I sometimes found myself in the harsh light of the bathroom, standing susceptibly in front of the mirror. I was approaching fifty. I looked older than I remembered myself the last time I looked. Did I have less hair? Despite the tennis and the running and even the feeble attempts at swimming, I seemed to be fatter. Not fat. But certainly bigger. I was yielding to the platitudes of self-examination.

It was around this time that I got offered a part in what my agent Julian Belfrage described as 'a very expensive B movie'. It was called *Alien*. I read the script and met the director, an Englishman called Ridley Scott who had made a name for himself in advertising and had directed a well-received film which I had not seen, *The Duellists*.

It was difficult to tell from the script what kind of film it would be, or rather what kind of film it would become. Scott told me that it had been through several re-writes (nothing new in that), but that he was now happy with it. He was young and wore a beard, which I didn't think particularly suited him. His clothes, the way he presented himself – all these seemed some-how secondary, artificially bolted on, and irrelevant to his curiously internal restlessness and energy. It was as if he was burning up with ideas and a kind of private imagery which he wanted, he needed, somehow to explain to you.

The script seemed very high-concept, though good in its way. Still, hardly Chekhov or Shakespeare, but I didn't much mind that. Anyway, I had done my share of flimsy, meaningless films. I was intrigued. And, unusually in projects like this, a star was not being used to act as a focal point for the financing. Normally, if there was no name attached, then a project like *Alien* was peopled with recognizable B-list actors, the kind of actors who would do a competent job and whose presence would signal what kind of film (i.e., shock-horror) it was going to be. But this was not the case either. Here, the cast seemed to be made up of evocative American character actors and a couple of respected British names. I think Jon Finch was mentioned as being the 'other one', though he was soon replaced by John Hurt.

I asked Scott about the casting.

'I want *Alien* to move those kind of films up to the next level,' he said. 'I don't want it to be one of those low budget sci-fi things.'

'You want me to play Ash, the science officer?' He nodded. 'And he's a robot?'

'Yes. A bit like the Mother computer in *2001*. But broken down into a person. Well – sort of. Do you know Kubrick?'

Well, of course I did. In a funny kind of way. So I nodded and changed the subject.

'Why the change into a person? A robot-person?'

'We were thinking that one day all computers will talk. It's an extension of that idea.'

In truth, I was prepared to do the film almost as soon as it was offered, though there was something that troubled me about playing a robot. I asked Scott about this, wondering how he saw the character on screen. I knew even then that he would have something to say about this. To him, ideas were an itch that begged for a scratch.

'I think Ash should be realistic.'

'How do you mean?'

'Realistic. Human. It's the same for the monster. The realism will make it work – not fantasy.'

This was the bit that worried me. When I'd done *The Lost Boys*, I had established an immediate, instinctive rapport with J. M. Barrie, or at least my own version of the character I felt Barrie to have been. And this was more or less how I did all my work. Playing a smuggler of secrets for the television production *Mirage*, I had met the real person on whom the drama was based and immediately *become* him, adopting mannerisms, transforming my face with his expressions and turning my hands round like him. I never felt this amounted to mimicry or mere imitation, though I do think that apery is a part of the art of the acting. But with the non-character of Ash, I had no leads, no way in. I suppose Scott meant that I should in some way fall back on myself and be 'human' in that way.

I accepted the part and brooded about a way to do it. Around then I was good at brooding. Part of the trouble was that I was spending too much time with my own thoughts and coming up against the unflattering mirrors they provided. And I had plenty of time to think. Bee hadn't yet moved out of Wassall House, but neither was she there all the time. There was the drive to and from Shepperton every day and then the hanging round on set. Usually I would have chatted with and observed the technical crew, but *Alien* wasn't turning out to be the right sort of film for this kind of easy association. There was too much tension and suspicion. And for several days, just before the filming of the scene where Ash is decapitated after being discovered trying to kill Ripley, I had to endure four or five hours in make-up. A false head was built up around my real one, providing a further opportunity for reflection.

I remember the special-effects team remarking how good I was at being still. In truth, I found it relatively straightforward. I had a great deal to think about, and when that became disagreeable, I thought about keeping still. It became, in a rather bathetic way, another means of showing off, of proving a point, of being *the best* at keeping still. 'Look! Look at me! I'm so good at being still.' But between the mawkish moments of triumph, dark thoughts and the unsettling experience of my self-scrutiny kept coming back to me unanswered like a non-deliverable e-mail.

As my therapist is now fond of reminding me, the route out of this disagreeable dilemma is to find an audience through talking, if not to others then at least to yourself. But talking to myself only begged the question, 'Who is doing the talking?' and frequently led to the more perplexing, 'And who is the listener?' In my case, the answer to both questions was always the same: 'I don't know. Perhaps *nobody*.' It was no different then.

So how was I to accomplish Ash's 'humanity'? What resources of my own could I call upon to create a generic sense of mortality? In some ways it seemed the wrong role at the wrong time. Always aware of my own bareness, I was then at my most vacant, and significantly, at my most self-consciously vacant. Perhaps a robot was the most appropriate role I could have taken on, though a robotic robot rather than the humanized android which Scott seemed to require.

One thing it did help me to understand was the difference that lay at the core of my own acting and Alec Guinness's talent. I had often assumed (and people had often assumed for me) that we were broken from similar moulds. But I began to realize that maybe I was confusing his invisibility with my anonymity. Not the same thing at all.

This is something he confirmed when we had dinner a few times six or seven years later. I think he liked my work, and obviously I greatly admired his brand of minimalism and the way that his startling physical transformations were complete but never conspicuous. They rarely drew attention to themselves. Whereas we both tended to change alchemically when 'in role', altering ourselves in the crucible of imaginative instinct, there was always a bit of Guinness left over. No matter what part he played, there was always something of him in there giving it a particular complexion. Exactly what is difficult to say. His evenness, maybe, or the ability to let a thought hang in the air. An abiding strangeness, a tactile mysteriousness. *He* would have known how to play Ash, perhaps investing the part with a hint of humour and a sense of his latent priestliness. In the end, I decided to cut my losses and play the part in a way that was literally human – quiet, helpful, civilized, unassuming – rather than actually so (pretty much the opposite of all the above). I played him as if I was attending an interview and therefore on my best behaviour, or as if I had some terrible secret which I wanted to conceal ... which was, of course, true. I worried that I might appear too conspicuously 'decent' in the claustrophobic tensions of the spaceship *Nostromo*, but the mix of characters Scott had assembled worked well, and in the final cut I sort of hovered around, rational and dependable and proper, until my unmasking.

I was helped in my diffidence by the atmosphere on set. It would be fair to say that *Alien* was not an easy shoot, and at times it was just bloody hard work, unpleasant and tense. Many of the crew worked eighteen-hour days, six and seven days a week. Shooting went on at Shepperton for sixteen weeks or so. The cast was split into distinct camps. Many of the American cast were method actors, and John Hurt and I found the intensity of it all quite hard to deal with on a daily basis. One of them, an enormous black man called Yaphet Kotto, was truly frightening. On several occasions I was sitting somewhere on set when he emerged through one of the cramped doorways, often hitting his head, and shouting, 'That's my chair!' or 'You're in my place!' He thought it terribly important that we were true to our characters even when the cameras weren't rolling, whereas I absent-mindedly plonked myself down in the most convenient seat. On several occasions, Kotto became so involved with his on-screen hatred of the alien that he tried to pick fights with the seven-foot Nigerian art student Bolaji Badejo, who played the monster.

This simmering ideological conflict was comically illustrated the day before John Hurt was due to play what has become known as the 'Chest-burster Scene'. Anxious that he wasn't preparing for this pivotal moment with the appropriate intensity and emotional fanaticism, director, producers and fellow actors formed a small huddle around him.

'Big scene tomorrow, John.'

'Is it?'

'Yes. You know. The thing-coming-out-of-your-chest scene.'

'Oh, yes. Of course.'

'So . . .'

'Yes?'

'So. How you gonna play it?'

'How do you mean?'

'Got any ideas? Anything you want to run by us?'

'No. I don't think so.'

Slight ripple of panic.

'Are you sure?'

'Oh yes.'

'Any ideas at all?'

John looked slightly quizzical. 'I thought . . .'

'Yes?'

'I thought I'd just use . . .'

'Go on, John, go on.'

'Just use my not-inconsiderable imagination . . .'

'We're with you, John. Go on.'

'I'd use my not-inconsiderable imagination and just DO IT!'

He turned towards his small audience as he bellowed, and looked directly at them. Each one took a fearful step backwards, genuinely startled by his sudden shouting.

'Yeah, that's very good, John. Well done. Terrific,' they chorused, though I'm sure they would have preferred him to say that he would swallow an orange whole and then lie on the floor for several hours trying to sick it up.

We all knew that when the actual moment arrived it would be fairly bloody, though nobody told us how extreme it was going to be. We thought something was up when we arrived on set to find the crew wearing protective clothing, with a huge vat of something waiting nearby. It had been on set for two days and the stench of whatever was in there was awful. Scott had decided that the shock on our faces and the disgust we felt should be as authentic as possible. Sigourney Weaver thought the hose with the gore (which turned out to be kidneys and livers and intestines and blood) was pointed directly at her, but when it all happened, Veronica Cartwright was the one who seemed to get hit by most of it. She was drenched in butchery. Her sodden clothes stuck to her body and, distraught, she had to be helped from the set. Veronica had been a child actor in Hitchcock's *The Birds*, and later told me that even the discomfort of that film was nothing compared to *Alien*.

As well as the different camps into which the cast seemed to split, there was a general undercurrent of petulant fractiousness.

There were rumours of arguments about the script, and crabby one-upmanship between the various special-effects teams and their creative masters. One of them, Roger Dickens, told me that he had never spent so much time on a set doing so little. He accused *Alien* of being a 'boardroom picture', where no one really knew what they wanted. Sigourney Weaver came to stay at Wassall and confided that she felt isolated and pretty miserable. She came from a well-to-do American family, had made a reputation for herself in fringe theatre, and clearly possessed both strength and intelligence. I think one of the producers took a shine to her, and though the bare facts of her eventual heroism are certainly present in the final shooting script, some of us were aware that the emphasis on her fortitude slowly shifted. During filming it became even more so. Ripley slowly became a star role and the film lost a little of its ensemble feel. Although *Alien* was good for her career, I think Sigourney felt used in a rather sly fashion, and that the way the picture developed – from its beginning, with the whole crew chatting over cups of coffee, to her near striptease at the end – was disingenuous.

Scott wanted to do everything himself. It was as though he was nervous of delegation, and this created ill feeling and a constant sense of strain. He was certainly skilled at psychological manipulation, a talent he had developed in the making of many successful advertisements, but stretching this over a full-length feature was a wearing, arduous process. Like the crew of the spaceship, I suppose we began to feel that we were merely skilled, well-paid technicians working within a narrowly conforming ideological work ethic. Generally speaking, actors like to feel more wanted than this. It was bearable – but only just. Also like the space travellers, we became prone to attacks of irritability and melancholy. Everything was done for us, and for most of the time there wasn't much to do. Then, at a sudden and given moment, we had to 'perform' our duties.

Scott drove us through the making of the film with impressive but remote and merciless explosions of energy. He told me that he wanted a film that was 'repulsive and scary as hell', and by sheer force of character he achieved it. Sigourney recognized the unmistakable imprint of the self-made man in all this, and one day, when Scott drove fiercely into the Shepperton car park in his Rolls, she asked him quite sweetly if his dad had bought it for him.

Being on set wasn't much fun, either. Scott was claustrophobic, and the *Nostromo* was built so that actors like Kotto had to duck as they walked along the low-ceilinged corridors and through the squat doorways. At one point, even I managed to hit my head. The enormous derelict ship control room came complete with a fossilized elephant-like extra-terrestrial pilot nicknamed 'the space jockey'. Much of the metallic-looking hull was actually constructed from old wooden apple crates, which we had to take care not to damage. Once I saw a couple of contortionists prowling round the set and bending their bodies into impossible shapes while Scott and his special-effects team estimated whether a monster costume could be built round one of them.

The whole shoot gradually began to assume a slightly surreal aspect and, though I wasn't much in the mood, humour was sometimes needed to help us get through it. It didn't help that for the part of Ash I had a whole body shave, so that a body cast could be made, which made me look like a glistening cherub. It also itched a great deal, especially when hair began to grow back in places where androids do not usually presume to have it. I wasn't very happy. John Hurt was very good in this respect, giggling his way through one of the Chest-burster takes as Roger Dickens moved the model of the baby monster beneath him (for the sixth or seventh time) on a specially constructed trolley. It began to seem a very silly way to make a living, and though he didn't laugh out loud, his eyes gave the game away. Small and raisin-ish anyway, they closed tight under the strain until they became nothing more than buttonhole slits.

In some ways, Hurt is a similar kind of actor to me, a 'sort of' character actor, though the eventual effects we achieve are very different. He may be more reckless, but like me he hates being asked how he acts, and has no answer beyond repeating Edith Evans's reply, 'I just pretend, dear boy.' There's a bit more to it than that, but I know what she means. During *Alien*, we both came to share an amused aversion to the method acting of the Americans. In addition, I now know that we both come from emotionally undemonstrative families and both of us have had three or more wives. There may be something here about becoming actors because we never felt loved as children, though I wouldn't presume to argue it too fiercely from his side. We did agree about *Alien*, however. He said to me that it was probably like all sci-fi films – incredibly dreary to make. 'You know, all you have to do is just walk around looking slightly concerned.'

Without it ever becoming an issue and without him necessarily knowing it, merely by being there John came to be a great help to me in just getting through the film. Bee was still at Wassall, though moving out in pieces, and I was at a pretty low ebb, all this aggravated by the rigours of filming.

There's a scene in the film when Ripley discovers that Ash is a robot working for the corporation which has instructed him to bring the alien back to earth. She announces that she will have to oppose him, and he goes berserk, but in a rather cool and even calculating way. He hits her and then (in what I took to be a kind of rape) tries to kill her by driving a rolled-up magazine down her throat. At that point, other crew members intervene and eventually manage to dislodge my head with, I think, the aid of a metal bar. I remember it as being a very uncomfortable experience. My real head was tucked out of sight somewhere beneath the prosthetic one, and keeping it that way involved all sorts of awkward bending and wrenching. The inside of the phoney head was packed with a mixture of organic and synthetic materials – plastic tubing mixed up with spaghetti and onion rings – to help confirm Ash's humanity.

Afterwards, when he has been subdued and his decapitated head has been electronically probed for information about the corporation's intentions, Ash's head is incinerated. Scott decided to use the 'real fake' for this scene and it was a strange sensation to watch my likeness go up in flames. For the purposes of this narrative, it would be felicitous to say that as I watched the blue-yellow blaze around my head I saw my own life being consumed. It's true I wasn't happy, but I reasoned that just as good things had happened to me, so I supposed it was only proper that over the years *some* bad things would seek me out. And the random shapelessness of it all could certainly not be explained or symbolized by a chunk of burning rubber filled with onions.

After the filming of *Alien* had been completed and I returned more or less full-time to Wassall, more or less by myself (unless you counted visits from children and increasingly infrequent ones from Bee, who would tease me about my so-called loneliness and what she termed my 'ladies-in-waiting'), I thought how love is more destructive than indifference and how in the end we all come to grief, one way or another. It's the price you pay for indulging yourself.

The writer Edward Upward said that the ageing process had led him to experience 'little failures of tolerance'. Well, I had never been much good at tolerance, and now – what? – my late forties was not a good time to start cultivating it. I'd never really thought about my age, but as it settled on me, heavy and invisible, I understood that I had choices to make. To carry on as before, doing much as I pleased and accepting the come-uppances which would doubtless come my way, or to somehow pursue a different sort of life, an unappetizing life of tolerated abstinence and thinned passion. For the first time in a while, I thought of my father (who had been dead for many years), and how the collapse of my marriages would hardly have been embraced by his own devoted temperament, and its resultant, dutiful slog through life with my mother. Undoubtedly I had crossed some sort of line – in terms of age, in terms of the way I lived my life, but also in terms of what my mother would have called 'comportment'.

I *think* my father used to wear striped pyjamas. The 'no-access' secrecy of my parents' bedroom extended even to what he might have worn there. But I fancied I could see him, in his striped pyjamas, rearing back from me in horrified conster-nation. And consternation is also what I think Lissy and Barnaby felt as Bee and I were separating, though it was more resigned than horrified. After all, we had been rehearsing severance for a while.

Even so, during the few times when we were still together at Wassall as a family, I sensed that they still hoped for reconciliation.

'All right, Dad?' asked Barnaby over the morning coffee which Lissy had dutifully prepared, the inquiry meaningful and symbolic.

'Toast?' asked Lissy, as if making the nest more comfortable could somehow make things better. 'And *marmalade*?'

But they knew that the game was up. They sensed the failure and went off up the lane to watch the cows being milked.

I still cried. Not much towards the end, though right at the start, when Bee had announced she was leaving, I'd shed tears by the bucketful and thrashed around like a lovelorn teenager. Or maybe like a ham actor. But she knew (as the doctor knew) that I had a strong sense of audience and of occasion and that I would survive. They were tears of delirium, intent, fear and influence, and they were spilt, as we all understood they would be, in vain.

11

CHARIOTS

Though I had behaved badly at the ultimate demise of the relationship with Bee (and I think I mean childishly rather than wickedly), the psychiatrist we both saw was right: I am a survivor. I continued to breathe, to function, to *work*, which, as Dirk said in one of his letters (to Bee only, now), 'I know is the most important thing to him'.

I didn't see much of Dirk and Tote after that. My friendship with Dirk was quite gladiatorial and I suspect that in some ways he was relieved not to have to continue making the disproportionately difficult effort to juggle two separate attachments. I was not much good at being in touch, writing letters, or keeping tabs, and so I simply drifted out of their orbit.

I think the only person I could honestly call my own proper friend – that is, someone met, befriended by me, and over an extended period of time maintained solely by me as opposed to any of my partners – was an actor called Laurence Davidson. We had met at Rada and he went on to become a very handsome matinée-idol type of actor who flourished in repertory theatre. He was, I suppose, a big fish in a smallish pond, though because he was a great Francophile and became bilingual, he also mopped up many roles which called for a Frenchman. However, he could be difficult to work with, and as he got older and his looks faded, so he got fewer and fewer jobs.

Openly gay himself, he was convinced that I would discover my own homosexuality by the time I'd left drama school. That may have helped to explain our friendship during the early stages, and I sometimes felt ours was an unconsummated love affair, though as time went past, we developed an understanding and a routine. I would nearly always contact him (he never called me), and the gaps between our meetings would often be six months or longer. But I never *didn't* call him, and each telephone conversation would sound much the same as the previous one.

'Hello.'

'It's Ian.'

'She's away, then. And you'll be wanting some food.'

'Tomorrow?'

'At eight.'

'See you then.'

'Yes. Goodbye.'

'Goodbye.'

It wasn't generally true that I called him up simply to get fed. Laurence grew weary of what he termed my 'parade of women', presumably having long since given up on the idea of my being gay. However, he did meet each one and I think liked them all; they certainly liked him, despite finding him curious. He lived in London, just behind the Hilton Hotel in Dartmouth Street, and produced the most magnificent meals from his tiny kitchen, using nothing but a Baby Belling. After he had done this, we would sit down, eat, drink, put the world to rights, say our goodbyes ('see you around'), have no contact for a while, and then do much the same thing several months later. He was available whenever I wanted to contact him, loyal, non-judgemental, constant, undemanding, and unobtrusive. These were probably the chief reasons our friendship lasted so long.

Laurence died quite recently and quite unnecessarily. He contracted leukaemia and initially fell ill in France, where he had been visiting a French air steward called Bernard to whom he was very close. Shy and secretive, he called me from University College Hospital in Gower Street, where he had suddenly become very frail. He thought there had been some mix-up over his notes and medication, though whatever the reason, his health deteriorated quickly and suddenly.

'What's going on?' I asked him when he called, detecting the note of feebleness in his voice. He was just able to tell me, though was dead twenty-four hours later. I helped a little with selling his house and spoke with a distraught Bernard; when he died I remember thinking, 'Oh dear. How sad.'

My father had died in 1955 and my mother in 1962. My father never saw me on stage, at least not in the professional sense, though had he lived longer I am certain he would have taken a considered and informed interest. Even then, perhaps in antici-pation of the direction my career might take me, he was busy reading Greek tragedy and wading through Shakespeare, then became an avid watcher of plays on an early black and white television. My mother, though, was cut from altogether different cloth. I think she saw maybe one play I was doing at Stratford, as Lorenzo in Michael Langham's production of *The Merchant of Venice*, which afterwards she described as 'beautiful'. I asked her about Peter O'Toole, wondering how she had responded to one of the country's most charismatic young actors.

'Which one was he?' she asked.

'Shylock.'

'And which one was *he*?' she inquired quietly.

I recall feeling slightly sad and even bitter that she was so much out of her depth. It wasn't really her fault, but to me, then, her reaction seemed to encapsulate the benign, passive in-attentiveness that had characterized so much of her life. I suppose it is from her that I have learnt – or inherited – my reluctance to take responsibility.

And so, when she died, I found the whole business of taking responsibility for my grief an impossible conundrum. She had been in a nursing home for a while, under the ungentle super-vision of a ghastly, unfeeling harridan, growing steadily fatter, her poor circulation and habit of grazing on such things as chocolates causing the generally uninterrupted inflation of her body during the last years of her life. By the time she died, her legs had become vast hams of accumulated, folded flesh.

She was interred in Worthing and I went down to see the body. An oldish man in an official-looking suit that wasn't quite a uniform stood outside her room, and gestured inside. It wasn't immediately apparent whether he was supposed to be stopping people going in, or perhaps ensuring that the dead didn't rise up and return to the land of the living.

'Your mother's in there,' he snapped. 'Knock on the door when you've finished.'

'Finished what?' I thought, though I nodded obediently and went through the door, not knowing what I should do, or was expected to do.

The room was gloomy and my mother's coffin was standing on a trestle in the middle of it. It felt like some sort of chapel, and on an impulse I thought that maybe I had better say the Lord's Prayer. I did this and wondered about leaving the room, only stopping when I thought that it might give the wrong im-pression. After all, I was meant to be grieving. This should take longer than the mere two or three minutes I had been in there.

I remember trying to think back to my father's death seven years earlier, attempting to find some kind of emotional cue for my feelings. The cause of his death had been something called 'angina pectoris', which is basically having a heart that is too big for your body. His condition got progressively worse, until in the end he couldn't get his breath and eventually stopped breathing altogether.

What had I felt then? Not much beyond a sense of inconvenience, the inconvenience of being expected to go through processes that one didn't necessarily feel. The nuisance of having to express a grief that just wasn't within me. Put like that, on paper, it sounds heartless – and it may well have been. May well be. But there is a principle behind it. How could I feel grief towards two people to whom I'd never felt remotely close?

Yes, they were my parents, but that didn't help. I was brought up by a succession of nannies while my mother and father remained remote, contained, isolated and distant. We met for meals, though generally in silence. My parents were as detached from each other as they were from me. Outside work, Dad (and even saying 'Dad' is slightly awkward) could find any number of tasks that would absorb him. Reading, mowing the lawn, later watching television; all accomplished with a solitary, self-absorbed determination that entailed shutting himself away for hours at a time. For him, books were not a subject for discussion, watching television not an activity to which others were invited. He made sure we knew our places and, accordingly, we kept our distance.

Mother (rarely 'Mum') used to annoy me with her sweetness and her cloying lack of intelligence and nous. I think Eric's death made things worse for her, prompting a further closing-down of her vital emotional faculties. She had no interests other than unobtrusively running the household and ensuring that there were meals on the table as and when my father desired them. There was no spark between my parents, or between them and me. One would have thought that the loss of

174

my brother would have brought us closer together, if only because there were fewer of us bidding for a share of the same emotional pie. But if anything it calcified us. Remember as well that when my father died, my mother didn't attend his funeral.

And then it was her turn to die, and I was in the room with her coffin, unable to muster any more anguish than she had done seven years earlier. I was sad, I wished that she was still alive – but she'd been getting on, hadn't been well for a while, and her time had come. After another five minutes or so, I turned away from my mother and tapped on the door, which I discovered had been locked by its elderly custodian. He didn't come to open it, so I knocked again, this time a little harder, a little longer. Still nothing. Impatiently, I rapped on the door again, and continued to do so for another five minutes, slowly increasing the volume of my hammering, mildly anxious that I was being punished in some mysterious way for not cherishing my mother – and by implication my father, too. There was a danger of it turning into a scene from a bad film, when the old man finally unlocked the door.

'Thank you,' I said, tartly and with heavy sarcasm.

He looked at me and smiled, and it was then I understood that if he wasn't completely deaf, he was somewhere close to it.

I would still, I think, be unable to grieve instinctively and in an uninhibited manner. I have never experienced the loss of someone to whom I felt very close. Laurence was a good friend (perhaps an *only* friend), but we were not close. All my children are still alive. All my ex-partners and wives are still alive. None of the above has cancer or any other life-threatening disease. *I* have cancer, though for the moment everything appears to be under control. Maybe my own death will be the first time I have to experience the death of someone close. And this year I will be the same age as both my parents when they died.

I do know, however, that I would be greatly distressed by the death of the woman in my life. That would, I am certain, leave me bereft, if only because a small voice inside would be saying, 'And who's going to look after me now?'

If all this sounds honest but rather brutal, consider that an actor I much admired, Derek Godfrey, once observed, 'Here comes Ian Holm, hiding behind his honesty.' This is something which, over the years, has rather perplexed me. It is true that I do find it difficult to be anything other than honest when, for example, asked my opinion about a script, though this inability to fake must seem peculiar in someone who makes his living from pretending, from acting. And yet I know what Godfrey meant. My lack of guile and apparent integrity frequently masks the fact that there is very little to back it up. It is an entirely hollow sort of honesty; an unfeelingly concentrated upright-ness. Everything I do on stage is an enactment of guilt or rage or comedy or whatever, but never the actual thing. There's very little I can call on to say, 'Yes, I've felt that,' and this helps to explain, I suppose, why I have some talent for acting: because I have to be *really* good in order not to be found out.

When Bee left I was authentically distressed, though in addition perhaps gave an inauthentically melodramatic display of heartache. But not long afterwards, and after *S.O.S. Titanic*, I met a photographer called Sophie Baker, and soon after that I moved into her house in Islington. And quite soon after that, in 1980, we had a son, Harry. That made five children with three different partners over a period of twenty years or so. Jessica and Sarah-Jane, Lissy and Barnaby, and now Harry. Lynne, Bee and Sophie – though she would not be the last. Is that success or failure?

I say that I 'met' Sophie Baker, whereas in fact Bee and I had known her for several years. She had even, I think, taken still photographs for *The Iceman Cometh*, and over the years had become a good friend. She laughed when I turned up in Islington with a strange, smallish suitcase containing two pairs of jeans (both frayed, both decorated with stars), two rather battered T-shirts, a tracksuit, a purple windcheater (with broken zip, repaired with pink cotton by Bee), and a book of poems by Alistair MacLean.

Almost immediately we went on holiday to Greece, where I spent some of the time learning lines for a BBC production of *The Misanthrope*. At the time, I felt this was a good role. The material was proven, the cast was good (it included Alison Steadman, Maurice Denham and Nigel Hawthorne), I liked Michael Simpson the director, and it was something I could manage without too much bother. It was also good to be working at a time when all the talk in the industry was of recession.

I played Alceste, a man filled with passion yet who was also something of a prig. At the end of the piece he goes away to live as a recluse, and there is something curiously unfinished, as if there is another play just round the corner. In a sense, it reminded me of Pinter's work, where there is usually something outside the room or the house of the main drama, something waiting for explanation or illumination. A part of me responded to that sense of a life happening or continuing elsewhere, of the drama not being a closed book. Maybe it relieved any responsibility I might have felt about life being in some way conclusively bound, about having to accept liability for its fixedness.

During *The Misanthrope* I grew quite close to Nigel Hawthorne, who was at the time a very good but underrated actor who could sometimes react quite sharply to what he perceived as a lack of recognition. He had not yet acquired the high profile that *Yes, Minister* would grant him, or at least had not converted it into national recognition on stage or in films. I think it was largely through his intercession that I agreed to do a production of *Uncle Vanya* at the Hampstead Theatre. This was the first time I had contemplated going back on stage since the *Iceman* crack-up four years earlier. Then, I had thought I would never get back on stage, but now it seemed a strong possibility. I discussed it with Sophie, who was very encouraging.

'You could do Astrov standing on your head,' she said.

'Well, yes – but can I do it *standing up* on stage in front of people?'

'It's Hampstead. A small theatre. It will be quite intimate – no great physical effort, no really big exposure.'

'I suppose so.'

'And you had a good time there in 1974.'

'Did I? What did I do?'

'*Other People* by Mike Stott.'

'So I did.'

'And much of the attention will be on Nigel. He's the "coming man".'

Sophie had an idea that my breakdown had been caused not merely by some chronic vulnerability to panic but by the wrong play arriving at the wrong time – i.e., gruelling material straight after the trials of *Jesus of Nazareth* – and exacerbated by problems in the domestic nest. She was right and had quickly got the measure of me, teasing me about methodical routines and the way that I would always try to create a calm space amongst any kind of chaos that might be threatening my need for stillness. She pointed out the obsessive way that I folded my clothes, did the washing up, weeded the garden, cut the grass and put the rubbish out. Even the habitual way I cleared away bathroom clutter to create my own toothbrushing space. I was forever tidying things away, and I would never cook or plant or do anything which involved the concoction of mess. I was particularly worried about my habit of mowing the lawn (something I did with fanatical enthusiasm at Wassall, usually perched on a small yellow tractor) as it reminded me of my father's zombie-like grass-cutting, though Sophie also observed that these methodical tasks were perhaps a form of self-discipline. In creating my own, controlled world I was also doing something which in different ways helped to define my acting.

I agreed to do *Vanya* and found to my surprise that going back on stage was not traumatic, although the experience was not especially pleasant. But it would be the last time I would work in the theatre for several years. My main memory is of difficulties concerning the American director Nancy Meckler, who was very good but whose working methods infuriated most of the cast. My agent Julian Belfrage had warned her gently beforehand that she shouldn't play games with us, though I don't know whether this was because he was protective of my 'comeback' or because he'd heard something about the way she worked. Anyway, we seemed to spend inappropriately large chunks of time doing things like learning how to write in the specific, shadowy darkness of candlelight, so that in the end Nigel Hawthorne exclaimed, 'Can't we just rehearse the fucking play before we forget its *title*?'

It all went pretty well in the end, I think, despite it not being an especially happy time. And then Sophie and I went to India, where Sophie photographed small villages for a piece on the caste system, an interest which would later lead to her writing a book on the subject. I was anxious that the sprawl and the sheer mess of the country, in addition to the fact that I didn't know the place, would cause me difficulties. After a problem with the flight, however, I found that I was enchanted by India. There was something about its simplicity which appealed to me, the sense of an underlying purity which transcended the physical disarray. And I was so well looked after by Sophie and the various people we met that I remember being very open and receptive to everything.

Through it all, Sophie was acutely aware that I was generally fine so long as I could plan ahead and knew that nothing untoward or unexpected was going to happen. The only problem came when she went off to the south of the country by herself for a few days and accidentally took my passport with her. When I discovered that I didn't have it, I recall feeling suddenly defenceless and exposed, even on the verge of another panic attack.

Years later, it emerged that our son Harry also suffers from similar symptoms. Although it strikes him in different circumstances, it does seem that there is something genetic in both of us being so prone to assaults on our equilibrium. *The Iceman* may well have been the wrong play at the wrong time, but it also acted as the trigger to a condition that must have been buried inside me long before that. Maybe my mother's lack of engagement with the world was actually a way of holding herself together; my father's habit of closing himself off from people a defensive mechanism designed to protect himself from otherwise disturbing incursions into his mind? My own shyness, my reluctance to take responsibility, my willingness to follow instructions, and my need to create alternative spaces through my work in which to live . . . all these things suggest a fundamental lack of respect for my own, given world. A fear that the 'nothing' at its centre is not up to the mark.

When we returned from India, there wasn't much work about. I remember getting by with voiceovers, in particular the BBC radio version of *The Lord of the Rings*, in which I played Frodo. This was an ideal project for me – there was a wonderful cast and a real sense of ensemble playing. The recording provided steady if temporary work which, unlike theatre, did not involve deadening repetition. Every day I walked to Broadcasting House from Islington. Walking provided me with an opportunity to create and live in my own world, so I relished the daily journey. I planned a route, more or less stuck with it so that it became a routine, and then set off – observing, looking around, slipping in and out of other people's physical identities, and just being by myself. I know that Dickens used to stride around London hatching plots and characters for his novels; my walking wasn't on the same intellectual or physical scale, of course, and the small worlds I created were momentary and instinctive by comparison, though I suspect the same kinds of forces were at work in both of us. Occasionally I would be recognized (though in general I don't think I am the kind of person who does get recognized), and someone would approach me and say, 'Aren't you an actor?' and I would say something like, 'Sorry. Not me. I'm a plumber.'

A couple of years later I did a Stephen Poliakoff play for the BBC called *Soft Targets*, in which I played a minor Russian diplomat called Alexei who is convinced he is being hounded by the British Secret Service. It was directed by Charles Sturridge (who had recently completed *Brideshead Revisited*) and starred Helen Mirren – as 'the woman with whom I get involved' – and Nigel Havers. I mention this now because Alexei always seemed to be walking the streets, suspicious and observant of everything and everyone around him. The part called for incessant watchfulness, or at least apparent watchfulness, and tapped into some of the things that define acting, such as observation and the need to be self-contained. Alexei's cautiousness and isolation from those around him made the part peculiarly appealing, and also reminded me that Ridley Scott had once told me that I should be a producer, and when I asked why, had told me, 'Because I can see your beady eyes watching me all the time.'

It was an arduous but rewarding shoot, and although Poliakoff wanted to show England as a foreign country in the film and to suggest the alienation of city life, it came out as a cross between John Le Carré and Lewis Carroll, a sort of gritty fantasia. I don't think this was unintended or unrelated to the play's more obvious themes; after all, Poliakoff was the son of immigrants, and on occasions England must have seemed both quaintly eccentric and unnervingly down-to-earth. This ambiguity was something I enjoyed exploiting, and I recall one scene where the Helen Mirren character and I were involved in a car crash. A passer-by wanders past and says something like, 'Looks as if she's in a bit of a mess,' and I, as Alexei, give Helen a sidelong glance, unaware as a Russian that the English sexualize their cars. Actually, it was something that Poliakoff and I had worked out beforehand, but it does suggest the kind of tension that was involved in playing the part.

It was around this time that Sophie suggested we stay at Wassall rather than selling the house and dividing things up with Bee, who seemed content to stay at Iverna and whose sense of independence did not in any case stretch to lawyers and complicated financial settlements. She is the only one of my 'wives' to whom I was never formally married – the reason, she tells me, why we are still on such good terms. I was character-istically unsure about what to do and was, as usual, waiting for someone to make a decision on my behalf. Sophie suggested it while we were walking along one of the lanes nearby, on the kind of warm summer's day when everything seemed right beneath an English heaven.

'You mean we'll live here?' I said.

'Well, why not? It's too big for a country cottage.'

'And you'll look after it?' I asked, suddenly sensing a very agreeable solution. It would mean continuity for my children, and Lissy could keep her pony. In any case Bee had said that she didn't want to live there.

We changed the house a little, moving the kitchen and adding a dark room so that Sophie could feel as if it was her own home.

This, I think, was also the time that a tennis court was built. I recall it as being a fallow period for work and spent the first weeks in our 'new' house weeding the garden with dutiful zeal, ignoring the temptation to use weedkiller and pulling out each stubborn root individually. It was also a time of fanatical lawn-mowing; I was driven to be occupied and involved.

And then two projects came up and I was able to do both. One was *We, the Accused* for the BBC, which was a fictional piece about a man who had murdered his wife and then run away with someone else. In the end he is found, caught, convicted and hanged. Albert Pierpoint's assistant came to advise us about the execution scene, and told us that England's last public executioner was a zealot who thought he was on a mission to rid the world of evil. He also said, with the lubricated ease of one who had already used the line many times, 'Don't worry, I won't keep you hanging about.'

Although this was an exhausting series, space was found to allow me to film *Chariots of Fire* at more or less the same time. David Puttnam flew me to and from locations, and as they were all in England, it didn't seem especially hard work. Usually I disliked dipping in and out of projects in this fragmented, inter-mittent manner, but because everyone was so accommodating I recall it as being a very happy experience. Puttnam was *very* professional; he knew exactly how to make me feel at ease, and the travelling did not seem intrusive or awkward. He was also one of the most adventurous film producers in the world at that time, winning prizes, doing well at the box office, and develop-ing valuable British talent. He was amiably disapproving of the American way of doing things and *Chariots* was exactly the kind of eccentric, curiously English project that would have appealed to him.

Despite never quite feeling as though I was a full-time member of the cast, I developed a good relationship with the director Hugh Hudson. Although he wasn't always effective at communicating with people and some thought him rather aloof, I found him easy enough. He was very good at painting a large canvas, though he was to get into difficulties a few years later with *Revolution*, which sank Goldcrest. In effect, he took the rap – unfairly, I thought. The film wasn't bad, certainly not *that* bad, and was burdened with a crappy script.

By then, there were unreasonably high expectations for 'a Hugh Hudson film'. But in *Chariots* there was a youthful buzz surrounding the whole project, a lightning flash of optimism that originated with Puttnam and animated the entire film. No one, of course, had any idea that it would be a hit on such a large international (i.e., American) scale, and Sophie and I were initially very disappointed when we attended an early screening of the film, before the Vangelis music had been added. It seemed somehow lacklustre and almost embarrassingly trite, and I remember us trying to sneak out at the end so we wouldn't have to confront David and Hugh.

I played a character called Sam Mussabini who was Ben Cross's running coach, and although he had an Italian-sounding name, he came from somewhere in the north of England, so I gave him a species of northern accent. His sister was still alive (though we didn't know that at the time), and afterwards she wrote to David Puttnam to say I sounded nothing like her brother but that she still enjoyed my portrayal.

I knew little or nothing of athletics coaching so relied on the script and went instinctively for the kind of stagy toughness that suggests it can be leavened by humour. A year or so earlier I had played a cowardly but pompously disciplinarian corporal in a re-make of *All Quiet on the Western Front*, and Mussabini was a more humane version of him. One of the final scenes, shot I think at a hotel in Harrogate, of me putting my fist through my straw hat at the news that Abrahams had won his Olympic gold, was almost an afterthought. As a professional (and perhaps as a half-Arab professional), Mussabini was not allowed into the actual stadium and had to wait for the playing of the national anthem before he knew that his tutee had triumphed. The moment was filmed while people were packing up and generally putting the film to bed, but caught precisely the picture's momentum. It was both a tongue-tied expression of joy at winning *and* the moment when the coach's tough-guy façade cracks wide open in the way that audiences had anticipated it might. Afterwards, Hugh told me he thought in many ways it was the unifying centre of the film. Mussabini was a very private man, yet manages to express himself *to himself.*

Puttnam's optimism struck a chord within the country. Margaret Thatcher's election was still fairly recent news, and Britain was still sore from the Winter of Discontent in 1979. People needed something to cheer them up, and the film's almost naive blending of nationalism and passion seemed to be what they wanted.

I was Oscar-nominated for Best Supporting Actor and the ceremony was held during the spring of 1982, while I was filming *Soft Targets*. Joel Grey, whom I knew very well, was reading the envelopes. When he came to my name, he announced it very slowly ('Eeeeee-annn Hoe-mmmm for *Chariots of Fie-ahhhh*'), though I don't know whether he knew in advance that John Gielgud had won for playing Dudley Moore's butler in *Arthur*. At the time Sophie was out in the Sudan working for Christian Aid, and she later told me that though I had tried to conceal it, she knew I was pleased to have been nominated.

A side of me that I didn't always much care for was the desire to win – to be good at something and to show off about it. I did wonder if my parents would have been proud of me. I could imagine my mother saying, 'Well it looks very grand, I must say,' and my father, having done his homework, recognizing the actors and correctly naming each one as he or she appeared on the television screen. By this time, they would have invested in a colour set. Something in me would have wanted them to be proud and something in them would have wanted to express pride. But something else would have prevented us from communicating even these quite straightforward emotions.

12

ON NOT BEING BRITISH

'Being competitive' was perhaps a more significant part of my make-up than I had previously thought. I had known for quite some time that one of the reasons for acting was to show off in front of others and thereby to receive their approval. I was good at acting and wanted the reassurance that came from the appreciation I accepted. I was not so good at tennis, though good enough to deceive myself into thinking that I was some good, and at this time good enough to want to play and win as often as possible.

Sophie bought me a John McEnroe Maxply tennis racquet when we got married, and by the end of the summer it was almost in pieces. I was as guilty of racquet abuse as the illustrious player whose name it bore. But whereas he would chuck the thing around for not being able to play a winning forehand pass by, say, Bjorn Borg, I would hurl it in the air for not being able to clear the net. Once it had to be rescued from a tree after I'd thrown it there in frustration.

I liked to win at tennis, at ping pong, at anything I did. And if I didn't do it, it was probably because I understood that

I wouldn't be able to win. Sophie had a very distinguished set of friends, many of them musicians or musical in some way, and I recall my delight – my elation – at beating the pianist Stephen Bishop Kovacevic on the Wassall court. The conductor Simon Rattle was another guest, looking rather like Brian May, the lead guitarist of Queen, and nattering enthusiastically about Shostakovich, Mahler and Birmingham. We liked each other well enough, though what I really wanted to do was get *him* on court, show him my backhand, give him the runaround, and then leave him (sweating, uncomfortable, unnerved) gasping in admiration.

I didn't play women at tennis very often, though occasionally there would be a game of mixed doubles. Somehow it was more important to win against a man. There's something which explains this. I once knew someone who liked watching Ann Jones play tennis. Ann Jones won Wimbledon in 1969. She was Amazonian with an extraordinarily athletic figure – though the wonderful body was crowned by a rather goofy face. While he was watching Ann on television, this person used to put his thumb over her face so that he could watch her body, especially (as I recall) her breasts. This isn't especially pleasant behaviour, but at its core is the sense that men view male and female tennis players in very different ways. For me, any sense of achievement on the tennis court came through the ability to triumph over someone of comparable endowment. There would have been no call for an obscuring thumb over the image of Stephen Kovacevic. At stake was not the matter of aptitude so much as resemblance.

Sophie nurtured any love I have of classical music. While Bee helped open my eyes and mind to reading (we read scripts together; we talked about them together), Sophie did much the same for music. One notable performance we attended was a prom at the Albert Hall conducted by Claudio Abbado. It was performed by the Youth Orchestra of Europe and all the musicians were young and inspired. The audience responded to their playing and became ecstatic, urging the orchestra to even greater heights of achievement. A curiously dynamic and irresistible bond was formed between orchestra, audience and conductor, each a component of a single whole, each a stimulant of the other. Urged into an excited but controlled frenzy, the orchestra played almost the whole of Stravinsky's 'Firebird Suite' as an encore.

However, if I could be animated and occasionally electrified by this exposure to music, I still kept a distance between me and the musicians (and painters and writers and journalists) that Sophie invited round to Islington or down to Wassall. There was no artistic rapport between us, for example, no especially rigorous interest on my part about how or why such extra-ordinary musical effects could be achieved. This was, I am sure, mostly my own fault. I don't think I was ungenerous or un-interested in them, or even unfriendly, but the exchanges between us were generally polite and uninvolved. I was shy – I *am* shy, though perhaps less so these days because there is less to lose – though I suspect that is not the whole reason. My reserve is very English in its manner, and is to do, I think, with an incapacity to see much beyond my own need for reassurance, a reluctance to give something of myself that would not involve getting something back. An inability, in short, to step outside myself. Stepping outside myself was for acting, though I needed a prescribed role. Real life did not offer the parts I wanted.

That sounds mean-minded, and is a mechanical and perhaps rather clumsy way of describing something which is a chiefly instinctive form of powerlessness. Feeling empty inside, a cipher, I also felt that I had nothing to give beyond, say, a wholly personal and self-entombed appreciation of music.

On the other hand, as I've already mentioned, it is precisely this blankness which allows me to act. Sophie often remarked on my absence of hobbies, by which I suppose she meant 'interests pursued with a passion'. Bee used to say that my inner vacancy caused me to become 'prismatic' while I was acting. By which I suppose she meant that any success I had with acting was based on a facility to project back to an audience precisely what it wished to see or hear.

Around this time, I was cast as Charles Dodgson, better known as Lewis Carroll, the writer of the Alice books, in Gavin Millar's *Dreamchild*. In addition to my playing of Napoleon at several points in my career (understandable), I have also netted two of the greatest writers of children's literature (much less understandable). Both Dodgson and J. M. Barrie enjoyed close relationships with young children, relationships that today may well have landed them in court on charges of paedophilia. Certainly Dodgson's photographs of young Alice would have created a storm. Both men produced classic texts from the sublimation of their repressed emotions (and some would say repressed sexual desires).

You would have to ask the directors and casting agents involved with both films to understand why I should have been cast in them. Each of the directors, for example, was very different; Birkin absolutely identified with Barrie – or Barrie's obsessions – while Gavin Millar was much cooler, more distantly intellectual. Maybe they thought it was something to do with size and children being less intimidated by someone who wasn't so tall as many adults. Maybe I was cheap. Maybe I was in favour at the time. Maybe they simply thought I'd do a good job, be reliable. Possibly I was developing a reputation for being dependable, which was fine as far as it went, except it came with associated baggage. If you were reliable, it also implied predictability, safety, and the worst kind of inflexible staunchness, and I certainly didn't consider myself an 'armchair actor'.

At best, casting is an imprecise science, and often a numbers game (male and female stars plus one or two reliable character actors), a stale equation of the reputedly glamorous and the apparently honest, the whole thing a mix of American and British or whatever, depending on the funding. Sometimes directors like to use favourite actors (Scorsese and de Niro spring to mind), and sometimes an idea develops into a kind of fetish, where there is a determination to cast *that* actor no matter what the consequences. Richard Attenborough told me at around this time that he had originally tried to cast Anthony Hopkins as Gandhi. Despite Hopkins's protestations (too big, too fat, too white), attempts were made to recondition him for the part. He was sent to a health farm, given a tan, and eventually wrapped in a loincloth. This was the point, about three months into the procedure, at which Hopkins began to insist that he was not right for the part. The role was passed to the far more suitable Ben Kingsley.

Dodgson had a bad stutter which disappeared when he dealt with children, the only people with whom he could identify. This, of course, was very different from me, who dealt with my now five children not very well at all. I remember one critic saying at the time, 'Poor Ian Holm! After his magnificent performance on television as J. M. Barrie, here he is again at the mercy of a dazzling and ruthless child.'

Dreamchild was very good, though small, British, and low budget. So perhaps *that* was why I was cast. It was written by Dennis Potter, who appeared a few times on set, always smoking, usually unpleasant, often ill. One had the sense that all these things were somehow related. Coral Browne played the elderly Alice, looking back on her early life with Dodgson as she sailed to America to receive an honorary degree. In the intervening years, life has caught up with her: two sons lost in France during the war and creeping cynicism. She flits in and out of her waking dreams and remembers the 'dreamchild' into which Dodgson/Carroll transmuted her.

Throughout the filming, we were watched very closely by the Lewis Carroll Society, which was fanatical about the film being authentic. Once, filming on the river at Oxford, there were problems about the light-coloured jacket I had been given to wear (it was hot, it was summer), because Dodgson apparently always wore the same rather gloomy dark-hued jacket.

At the time, I remember thinking that if Dodgson's repressed, unexpressed sexuality could resurface as two uniquely sexless masterpieces, then maybe acting, or my acting at any rate, was based on the same principle of being able to effectively redirect muffled, subdued emotions. Of course, I do sometimes wonder why I can act (and how), though instinct also warns me that too much inquisition could bring the whole thing crashing down. But the alter ego aspect of the Dodgson/Carroll relationship did make me wonder.

And here I was, playing a man who brought a young girl under the spell of his imagination. In effect, he projected on to her a dream of innocence, realized in the world of his books where Alice enters 'the wood . . . where things have no names'. Gavin Millar told me that he wanted to make a film about 'anxiety and the illusions of love', presumably the illusions thrown up by the relationship between Dodgson and Alice and how time qualified it.

Dreamchild prompted all sorts of questions about the nature of unconditional love. It also invited a more nagging, directly personal one. Was I a good father? You would have to ask my five children, though I suspect that for much of the time the answer was probably 'no'. When Bee and I separated, Lissy and Barnaby were old enough to realize and possibly understand what was happening. That could not have made it any easier for them, but when I had left Lynne, Jessica and Sarah-Jane were much younger and more vulnerable. They must have felt abandoned, and to a degree, they were. My relationship with them over the years has been built in an erratic, haphazard manner, none of us entirely confident of its true basis.

My relationship with Jessica, my first born, has been particularly capricious, and at several points during my changeable domestic situations she has held me to account for my 'incredible behaviour'. Probably each new bout of unreasonableness on my part merely reminded her of the unreasonableness I had practised on her, her mother and her sister. This is understandable, and has resulted in splits and silences between us, sometimes lasting for several years. However, a year or so before *Dreamchild*, I had invited Jessica to travel with me to Africa for the making of *Greystoke: The Legend of Tarzan, Lord of the Apes*, a twenty-seven-million-dollar film that became quite affectionately known as 'Staybroke'. Jessica was a zoologist and not much interested in the making of the film, though very keen on being able to visit rainforests and so on and so forth. She took time off from her job to join me, in the end taking such a long time off that she put it in some jeopardy. As she explained, it was the chance of a lifetime and well worth the sack, should it come to that.

Sophie was instrumental in the invitation being issued. During our time together, she tried to bring the disparate strands of my family together, tried in effect to make me feel like a normal family man. She and Jessica became very fond of one another, and it turned into one of those periods when father and daughter were close, though both of us knew that it probably wouldn't last for ever. That, somehow, was the uncomfortable but irresistible nature of our relationship.

After filming had finished, Sophie told me that Jessica had

only been able to afford to bring out a hundred pounds to Africa and, seeking to please me, had spent sixty of this on a bottle of Morgon wine. Apparently, although I was grateful enough, I was less demonstrative in my appreciation than she had anticipated. The subsequent feelings of disappointment she experienced were representative of the underlying tension and sensitivity of our relationship. I suppose that by keeping her distance at certain times, Jessica has sought to protect herself, to keep at bay possible hurt and any disillusion with me. For the moment, however, and despite the relatively unappreciated bottle of wine, we were both happy enough, she finding contentment in her exploration of the African rainforests, and me in the making of the film.

Greystoke was directed by Hugh Hudson who, after *Chariots*, was something of a hot property. I think he asked me to read the script very early – before even Tarzan was cast – and asked me to consider the part of d'Arnot, who was a kind of father to Tarzan, someone who knew him in both states, wild and tamed. Like a proud father, he teaches Tarzan to speak and introduces him into the world.

I greatly enjoyed making *Greystoke*. As well as sharing the same perspective as Hugh on d'Arnot – that he lives vicariously through Tarzan and is sad at having to let his man-child go – I think he also saw me as an ally or a kindred spirit in a wider sense, and began to involve me in much of the film-making process. From being the quiet but genial bloke who pottered around the set observing it all with quiet but focused intensity, I was suddenly more enmeshed in the whole operation.

While Jessica was away studying the wildlife and the geography of the place, I found myself giving occasional notes from behind the camera, looking at rushes, and generally acting as a sounding board for the director's ideas. For me, it was the perfect scenario: involvement without responsibility. I even recall helping in the casting of Christopher Lambert when Hugh wanted someone feral and intelligent-seeming while the studio attempted to foist on him any number of over-muscled, walnuts-in-tights, Mr Universe types.

There are many different ways to direct a film, and Hugh's was rather cool and detached. Lambert complained that he didn't speak to him more than four or five times during the first four months of filming. When this lack of communication was pointed out, Hugh explained, 'You were an animal in that part of the film, and animals don't talk.' I don't know how Lambert took that, but they had a row, made up, and got on pretty well after that, even gossiping away in French together.

I enjoyed being in the jungle. I even liked being hot, and being on good terms with Hugh and John Wells (who played Evelyn Blount, the hypocritical scientist) made it even more satisfying. Hugh, though, was increasingly in trouble with the studio. When Blount shot dead Tarzan's ape-father in London, for example, Warners wanted the impact softened and requested an alternative storyline, one where the ape survives, is transported back to the jungle and released into the wild. 'This isn't fucking *Disney*,' I remember Hugh saying. 'The monkey stays dead. That's what happened. That's what I'm going to show.'

Occasionally, he would inadvertently contribute to the friction, often heading off into the jungle with his cameraman, the brilliant John Alcott (who tragically died shortly after the completion of the film) and leaving everyone in limbo. Once, he went to Chad to shoot a tribe which boasted extraordinary horses and riders. He had a notion that if he could film them, then somehow the footage could be shoehorned into the movie. The horsemanship was indeed impressive. Hugh came back with astonishing pictures of men riding teams of magnificent horses at full tilt and then turning them on a sixpence. However, the images never found their way into the finished product, and the studio swallowed hard while an expensive week slipped by. The film's 1983 release was postponed, and then twenty minutes were cut from the released print, both sure signs that there had been further disagreements.

Greystoke had in fact become an entirely predictable sort of misfit. Having given a lot of money to a relatively untried director on the basis of a single hit film, Warner Brothers was increasingly anxious about its investment and attempted to influence the way things were going. One of the producers – decent, hands-on – got 'bumped upstairs' just after we'd begun shooting, and overnight became a different character – monstrous, distant – and this only served to destabilize things. Warners wanted an action film, whereas Hugh was more interested in the human side of things, though there was action in it. The result was an inevitable muddle. The film wasn't at all bad, but it eventually satisfied only a few people.

For much of the time, we stayed in the Atlantik Beach Hotel, which was run by a German who obediently conformed to all kinds of national stereotyping. The French community which worked at the vast petroleum works nearby took over the complex at the weekends. Good food was flown in from France on a daily basis, so few of us had much exposure to the dis-comforts one found outside these kinds of European enclosures. In fact, the only irritation I can recall was the almost daily appearance near to the set of a man with a chainsaw, apparently engaged in cutting down trees, though I doubt he actually felled many. Every time the camera was about to start turning, this man would crank up his saw. The first time this happened, and after the third or fourth ruined take, Hugh sent someone over with a small amount of money. The man stopped, took the money, said thank you, and left. But the next day he was there again, and the whole routine started over. Hugh sent the same man over with the same amount of money. He returned five minutes later.

'It's no good, Hugh.'

'What do you mean *it's no good*?'

'He wants more money.'

'How much more?'

'Not much. Just more. Then he'll go away.'

And so it went on. The chainsaw man's price increased every day until, eventually, he was making a relatively tidy sum out of his mischief.

I daresay the total amount of money which exchanged hands was not large, at least not in our terms, but the whole thing made me feel uncomfortable. It wasn't the actual blackmail that rankled, more the gathering awareness that we were being pushed into playing the role of wealthy colonialists who, through this act of bribery, were somehow patronizing the corrupt and poor Africans. Though on a diminished scale, there was something Orwellian and a bit 'Shooting an Elephant' about it all – the colonizing white men being expected to behave in a certain way and doing so. Would the same thing have happened if we'd been filming at Shepperton? Of course not.

During the first few years of the 1980s, I was involved in several films which sought to define the national psyche or played on the idea of Britishness. The mini revolution of British films about being British had been sparked by the success of *Chariots*. Remember Colin Welland's triumphalist, even notorious Oscar-waving speech, when he proudly if perhaps prematurely proclaimed, 'The British are coming!' after receiving his screenplay award? Suddenly, inspecting one's national navel was all the rage. Even *Dreamchild* – with its re-creation, testing and despoiling of Edwardian England – paid lip service to this tendency.

I suppose it was a time (post-Falklands, post-economic

depression, post-union-dominated industry) when a swelling of national pride prompted questions about such things. In 1985 I went to an exhibition of Francis Bacon's paintings at the Barbican, thought about buying the newly published edition of *The Domesday Book* (but did not actually do so) and watched on television the Heysel Stadium disaster a year after Liverpool had won the European Cup. Greenwich Mean Time faced termination through lack of funds . . . and it was British Film Year. Supposedly, British film-making was on the crest of a wave. That year, I recall *Wetherby* and *Dance with a Stranger* coming out at more or less the same time, both in their own ways good films, both concerned with questions of national identity.

I've never much liked the uptightness of Britain, probably because it reminded me too much of myself. Yet in *Wetherby* I played a character called Stanley Pilborough, whose only real appearance in the film is at a dinner party. Mrs Pilborough was Judi Dench, whom I had known since the early days at Stratford, so I knew it would be rather jolly. David Hare's script was carefully and sharply honed to be representative of England. Vanessa Redgrave's cottage was on the edge of a town rather than a village, and the library where the suicidal John Morgan (played by Tim McInnerny) worked was no normal library. It was home to the British Library Lending Division, the significance of which was its decentralized, cold, glassy smugness and, crucially, the fact that it didn't lend books to individuals – only other institutions.

Wetherby was set in Yorkshire but filmed in Hertfordshire, a 'Yorkshire of the mind' as one of the carpenters said. Because all-round views were wanted, a cottage was built in a field just outside London. Polystyrene trees were brought in from the recent Disney production *Oz*. I recall Judi Dench wandering around after shooting had been completed, helping to pack them away, walking round the field piercing and picking up litter with a sharpened stick and saying how happy the whole thing made her. 'I could do this,' she twinkled, 'it's so satisfying.' Also, as most of the cast and crew lived in London, they had the benefit of a short commute out to the set every day, so the atmosphere was quite relaxed. I later heard a story that someone had appropriated John Morgan's coffin for Andrew Birkin and driven it to his house in Wales, where he spent the night in it.

My role was pretty straightforward. I remember being asked as Stanley Pilborough to explain what Margaret Thatcher had done to Britain and why she had done it. He said, 'Revenge!' At another point, he gives some advice to the spinsterish character Jean Travers that Vanessa was playing: 'If you're frightened of loneliness, never get married.'

When the shooting finished, the producer presented Vanessa with a gift. After she had accepted it, she put it down and brought out a piece of paper from which she read a ten-minute speech about the plight of the miners. Actually, although I don't believe acting is much about identifying with a role, it was the character of Jean Travers that most intrigued me. In the film, the desperate student John Morgan comes to Wetherby to commit suicide. He is looking for an audience and picks Redgrave's character not merely because of an earlier relationship between them, but more, I think, because of the disfiguring emotional blankness within her which acts as a magnet for the obsessions and desires of other people.

When I first read the script, I wondered about the reasonableness, the credibility, of this procedure. But now I understand what David Hare was trying to say, and can unnervingly glimpse something familiar in the relationship between Jean Travers and John Morgan. I reckon that personal blankness was what enabled me to act, working like a magnet for the characters I took on, providing them with a sort of internal audience.

Vanessa played the part brilliantly. In her own life, she is such a strong and involved character; the speech she made about the miners would have been impossible for calm, detached, uninvolved Jean Travers. She had the opportunity to be a movie star in the 1960s, but something always held her back and pitched her as someone who wasn't a star, yet was not quite a character actress either. Her politics attracted many enemies, and she could be awkwardly outspoken, but she is an extraordinarily skilled and versatile performer.

Watching her in *Wetherby* was a strange experience, because off screen she was a charming but insistent political activist and campaigner for all sorts of causes from feminism to denouncing Zionism. What I remember feeling most, I think, is *How is it that somebody can feel so strongly about things?* Vanessa is a member of the Revolutionary Workers' Party. By contrast, I have never even voted. Not necessarily from apathy, or not merely from apathy, but also because I am vulnerable to persuasion about the relative merits of most political codes, and therefore find it difficult to make a defining decision whenever the opportunity comes round. It is fair to say, therefore, that I hold no strong political convictions.

During those years, I never felt that I was involved in some orchestrated attempt by the film business to investigate the state of the nation or whatever, though I'm sure some did. If anything, I have tried to throw away my Englishness. If pushed, I will sometimes say that I'm a Scot, though I understand how bogus that may seem. Recently, I have spent a fair amount of time in New York and become seduced by the city's openness and pugnacity. I have put myself through therapy in an attempt to peel away my habitual reserve and detachment, to – as they say – 'open myself up'. Yet I also know that these are diversions, borne of circumstance rather than propelled by desire. Still, there remains an habitual reticence about all that I do, a sort of unforthcomingness and restraint that precludes commitment to much more than passing impulses or fancies. An empty or emptyish vessel waiting for a character.

When *Dance with a Stranger* came along – more or less at the same time as *Wetherby* – I did not have to wait long for the character I was playing. Desmond Cussen was the much-abused friend of Ruth Ellis, the last woman to be executed in England, for shooting her lover Blakeley outside the Magdala Tavern in Hampstead. The film re-created London in the 1950s (packet of Dunhills 3s 7d for twenty, debate about the abolition of the H-bomb, Ted Heath swing bands etc., but most important was the unforgiving fabric of the British class system), and Cussen is Ellis's only true supporter and the person she endlessly betrays. There remains an unresolved question about whether or not Cussen provided Ellis with the murder weapon.

The director was Mike Newell, a very good, solidly professional man who had learnt his craft in British television and could turn his hand to almost anything. I asked him early on whether there was anything on tape of Cussen that I could see, something that might help me find the character.

'Only one thing,' he told me, 'but it won't do you much good.'
'Why's that?'
'It was something he did quite recently. It's shot in Australia. There's a beach and sea in the background. He's got an Australian accent. He's a broken man.'
'Oh – in what way?'
'He remarried, but his wife died of cancer. Business failures. That sort of thing. Bears no relation to the man you want to see thirty years ago in London.'

I asked to see the footage anyway. Cussen did indeed have the look of a resigned and even pathetic man. Physically he had changed; in 1955 he was six foot three, whereas now he looked somehow shrivelled. Behind him, as Mike Newell had described, waves broke on to a virtually empty beach. Then came the question I had been hoping for: at the end of the interview, he was asked whether he had loved Ruth. Cussen took off his glasses, wiped a tear from his eye, and said, 'Yes. I still do.'

I turned to Mike and said, 'Thank you very much. That's all I need to know.'

Just as when I heard J. M. Barrie's voice, everything seemed to drop into place. Cussen could well have given her the gun (I tried to play him with both possibilities kept open), but as far as I was concerned, that wasn't the issue. I saw something pitiable and tender in Cussen, certainly something more affecting than in Blakeley, who thought that with Ruth he was slumming it. She was, after all, a married woman. Cussen may well have been a dapper nonentity, but he was a dapper nonentity who longed for Ruth and supported her despite the impossibility of love. Once that became apparent, it was a matter of finding the appropriate emotional note around which the rest of the character could take form. On the one hand he was the model of a lonely man entering middle age, but there was in addition a desperate, almost dignified integrity about him, an inner energy that suggested he might explode at any moment, and *that* was the note to find.

This was something that Mike Newell and I talked about and worked towards. At one point during shooting I gave him a lift to Southend and he teased me about being, like Cussen, a Chigwell man, 'homo-Chigwelliansis', i.e., a middle-class man from a north-east London suburb. We had worked together before on *The Man in the Iron Mask* and before that in television, just after the *Iceman* crack-up, so I knew how seriously he approached even the slightest-seeming projects. For someone involved in the film business, he had a refreshing lack of self-importance and pomposity, and not much tolerance for those who were bumptious or strutting. He coaxed an excellent performance from Miranda Richardson (as Ruth, and in her first film), but fell out almost immediately with Rupert Everett, who played Blakeley, and who in anticipation of a bedroom scene preferred getting his body 'right' to attending rehearsals, a discipline upon which Newell insisted.

When the film was released, many praised it for its sharp portrayal of England in the 1950s, and especially of lower-middle-class England, and of lives filled with secret passion doomed by social convention. But I never felt that I was contributing directly to this effect, I suppose because I have never felt that I belonged to England, or at any rate belonged to it closely. But then my remorseless detachment had always been apparent. Even the acts of falling in love and being in love seemed, ultimately, to develop into medium-term preparations for eventual expressions of indifference. And the rash of good and goodish films in which I appeared at this time – made by Britons in Britain about Britishness – only served to remind me that I didn't much feel British. Didn't much feel anything, in fact.

13

RETURN I WILL TO OLD BRAZIL

Around this time, Sophie's sister Charlotte committed suicide. We were at Wassall when Sophie received the news. I recall her taking the phone call, becoming very quiet, and then hurrying to tell me what had happened before rushing out to her car and driving to London. I was in the bath and received the information she had given me with a mixture of concern for Sophie and a twinge of bewilderment. It was the kind of event which asked difficult questions of me. How was I supposed to behave? What was I supposed to do? The situation seemed to call for something decisive and humane, yet I was awkward and apparently paralysed by it.

I watched Sophie drive away and thought about it for a few moments. I did not know her sister very well and actually felt very little; certainly not grief, at any rate. The idea of suicide did conjure several images in my mind, none of them pleasant, and I suppose there must have been sensations of regret and alarm at the awfulness of Charlotte's death. I wondered what Sophie would *want* me to do, if she wanted me to do anything, and eventually decided that she might – only 'might' – want me to be with her in London. Out of a sense of delayed but purposeful and well-intentioned duty, I therefore jumped into my own car and followed her towards Bloomsbury, where the dreadful act had occurred.

The room in which Charlotte had been laid seemed unremarkable apart from the fact that it contained a dead body. Except for my mother's, it was the first corpse I had seen. She looked to be asleep, apart, I remember, from her feet, which were already turning a pale-bluish colour. A nervous and rather embarrassed policeman guarded the scene, perhaps as uncertain as I was about how he should be behaving in such dire circumstances. Meanwhile, I hovered in the background, my favoured position at such moments, trying to look 'on hand', attempting not to look embarrassed or inconvenienced, balancing concern with uninvolved, reliable steadiness.

I felt very sad for Sophie, yet found it difficult to empathize with her. I thought back to my father's death and my mother's refusal to attend his funeral. Not so much a refusal, in fact. That word is too dynamic. She had simply disregarded the occasion of her husband's death. 'Och, that's all over with now then,' she'd said, though saying it didn't mean she didn't love him. Death for her was something you didn't tamper with. Maybe it was something to do with her Scottish Presbyterian outlook, and undoubtedly she was scared of showing her emotions. Most likely the one went some way to explaining the other, instinct and belief coming together in complementary fashion.

Besides, all the grief she'd had in store had been expended on Eric. Then, she *had* mourned, and I think mourned hard, though the actual lamenting was done on the other side of a heavy wooden door. I never witnessed her anguish, and possibly she emerged from her relatively brief but no doubt bitter incarceration with an even more defined sense of its futility. It did no good. Eric was gone. He was not going to return. No amount of tears or distress could change that. So when my father died, she knew the score. 'Och, that's all over with now then.' It was a gentle but firm acknowledgement that life was finite, death was inevitable, it came to us all, and there was no need to make a fuss about it.

My parents never went to Egypt to see Eric's grave. I have never been to Egypt to see Eric's grave. It feels to me a little like unfinished business, though only business. A duty I should at some time discharge, like standing at the back of a small room in Bloomsbury, looking at Charlotte's feet and considering my demeanour.

Now, I wonder whether this inability to feel grief is my biological disposition or circumstantial. When the right moment arrives, when the appropriate circumstance presents itself, will I feel mournfulness and remorse? I would like to think so, though I have the uneasy sense that I am by temperament an unaffected man.

Bee once told me that she thought I looked at life through an inverted telescope. By this I suppose she meant that I could see things clearly enough, but at a distance and in a curiously self-contained, unimpinged way. I know what she's driving at – what she perceives as my sense of sense-deprived oblivion and emotional distance – but I don't know if it's entirely true. In many ways, the foreground of my life *is* crowded, so much so that I have difficulty concentrating on much beyond its immediate details. I respond quickly and intensely to people, habitually picking up their speech, their mannerisms, their characters. I can't settle to read novels. My conversation is littered with non sequiturs. My mind is constantly turning cartwheels, though, alas, not of the intellectual kind. My tastes are shaped by others. I am at once irritated and pleased by the momentarily encountered minutiae of life. My vision of life is in fact so blurred that it cannot even settle upon a rational number of marital partners.

The one thing that steadies this solipsistic dizziness is work. That is the sole focusing point of my life and lately I have begun to realize how important it is. I recently watched a tape of the artist Frank Auerbach talking with a stern, steely brightness about his work – albeit *reluctantly* talking about his work. He paints for 364 days of the year, and then takes a one-day annual holiday in Brighton, where he plays arcade games on the pier. For him, there is no real life outside work. My existence is not as extreme as Auerbach's, though if I had his relentless self-discipline (I can be lazy) and the opportunity (actors are often out of work), who knows?

I dislike being out of work. I dislike it intensely. Acting is what makes me complete. Without it, I am undoubtedly a diminished and decidedly unfinished person. Like Auerbach, I find it difficult to talk about work, and don't see that much point in such discussion. Expressed simply, acting seems to me the only plausible reason for my life, the only element of it with which I can completely identify.

It is difficult to explain how something can become so consuming that it is not merely a way of life but stands in for life itself. Stands in to the extent that it almost *becomes* life. I don't think this expresses the situation too strongly.

Money does not motivate me. It interests me only in the sense of allowing me choice, and in the sense that not having it might stop me acting. I have an untroubled attitude to money. For most of my life I've had some, and despite a couple of occasions when I came close to being broke, there's always been enough.

Things, possessions, do not interest me. I have bought and sold and handed over numerous properties during my life. The flat I live in at the moment is relatively modest: it has only one bedroom and is quite sparsely furnished. Most of the cupboards are bare. The kitchen looks sharp enough (in the modern manner), but is poorly equipped. A few goodish paintings hang on pale, neutrally painted walls. An expensive television squats in one corner. If you were to come through the keyhole, I suspect it would be difficult to piece together the person who lived here. No theatrical memorabilia, no nostalgic photographs of me or anyone else upon a stage, no film posters, no books, no tell-tale videos or DVDs, and no music. A lacuna of interior design without even the compensation of a Zen-like ambience.

Naturally I act for praise or recognition, evidence that I am doing my job well and a sign that I am liked, but other than that there is not much beyond work itself which interests me. So when I think about the lack of grief in my life, I am usually led to ponder its unbalanced impropriety and to ask myself whether it is a good or a bad thing. A part of me, of course, recognizes its unseemly nature and seeks to cover it up, somehow to conceal it. The genuine experience, however, eludes me and I now think that not having the capacity to feel grief indicates a sense of not belonging, or at least of not belonging *close* to someone or something. Furthermore, I am sure that the general absence of such an unpleasant experience helps to account for my essentially congenial and bland approach to life; and it is this, I suspect, that allows acting to do to me what life should be doing.

When Sophie lost her sister, therefore, I did not feel empathy having, through Eric's death, been there before, but felt rather a sense that I had *not* been there before. And it made me wonder how long her anguish would last and how she would accommodate it into the rest of her life. I felt that we were very content together. She was a very forceful character whose cheerful social gaucheness seemed to complement my own grumpy reticence. Sophie was unguarded, frequently saying the first thing that came into her head. This was rarely unintelligent or dull, though was often said regardless of social protocol. She had a talent for bringing people together and for staying in touch with a wide circle of friends and acquaintances. All this was an effective foil for my habitual discretion.

In retrospect, the parties and the events she organized, in Islington or at Wassall, when the house was suddenly full of musicians and journalists and photographers or whatever, were very entertaining. And being amongst other artists was intriguing. It made me think a little about my acting, whether it changed depending on whom I was with, and decided that probably it did not. Part of me would have liked that not to be the case, but generally I don't think environment or circumstances have any tangible bearing at all. There were obvious moments of crisis like the *Iceman* crack-up, but once I was actually fit to work and was working, nothing else mattered.

This was something I had discussed briefly sometime in the 1970s with Alec Guinness, who after seeing me in Edward Bond's *The Sea* sent me a card inviting me for a meal. It had often been remarked that our acting styles were similar, and I suppose a meeting between us was bound to happen at some point. He agreed with me about the lack of influence one's partner exerted on acting, and confided that at one time he had engaged in sexual relations with men and then given them up when he got married, so he had probably been exposed to the possibility of that influence on a wider scale than I had. 'But you're right,' he said. 'It makes no difference. Not really.'

Dinner with Alec Guinness was a curious affair. He drank – we drank – a considerable amount, starting with cocktails, then going through the wine (red and white), followed by some kind of liqueur, and even finishing with a bottle of beer. He talked quite openly without giving away too much of himself, and was friendly without throwing off a manner of quiet, watchful reserve. He talked about sex without seeming to be particularly interested in it, and was keen to talk about Charles Laughton, with whom I'd acted at Stratford, and whom Guinness admired a great deal.

He did not care much for what he perceived as Olivier's shoddy treatment of Laughton and also made it clear that he didn't care much for Olivier himself. He thought Olivier was vulgar (in particular about homosexuality) and I suspect this helped to colour the prejudice he voiced against his acting. It was easy to see why he disliked Olivier's way of doing things, as the two men had such antagonistic approaches.

'Sometimes after watching him I would wonder what was going on, wonder what on earth he was up to,' he said.

'How do you mean?' I asked, instinctively defensive about one of my heroes.

Sir Alec considered and took another largish but polite swallow of wine. I thought he had actually become rather portly.

'For example . . .' he continued, now actually quite angry though still measured, and puffing away on a cigarette, 'for example, he would make a point of stressing a line, or just a word – something at any rate that didn't warrant the stress. He would distort meaning for *effect*.'

I could see what he was saying – Olivier was, after all, a magnificent show-off, occasionally wringing impressions from the text that emphasized his own virtuosity rather than being based on any interpretation.

'I see what you mean,' I replied with characteristic non-commitment, though seeing what Guinness meant didn't necessarily imply that I agreed with him, and I think he sensed that. I could forgive Olivier for his moments of operatic whimsy, especially as they seemed to be a part of the way he functioned as an actor, a sort of flamboyant preface for something irresistible which might be just round the corner.

I later heard that when he delivered the oration at Olivier's memorial service, Guinness recalled the tendency to over-embellish as being characteristic of his genius, so he either reconsidered or was making mischievous conversation – though I don't doubt that his aversion to Olivier's spasms of crassness was real enough.

Coral Browne was also in the production of *The Sea*, and I told Guinness her opinion of Tom Conti when he asked who of the younger actors coming through was worth watching. Conti had been appearing in Christopher Hampton's *Savages* and had shown what a brilliant all-round performer he could be. Coral's verdict? 'Well, he must be a lousy fuck – he can do too much.'

I liked Guinness without quite understanding precisely *why* I liked him. Though we seemed to care about the same things as far as acting went, we were actually very different. I'm not sure, for example, that he needed a role to make himself complete. He was certainly a brilliant alchemist, but he proceeded, I think, from a place of inner calm and repletion. Poetry and painting, for example, were great loves, and occupied his mind in a way that nothing ever occupied mine.

We talked as well about roles that we wanted to do but were afraid would never happen. I told him that I should have done Hamlet, though by then I was probably too old. Also, I felt (and still feel) that, if given the chance, I could do comedy quite well. Although I couldn't complain about the variety of roles I'd been given, I felt that I was still considered by casting agents to be a 'classical' actor rather than a 'funny man'.

Guinness surprised me with his response, saying that he liked playing clownish parts (you only have to look back to his work in the Ealing Comedies to see how good he was), but ideally would like to find something unrealistic and strange to do. I mentioned Obi-Wan Kenobi in *Star Wars* and he waved me aside and said, 'But I played him as a real person.' Then he smiled. 'It was the *only* way to play him.'

I still wasn't sure I understood what kind of roles he meant, and tried to press the point.

'Oh, fantastical men. Maybe parts that haven't been written yet or aren't available. I don't know, quite –'

Light flooded his face as he spoke, and then, for a brief moment, I envisaged the kind of chimerical, visionary man-magic being he had in mind. He had done some of this with Fagin in *Oliver Twist*, effectively bringing Cruikshank's cartoon to life. Given his interest in poetry, maybe he was thinking of someone like William Blake, though I sensed that in some way he wished for a role that would enable him to escape from himself, or at least escape from his stout frame and the sense of earthly mortality that was creeping up on him. Even with the grave Smiley there had always been a hint of fantastical whimsy, and I see now that his acting often lay in the balance or *frisson* between these qualities. When it went wrong – which was not often – it was usually because there was a lack of poise in his performance. Thus, with Godbole in David Lean's *A Passage to India*, when there was too much fanciful eccentricity. I know that he recognized this, and had heard that he was mildly ashamed of his exhibition in that film.

I found Guinness fascinating, not least because professionally we were supposed to have things in common. But his brand of invisibility was different from my own. It was, I think, a reflection of a kind of loneliness. He was no blank space, no man who wasn't there. Also unlike me, I didn't feel that he wanted to be liked. He didn't *mind* being liked, but showing off and a desire for acceptance, both to some extent ingredients in my own acting, were wholly absent from his.

Guinness's inscrutability was also unlike Dirk Bogarde's, whose career and style evolved into a gradual exposure of the quite venal appetites that lurked beneath the surface of the smooth identity that had been formed for him by the Rank

MY NAPOLEONS: 1, *Napoleon and Love* (1974); 2 & 4, *Time Bandits* (1981) and, most recently, 3 & 5, *The Emperor's New Clothes* (2001). Though seventeen years had elapsed between the filming of the first two, I found myself slipping into literally the same costume.

On the set of *Greystoke*: with Christophe Lambert, Hugh Hudson and Jessica. And (**left**) as Sam Mussabini in another Hudson film, *Chariots of Fire*.

With Sophie at the birth of our son, Harry. And again at our wedding in 1982.

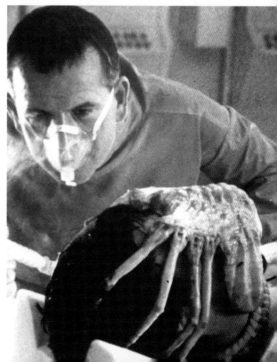

With Harold Pinter. At this time, I was still suffering from 'stage fright' and doing exclusively films and television work, though it was somewhere in my mind that a Pinter play could get me back on stage.

As the android Ash in *Alien*. John Hurt is under the claw.

All my children on a fence: Barnaby, Sarah-Jane, Lissy, Jessica, Harry.

Left: Judi Dench and I have been acting together since Stratford; she is always sparky fun. Here we are in *Mr and Mrs Edgehill.*

Right: Awarded the CBE in 1989. Outside Iverna Court with Fido, Lissy, Barnaby and Sarah-Jane.

Above: With Penelope Wilton. A couple in real life and on screen – here in the television series *The Borrowers*. And (**left**) in *Laughterhouse*, where we met.

Above: Finally back on stage, in Pinter's *Moonlight*. With Anna Massey (1993).

Left: As Frankenstein's father in Kenneth Branagh's *Mary Shelley's Frankenstein* (1994).

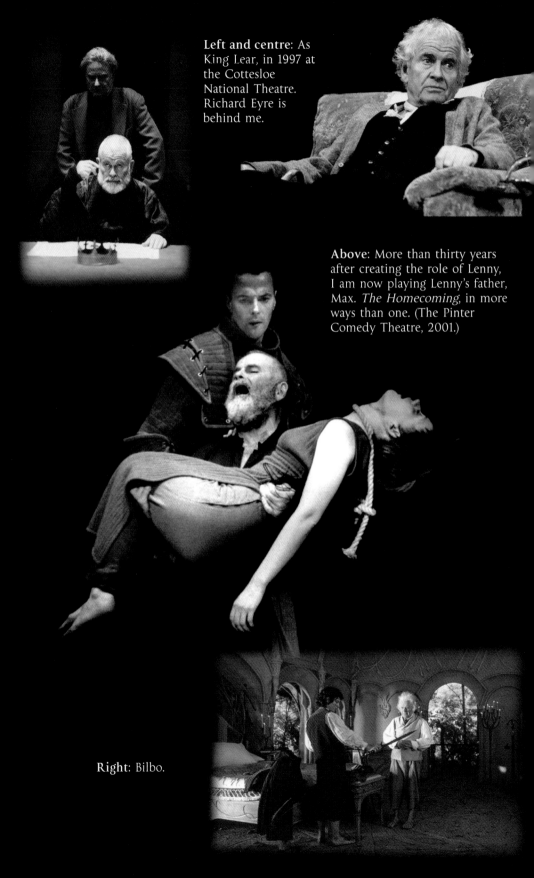

Left and centre: As King Lear, in 1997 at the Cottesloe National Theatre. Richard Eyre is behind me.

Above: More than thirty years after creating the role of Lenny, I am now playing Lenny's father, Max. *The Homecoming*, in more ways than one. (The Pinter Comedy Theatre, 2001.)

Right: Bilbo.

Christmas 2000, Iverna Court. Sarah-Jane, Archie,
Sarah-Jane's partner Paul, Harry, Talulah, Lissy,
Poppy. I'm between Sarah-Jane and Archie: father
and grandfather.

Sophie and me. 2004.

At rehearsals for *King Lear*, somewhere in a National Theatre corridor. 'Whither now?' or just 'wither'?

Organization. We were all in our own ways, I suppose, difficult to know and self-effacing, and our enigmatic personalities were reflected in the diverse ways we played our parts. Though I never met him, I think Peter Sellers was another unfathomable, but his manic disguises tended to conceal panic at his emptiness. I, however, was merely grateful to be someone else, though thankful rather than distressed.

I can't say that I was friends with Guinness or even, really, much of an acquaintance, though every now and then you do meet someone who seems to carry some kind of weight in your own life. We ate supper, drank, and circled one another with cautious but polite respect, both wondering how it was that we had been classified together as men who hid behind masks. I knew the line from T. S. Eliot's *The Cocktail Party* which Guinness had said when he appeared as the Unidentified Guest in the original production of 1949, when he became the mouthpiece for the writer's thoughts on the malleable nature of identity: 'Nobody likes to be left with a mystery. But there's more to it than that. There's a loss of personality; or rather, you've lost touch with the person you thought you were. You no longer feel quite human.' I think in the end we were both as clueless as each other about our relative inconspicuousness. We appreciated and used it without necessarily understanding it.

I was reminded of Guinness when Terry Gilliam asked me to be in *Brazil*. Despite its surreal and spectacular nature, much of the script was somehow very English, and I don't mean in the way that it is in some respects an acidic Orwellian parody. A significant part of the film's story involves the blind malevolence of a bureaucratic society and the cowed, almost grateful obeisance of its workforce. It all reminded me of the world depicted in several of the Ealing Comedies, a world with which Gilliam was very familiar. I thought of Guinness's portrayals of trembling employees in *The Man in the White Suit* and *The Lavender Hill Mob*, where he played men who eventually strike out against the lumbering indifference of the institutions which pay them.

I think Gilliam is one of the directors with whom I've most enjoyed working. He once told me that he thought he directed 'like an actor'. Initially, I thought this was an odd claim. To my knowledge, he had never acted – not unless you count the leering grotesques and mumbling fools he'd occasionally done in *Monty Python's Flying Circus*. But I'd learnt in *Time Bandits* that he was relaxed, slightly mad, very funny and – important for an actor – open to all kinds of suggestion. He operated a sort of receptive open-door policy and invited everyone (and I do mean everyone – cast, crew, and sometimes even casual observers) to say their piece and not to feel intimidated if they could think of a better way of doing things. Having said that, you always felt you were in the presence of an able, very bright man who knew exactly what he wanted to achieve. Consequently, there was a carefree, happy atmosphere on his sets.

Four years before *Brazil*, when I had been wheeled out in *Time Bandits* for one of my occasional Napoleon outings, Gilliam's freewheeling chaos-as-order style suited the hectic manoeuvrings of the film. He told me that I had been cast because he had seen me in *The Misanthrope* on television and thought me very funny.

'Being small didn't help, then?' I asked.

'Well, that as well. And you showed me you could do "French",' he added, with a characteristically fruity chuckle.

Afterwards, I was informed that at one point (during the banquet scene, I think) he had left the set because he was giggling so much. Whether this was because I had done something which was intentionally or unintentionally amusing I do not know. It is often difficult to tell with Gilliam. His mind is so epically eccentric that it is often hard to understand its motivations.

He cast me as Kurtzmann, who was in real life associated with MAD comics and was a big influence on the schoolboy Gilliam. In *Brazil* I was the lily-livered boss of the Ministry of Information who makes a mistake and is saved from disgrace by Sam Lowry. Lowry was played by Jonathan Pryce, a fine actor whose quiet understatement made him ideal for the clever, unambitious, mother-dominated man who was all for keeping his head down until events compelled him to act.

There was something topsy-turvy about Gilliam, as if he was irresistibly programmed to see the world upside-down, to make serious fun of it. Just as he was prepared to take intelligent risks with ideas, so he was always alive to the possibilities of strange casting. The ever-pleasant Michael Palin appears, therefore, as a psychotic plastic surgeon, while Robert de Niro was satisfied with (for him) a relatively modest role. *Brazil* revealed a fascination with both cruelty and humour, and Gilliam appreciated that in England – especially in England – being funny is a defence mechanism, a way of saying things without exposing yourself. He brought American scale and charisma to a film of essentially English preoccupations.

During *Time Bandits*, Gilliam had told me that I had given the kind of performance that could only be messed up in the editing, and a certain trust had developed between us. This, I think, gave me the assurance to take more chances in *Brazil*, though I think at first he was bemused by this. He thought some of the takes were uneven, though as the Kurtzmann character grew into the lisping, cunningly ferret-like mercenary who eventually arrives on screen, he seemed pleased. And relieved. He saw this as a kind of payback for having gained my confidence in the earlier project.

'Connery doesn't work like that,' he offered. Sean had played King Agamemnon in *Time Bandits*. 'He's very, very good – but he knows exactly what he can and can't do.'

'Those are useful things to know,' I replied, rather weakly and in the vein of someone who had never quite fathomed his limits, upper or lower.

'He'll say how he should be shot getting on a horse, which side of his face the camera should be on when he's walking . . . and so on.'

'I suppose that's because he's a star.'

'He knows what he's got and he knows how it should be shown. He was always right, of course. But he wouldn't try things.'

'Did you ask him?'

'No. I wouldn't dare.'

Of course he wouldn't. Who would? Connery has become one of the great old men of the movies, offering an uncompromising and rather daunting, scary sort of charm

Another actor we talked of was de Niro, whose trusting and clearly strong relationship with Martin Scorsese, Gilliam thought, had given him the confidence to really test his limits as an actor.

'Trust is important,' he said, 'so that actors don't mind looking like fools some of the time.'

I agreed, though I was beginning to wonder whether I had looked a fool during the shooting of *Brazil*. I was all for flexibility, though the aim, of course, was never to look inane or absurd.

Robert de Niro was interesting to work with, though a difficult man to know. Part of the problem was my own taciturn shyness, and part of it was de Niro's taciturn heedlessness of other people. Apparently oblivious to charm, he is as threatening in real life as he is on screen, though this may be because he is so immersed in his character preparation that he has neither time nor opportunity to be chatty and sociable.

At one point in *Brazil* he had to be seen to pick a lock. It was something which needed to be done, but was only a pick-up shot. It should have been a matter of a few minutes, but de Niro insisted on playing the shot for real and on picking the lock perfectly. He didn't manage it and, even though it wasn't necessary, wanted another take. Fifteen takes later, he failed again. By this time, the English crew were becoming impatient.

'Take Sixteen!' Bob the jolly focus-puller shouted. 'And stii-iill trying to pick up.'

De Niro whipped round, momentarily out of character, angry as a scorpion, and said, 'Whaaaddya mean?'

'Sorry, sir,' Bob replied. 'English humour.'

Brazil had arrived after a relatively quiet period when I seemed to be at Wassall doing not much more than mowing the lawn and weeding the driveway and the garden. And afterwards – after the suddenly mad time of doing *Brazil* and *Wetherby* and *We, the Accused* and so on – I continued to do much the same.

'Why don't you ever *plant* things?' Sophie asked.

'It's never occurred to me,' I answered. I liked tidying up the garden and pulling things out of the ground. On the other hand, putting *in* plants and bushes, actually creating a garden, never appealed to me. Sophie thought it was to do with self-discipline and the manufacturing of my own intense, roped-off world. Defined, if limited tasks were a part of the process.

Three or four years earlier, the last letter I received from Dirk Bogarde ('the last' signifying nothing more sinister than that we merely stopped corresponding) had included something on his garden. He talked with considerable enthusiasm about a 'vast' jasmine plant given to him by Hugh and Sue Hudson. 'It's taken days to find out what KIND of jasmin [*sic*] it is . . . and how to plant it and just where. Now I know. And the pot and the soil I've bought would have paid for one night at the Connaught.'

I knew that Dirk and Tote had invited some of the *Chariots* cast round to Le Haut Clermont. As I lay in the bath after one of my gardening frenzies, I was reminded of the letter, of the times that Bee and I spent with them, of *Chariots*, and of the impossibility of going back, of turning back the clock on an older world that time has inevitably made sentimental. In a sort of Proustian moment, I lay there and recalled the letter quite clearly. 'Lunch . . . lots of wine and great mixing of chums. Sun and all, under the olives . . . Havers and Charleson came and were super, but not Cross. Who, I gather, was. Which was v. sad because I thought he was smashing in the fillum . . .'

I lay back in the bath, soaking myself, thinking also of the two films I had just been offered. One involved a bit of money and was about Scott of the Antarctic. The other (involving almost no money) was a small English film about geese. I didn't really know what to do. I wondered what Bogarde would have done and thought that he would have probably trusted to chance. Then I heard the sound of geese in the field next to the house. I was in what was for me a visionary mood and felt strongly that this was some sort of sign. So with uncharacteristic decisiveness I agreed to do *Laughterhouse*, the goose film with no money, unaware how much life could turn on such moments.

14

SLAUGHTERHOUSE AND ANOTHER WOMAN

Laughterhouse (1984) was written by the wrestler turned actor-cum-writer Brian Glover, with whom I had worked several years before in *Bequest to the Nation*. The story is very straight-forward: Ben Singleton, a goose farmer, has a misunderstanding with the TGWU and finds himself and his geese without trans-port to London for the annual Christmas slaughter. He decides to walk his flock from Norfolk to Smithfield. He arrives with the geese intact. That, more or less, is it. I was cast as Singleton. Penelope Wilton played my wife, Alice. Bill Owen was Amos, a curmudgeonly farmhand. Sophie was contracted to do the stills photography. Richard Eyre directed the film, having had some success with Ian McEwan's *The Ploughman's Lunch* a year earlier.

I liked the script and I liked the people who were involved in the making of the film. Brian Glover told me that *Laughterhouse* was based on a western called *Red River*, which involved John Wayne taking a huge herd of cattle to Missouri. I played the Wayne part and the East Anglian countryside stood in for the wild west. In other words, everything was miniaturized.

The shoot suited me very well. Although everything was

done quickly and cheaply, there was a brisk, focused efficiency about it all. Cast, crew and geese moved through the landscape together as a sort of extended family. In addition, there was a firm political commitment to the film. *The Ploughman's Lunch* had been about cynical opportunism, and now *Laughterhouse* was revealing a more human dimension to Eighties England. Singleton's successful walk was a throwback to a time when the country was less in the grip of making a quick turnover and people put themselves to the test in other, less inhuman ways.

Even I, pretty agnostic about such things for the most part, felt myself becoming vulnerable to the charms of the countryside and the more sentimental claims of the film. And the entry into another world – the world of the goose – was full of irresistible details. During our walk, the geese faithfully followed the farmer's daughter who had been given the job of leading them. They trailed her because the farmer had ensured she was the first thing each of the geese had seen after they hatched; they therefore assumed that she was their mother. They were 'shod' by walking through tar and sand. I discovered that England was still full of drovers' trails and fields round London which had been put aside for fattening birds after the exertions of their walk. And as we moved through the landscape I was made aware of a vanished and ruined country, of vast poultry farms that echoed to the sound of canned music, of boarded-up farm cottages, of vulgar village pubs, shabby shopping precincts, and remorseless arterial roads.

That I was seduced by a sense of nostalgia was not altogether surprising. Before the completion of filming I had fallen in love with Penelope Wilton, and she with me. We had met a few years earlier at Julian Belfrage's annual Grand National party. At that time she had been with the actor Dan Massey and I remember that we had liked one another and talked, I think, about *Othello*.

Even earlier than that, I had seen her and Dan in a brilliant stage production of Pinter's *Betrayal*, though (strangely, I now feel) the fan letter I had written was specifically to Dan. When she arrived for *Laughterhouse* I asked her if she was nervous, and she answered rather crossly, 'I can't afford to be nervous – my daughter has chickenpox.' As filming progressed, however, we drew closer to one another and it gradually dawned on both of us that we wanted a relationship. Well before the first sudden, electric touching of hands, we were aware of our developing emotions.

Though the weather was unbelievably cold, this only contributed to the sense of camaraderie and dogged insularity which doubtless made the circumstances even more cosy. At the end, when everyone was saying their goodbyes and travelling back to London, Pep and I acknowledged that something had happened between us and headed instead in a different direction, for one of the more picturesque pubs we had found en route. And there we stayed, until we were certain that we both wanted the relationship to continue.

The experience of *Laughterhouse* would have been a happy one even without falling in love. The friendly, funny, mainly Scottish crew, the pretty outdoor locations, the sense of doing something worthwhile, the lovely producer Ann Scott, even the geese . . . it all amounted to something odd and beguiling. Every night, the geese were led into a lorry by their 'mother', bedded down and fed, doing both with no tantrums. It was as if they too could sense an atmosphere of contentment. One of the final shots is of me and the geese in front of St Paul's Cathedral, an image of achieved, mutual togetherness that in its own way was worthy of Humphrey Jennings.

Brian Glover's script was, I think, very funny, though some have judged it 'slight'. There's some truth in this, though being slight need not necessarily be a drawback. The film received a polite pounding in the press – I believe people *wanted* to like it – with many critics judging that the characters were not sympathetic enough. Some thought this was Richard Eyre's fault, and it is true that he could be rather distant and removed. Like Peter Hall, he always seemed to be on the verge of nipping off and doing other projects. But that was his manner. As a director he was shrewd and very committed to *Laughterhouse*.

Bill Owen's cantankerous, slightly choleric, down-to-earth presence as Amos should have provided an opportunity for us to play against his crabbiness, but somehow that didn't work either. Though I didn't get to know him very well, I also had the suspicion that Owen didn't much want to be known. He was as cranky and difficult in real life as he was as Amos, or indeed as the seedy character Compo he played for many years in *Last of the Summer Wine*. His career, mostly in television, stretched way back, and he carried with him an air of tramp-like, this-is-what-I-do-and-how-I-do-it stubbornness.

Still, the movie's end product could certainly have been lighter. In retrospect, I wonder if we didn't rely too heavily on the inherent comedy of the film's situation rather than developing it for ourselves. It has since been put to me that I might have *under*played Ben Singleton's lightness as an unconscious reflex to the euphoria of falling in love. That is, I didn't want people to think he was having too good a time of it; I was being deliberately glum so that I didn't over-emphasize the levity. Well, maybe. But as I've said before, beyond the idea of acting out of a secure nest, I don't think one's personal situation has any direct, tangible bearing on the way one acts.

Who can say whether or not my professional life changed as a consequence of developments in my domestic situation? I suppose the fact that Pep is an actress, and a very fine one, could have affected me, though if it did I was unaware of it. Later, when we were married and living together, the fact that we were both involved in the same kind of life meant that we were able to take short cuts with one another. In some things, we just knew and understood what the other was going through. I don't think it would be too strong to say that it was Pep who got me back on stage in 1993. She also had very shrewd insights into the way I worked as an actor.

However, all this lay somewhere in the near future. Immediately after *Laughterhouse* I went back to Sophie and Harry, though was unable to keep my mind off Pep. We had fallen in love and in characteristic fashion I went with the momentum of the situation. Pep rented a cottage in Battle, just along the road from Wassall, and in a way that was reminiscent (though more sedate) of the fevered farce I put in motion when courting Bee, I scurried between two houses.

The situation could only last so long. One night I went up to London to see Jessica – I think she was receiving an award – and Sophie, who by then had an inkling that something was wrong, called her and asked whether or not I'd been at the party. I had, but only for thirty minutes or so. Then I had gone to see Pep.

After this there was a confrontation, an argument, and then an admission. The subsequent split with Sophie was not pleasant. She told me of her distress at discovering that our marriage was just like any other marriage, by which I suppose she meant any other marriage that ends badly after adulterous revelations. She had a point.

Sophie and I had been together for four years. One afternoon, she moved out of Holland Park Mews, our place in London, taking with her most of the house's contents. She sold Wassall and bought a smaller house almost opposite, in the same road. Pep moved into Holland Park Mews, but quickly felt uncomfortable about it, so we bought a flat in Stonor Road, close enough to Kensington High Street, which had developed into a sort of stomping ground.

And how did my family – my two daughters from my first marriage, my son and daughter from the time with Bee, and Harry, still only a small child – respond to their father's fickle life?

Jessica, I think, was the most hurt. She and Sophie had become good friends, and her stepmother had been instrumental in bringing her back to me and healing wounds that had been untended by me since I'd abandoned her and Sarah-Jane in Stratford. She took it very badly and more or less refused to speak to me for the next five years. For her it was not merely a case of history repeating itself but of apparently malicious damage being done. Who, she must have asked herself, was her father, this elusive and seemingly erratic figure who seemed determined to keep destroying the possibility of any kind of constant relationship? She may have also been put out by the fact that I had used her as an excuse – a partial excuse – to see Pep. She wrote me a strong letter saying that she never wanted to see me again. Sophie had become an important part of her life, even something of a role model, and my relationship with Pep was perceived as being a betrayal of both wife and daughter. I replied with what I thought at the time was civilized, even formal restraint – saying that I quite understood the way she felt – though such stiff-backed acquiescence, I now recognize, was probably the worst way I could have responded.

Lissy and Barnaby were more philosophical about it all, though there was also a certain amount of eye-rolling and good-humoured, tolerant disapproval. They had not been left in the same way as Jessica and Sarah-Jane, and by the time that Bee and I separated they were in any case old enough to understand something of what had occurred.

Harry was more difficult. I remember him running around at that time in a Spiderman costume and obsessively wearing the same pair of trousers for days on end. I'm not sure how much he missed me, but he did miss Anno, Bee's son with Andrew Birkin, who was more or less the same age and was a regular visitor to Islington, then Holland Park Mews and Wassall. 'Where's my family gone?' he asked, referring I think more to Anno and the Iverna connection than to me. In the immediate aftermath of the split with Sophie, the visits from Anno had come to an end – not, I think, from the implementation of any judgemental embargo, but perhaps because people wanted to see how things would settle down.

Years later, when I had been persuaded to put myself through therapy in New York, my therapist told me that I was a 'border-line love junkie'. There is some truth in this, notwithstanding the unsavoury implication of addiction which her estimation suggests. Maybe there is a part of me that enjoys the drama of being in love. Isn't there a part of everyone which enjoys the drama of being in love? My difficulty, I think, is that I am com-paratively autistic about the consequences of maintaining the habit; that is, by being chronically self-absorbed. All separations are awful, the one with Sophie perhaps more so than the others. And I don't enjoy them. I don't enjoy the hurt and the trauma of upsetting people. But I still do it, caught up in the theatre of it all, not able to resist, though still wanting romance to exist concurrently with the nest.

Maybe some of this is an excuse for giving in to momentum and allowing things to happen, situations to develop to the point where something has to give. It fits with my not believing or necessarily *un*believing in anything like fate (or Fate), and passively authorizing the way that life unravels. Does this make me unprincipled and lethargic? Or is it in part a naive acknow-ledgement that things happen and everything can seem to have some kind of purpose?

Back in the real world, there didn't seem to be much work available after *Laughterhouse*, and this allowed Pep and me to settle down and build a life together. She worked – I remember her carrying John Cleese around a muddy field during the filming of *Clockwise*, an ant hauling a log, her slender, tight body disguising enormous physical strength – while I seemed to make do with voice-overs.

I had discussed voice-overs with Brian Glover, well known among other things for his work with Tetley. Like all actors, I suppose, we weren't quite certain of their value, but knew that doing them made deafening financial sense. However, I was perhaps a little disingenuous with Glover, as I actually *liked* doing voice-overs. They appealed to the lazier side of my nature. Although there may have been some things I wouldn't have advertised, either due to moral or political reservation, I don't think any undesirable products ever came my way. I was, for example, the voice of BMW and then the voice of Nurofen without ever quite understanding the connection between luxury cars and painkillers or why I should have been cast in such roles.

I never took much interest in the product, preferring merely to turn up and do the job, indolent to the point that, given the choice, I would even ask someone else to turn over the autocue so that I wasn't responsible for the pace of my own voice. Occasionally, an intrusive producer would try to direct me ('Ian, could we have just a little more *oomph* on "unique", please . . .'), but by and large I was trusted and allowed to get on with things in my own way. One actor I know – a brilliant mimic but actually not a very good actor, thereby inviting interesting questions about what 'acting' is – made a great deal of money by pretending to be well-known people, and seemed to advertise everything from cars to washing powder.

The relative lack of work meant there was a chance to travel, and Pep and I took two holidays to France, one to Bordeaux and the other to the Loire, Lissy accompanying us on both occasions. These were, I now realize, important milestones in Pep becoming accepted by my immediate family. Her qualities as a generous and very funny woman could easily have been obscured by the manner in which our relationship had begun. Lissy, who was about twenty years old at the time, was exactly the right person to appreciate Pep. She has inherited her mother's talent for convivial inclusiveness and was perhaps the only person who could have brought Pep into the family circle while at the same time maintaining connections with Sophie and Harry. Pep became friends with Lissy, their goodwill towards one another reinforced during both holidays, and perhaps most explicitly celebrated during a meal at Bagnoles de l'Orne, a neat German-looking spa town in Normandy where the restaurant in which we ate served only trout. A postcard advertising the spa caused great hilarity. It featured photographs of naked men relaxing in whirlpools and large baths, one of whom bore an uncanny resemblance to Peter Hall.

Otherwise, Pep did film work in Venice and I did some television, including *Mr and Mrs Edgehill*, which reunited me with Gavin Millar and Judi Dench, and *Game, Set and Match* for Granada, which was a multi-part serial and filmed all over the place. The story was from a trilogy of books by Len Deighton and in some ways echoed the exploits of George Smiley. I played an espionage character called Bernard Samson, a loner who had been retired to desk duty but who is called back to discover the identity of an infiltrator.

During filming for *Game, Set and Match*, I received a phone call from Woody Allen asking me to be in his next film. Instinctively I wanted to be in it whatever it was – this was, after all, Woody Allen – but out of habit I asked him to send me a script. Apparently, Allen rarely did this. He preferred that only his leading actors saw the entire script and that the others knew their own lines, understood the general arc of a film's story and their place within that arc, and then made the best of it. Therefore, when I asked him for a script, all I heard at the other end of the line was a heavy, rather surprised silence.

'Hello?' I said, not wanting to call him 'Mr Allen' but feeling that 'Woody' was somehow impertinent. Within only a few moments I sensed how fragile and touchy he seemed.

'Ian . . . well, I . . .' he eventually replied. 'I'll tell you what I'll do. I'll send my costume man Jeffrey Kurland over to England and he can let you have a look at the script. If you like it, he'll take your measurements and bring them and the script back to New York. If you don't like it, he'll return with just the script. OK?'

'OK.'

Jeffrey Kurland duly arrived. I liked him and I quite liked the script. At any rate, he took both script and measurements back and I agreed to do the film. Pep was delighted when I told her. She was a great admirer of Woody Allen's work and asked me what the film was about.

'Well, I don't think it's very funny,' I said gloomily.

Allen had lately been developing his work, which had become more intense and melancholy. The last film, *September*, was a dark one in the style of Ingmar Bergman, whom Allen revered. Critics had already identified this change of direction and the apparent aping of an icon as an arrogant attempt to be accepted as a serious dramatist. Allen himself was on record as saying that he hadn't yet produced the masterpiece he craved. Perhaps this would be it, though I'd heard that *September* had left audiences depressed and dismissive in America.

'Well, what's it called? What's the story?' urged Pep.

'It's called *Another Woman* and it's about a woman called Marion who's a philosophy professor. She rents an apartment in order to write a book. Through the walls she hears another woman confessing awful things to her therapist and this prompts her to re-examine her own life.'

'So who do you play?'

'I'm Ken, her husband. I'm a cardiologist. The passion has gone out of our marriage. I'm seeing one of her friends.'

'Behind her back.'

'Behind her back.'

'Mmm. Sounds a little familiar . . .'

Still, I was committed to the movie and wanted to do it, as much for the experience of working with Allen as anything else. The project sounded interesting, no more than that, though I was pleased to hear that Gena Rowlands would be playing Marion, Mia Farrow the woman she hears through the walls, and Gene Hackman was down as Marion's ex-husband. I also looked forward to spending six weeks or so in New York, a city I liked but had not visited since the production of *The Homecoming* twenty years earlier.

Something nagged at me, so I spoke to Denholm Elliott, who had been in *September*. He was a brilliant actor, full in equal and delicious measure of decency and decay, who because of his technique and sensitivity could play in almost any film. He didn't exactly set my mind at rest, frankly explaining that the experience had been a nightmare.

'I'd done all my lines and was in my hotel room packing up, you know, to get the plane back to London. Then Woody phones me and says that I haven't finished. I said I have finished. It says so in the contract. And he says that's all been taken care of and there's more to do. So after all it seems I hadn't finished. And all I wanted to do was get home and ride my motorbike. Anyway, I did an extra three weeks playing – it seemed to me, and *still* seems to me – a character totally unrelated to the one I had been doing for the previous month or so. I was absolutely bemused by it – I had no idea who I was, what my new role in the film was, or how it connected with what I'd already done. Anyway, I was so put out by it all that I never bothered to see the film. Did you see it? And if you did – who was I?'

I hadn't seen *September* and couldn't help him out, but what he said made me uneasy. I also found that the part of Ken had been offered to George C. Scott (who refused even to read the script, which, quite surprisingly I thought, meant that he must have received one) and Ben Gazzara (who was eventually thought to be unsuitable). I didn't mind this – actors are always being cast and un-cast for all sorts of reasons – but it did add to a vague feeling of anxiety.

Shooting for *Another Woman* started in October 1987 and I was contracted to stay in New York, at Wyndham's Hotel, for six weeks. Despite Denholm Elliott's story, I had no reason to think I would be there any longer than that.

I found Allen chronically shy and secretive, and he would often speak through other people, even while he was in the same room as you. This isn't to say that I disliked him, more that he was impenetrable. And it was the same while he was directing. He offered vague, insubstantial instructions, which meant I never quite knew what was happening or what was expected of me. More than once he would say something like, 'Just move over there a bit. Or even over *there* if you feel like it.' He rarely said exactly where 'there' was. 'And maybe do something with your tie. Or maybe your hair. And if you can think of something better to say than your lines, maybe go with that.'

On occasions, you weren't entirely sure whether what you were doing was being filmed. And it wasn't unusual for Allen to seem entirely bored by the whole process. He would sometimes open a book – Chekhov short stories at one point, I seem to remember – now and then glancing up to see what was happening, once in a while saying 'Cut' or just nodding to Tom Reilly, his assistant director, who would then shout 'Cut!' on his behalf. When the weather turned nasty he'd decide that he'd had enough and go home. One scene had to be filmed in a local theatre, and I recall an actor being uncertain which character he was playing.

There was, I suppose, a certain kind of collusive looseness about the whole process, though it wasn't the kind of collusion or openness I was used to. I thought back wistfully to the days of Peter Hall at Stratford, where one always had the impression that one was involved and being consulted, but that generally there was a firm and even ruthless hand on the tiller.

Remember that I was the kind of actor who liked to be given a role, to learn his lines, and then get on and do it, never quite sure of how the actual inhabiting of character worked, but always trusting that so long as one had some talent and was prepared to work, something (in Micawber's words) would always turn up. This apparently prosaic approach must have seemed very dull to the method actors, especially American method actors who relished looseness and the subsequent opportunity to really express their characters. Brando, for example, had everything written on his cuffs. When he was asked why he didn't just learn his lines, he said tartly, 'How the fuck do I know what the other person's going to say?'

I had a conversation with Gene Hackman, a fine actor who somehow manages to be both gruff and decent, during which he expressed concern about his double chin and the pain in his knee, and in between asked whether I would ever want to work with Allen again. I sort of rolled my eyes in a way that didn't commit me to a specific answer, but (I hoped) indicated a degree of polite uncertainty.

'I would,' he said unequivocally, 'like a shot. I'd work with him again for sure.'

'Why's that?' I asked, it being the question I felt Hackman wanted me to ask.

'Not many takes. That's good. I don't like too many takes.'

Observing the slightly fishy look in my eyes, he obviously felt more information was required.

'And because he leaves you alone. I love being left alone.'

I nodded. He was right. Allen certainly left you alone. But I was no Hackman.

I felt especially put out when, on the third take of one scene, a woman with whom I was meant to be having an argument suddenly, and unexpectedly, pulled her hand back and slapped me hard across the face. Very hard. If she wanted to achieve realism or authentic shock from me, she certainly succeeded. The moment may have looked very effective on screen, but the time had come when I thought I ought to have a word with Woody.

I hit upon the not very original idea of inviting him out for a meal, to break the ice as it were, and put this to one of his assistants, calculating that as Allen tended to use conduits to communicate with the outside world, maybe this was the right way to approach him.

'Does Woody ever eat?' I asked.

'Sure Woody eats. Every day.'

'Do you think he'd eat with me?'

'Sure. Why don't you ask him?'

'What? You mean . . . just ask . . . ?'

I was astounded at the simplicity of it all.

'*Sure*. I bet he says yes. Woody likes to eat.'

He did say yes, and without fuss, so we went out to Le Cirque, a very expensive restaurant where he often dined. I say 'often' when perhaps I mean 'habitually', because Allen is famously a creature of habits – playing his clarinet every Monday night at Michael's Pub, for example.

We had a very pleasant meal, chatting affably about families, the fact that Mia was expecting a baby towards the end of the shoot, how he was going to cope with that (the shoot – not the baby), London, baseball, and so on and so forth. He also told me how much he disliked group activities and that, for him, this was the worst part of directing a film. That, at least, explained some aspects of his, to my mind, erratic behaviour.

While we ate and talked, he dealt patiently with the pretty constant stream of autograph hunters who approached our table. Apart from being a fine film-maker, he was also a big star in New York, and made several jokes at his own expense about hating celebrity at the same time as being quite prepared to sit in expensive restaurants and sign autographs. I felt as if we had made some kind of connection and hoped that this would be apparent in the way we related on set. But the next day the shutters came down again, and he became his usual grumpy, discomfited (though never actually angry) self.

The film was photographed by Bergman's cameraman Sven Nykvist, a great bear of a man who, unusually, only worked with three lights. I chatted to him about Bergman and the relative lack of lighting. He chuckled and said, 'Ian, as you get older, you make do with less.'

He also told me that Allen had instructed him always to shoot out of direct sunlight so that *Another Woman* became a very dark-looking film. I asked him about the parallels with Bergman, even going so far as to say that, like Bergman, Allen made films which were essentially about himself – the anguish in both cases is central – and that, like Bergman again, to make those films he had to stay close to home.

Sven laughed, but was becoming used to fielding questions about his old master and the new pretender. He did however observe that both directors had built up round them loyal teams of people on whom they could rely, and who had become virtual families, though both Bergman and Allen still retained the right to be distant and unknowable. Allen, for example, would sometimes play chess with his technicians between shots and would let crew members use his seats for the New York Nicks basketball team whenever he was unable to attend matches. He was friendly enough, without ever being a friend.

On several occasions I spoke with Mia Farrow, who seemed disenchanted, if not to say disinterested in the whole business. She turned up on time, spoke her lines, and then went home. She was, of course, seven months pregnant when shooting started, but I don't think this accounted entirely for her detachment from the project. In contrast to her usual ethereal self, she seemed rather lumpish and curdled, muttering about her size and how exhausted she was. In addition, her relationship with Allen was strained. Both had been surprised when Mia became pregnant (there were rumours on set about that side of their association), and he had declined the opportunity to be her Lamaze coach. Part of the explanation for this no doubt lay in his extreme aversion to all forms of physical unpleasantness – physicality in general – though the stand-off between them was aggravated by Allen's wish to call the baby Ingmar. After the December birth, Ingmar was named Satchel. And less than a month later, Mia was back on set for reshoots, heavily padded with a cushion so that she looked more or less the same as she did before. She never went to see the finished film.

This stand-offishness was not because the material did not interest her. 'Woody and I used to spend time speculating on people's lives in apartments,' she told me. 'We were fascinated by them, by all the different kinds of existence.' So I imagined that the framing idea for *Another Woman* had been conceived during a time of animated, voyeuristic musing between the two of them, but somehow the whole thing felt listless. At first, Allen seemed happy enough with the dailies, though there was an occasional mumble of regret at not doing it as a comedy. Then he worried that the scenes didn't look exciting enough, and then he began to think it was cold and boring. Gradually, one felt, life was draining from the project. The anticipated masterpiece wasn't working out.

At the end of my filming I called Pep and told her that I would be coming home on schedule. There would be no tinkering or much attempt to transform the material already filmed. Allen said, 'There's no need to sit down and beat a dead horse,' which was harsh and perhaps unfair on himself, though I could see he was disappointed. His increasingly melancholy attitude was at least tempered by an understanding that the bottom wasn't about to drop out of his artistic world. His reputation and the way in which he had things set up in New York meant that, success or failure, he would still be making films next year. One film a year, in fact.

While actors move from role to role, each role arguably assimilated into their cumulative present until later in life they drag into every part echoes of their earlier screen roles, Allen has become famous for films about the same archetypal character. With his acting, it's difficult to think of any performance in isolation from others, and the deeper he sinks into that role (if it is a role), the more of a burden it seems to become. In some ways, he has turned into one of the starry celebrities of whom he is so suspicious, embracing the same kind of comforting predictability on which they depend. This may have confounded him.

It was therefore refreshing to have dinner with Gena Rowlands towards the end of the shoot. Her husband, John Cassavetes, was seriously ill with liver disease in California, and yet she still gave an unfussy, powerfully focused performance as Marion. Maybe she was used to working with directors like Allen (Cassavetes, after all, was a sort of wishfully tyrannical liberal) and knew exactly how to deal with them. She has a straightforward, unselfconscious energy that seems to neutralize any kind of affectation or insecurity. When someone wandered up to Gena at our table, recognized her and said, 'I know you,' she merely replied, uncomplicated and unashamed, 'You probably do. I'm an actress.'

15

A FILM ACTOR

Another Woman was received with indifference in America. Though admired in Europe, it did not do particularly good business. One critic called it Woody Allen's *Wild Raspberries*, an impolite and mocking reference to the Bergman classic *Wild Strawberries*. I thought this was unfair. In the end, despite my misgivings, the film was decent enough and in its own rather peculiar, muted way, very ambitious. There were some fine performances, notably by Gena Rowlands, and somehow during the edit the ramshackle story about which I had felt so uncomfortable had acquired shape and coherence.

Later, I learnt that Allen used an editing machine like a man on an emotional rollercoaster. He was very exacting and hated the idea of a finished product. I suspect he disliked the notion of a product as much as the idea of anything being finished, the blocked-off finality of an edited film implying contentment and a sense of achieved perfection that his fidgety temperament could not tolerate. But with another film already being made – one film a year, regular as clockwork – he had somehow to bring the thing to a close.

I don't think he worried too much about a film's critical reception. He was in fact very suspicious of praise or acclaim, and especially where it originated. He told me that if Hollywood ever praised one of his films then he would have to re-evaluate it. 'I mean, if it was really so good, so wonderful, they wouldn't be that interested.' He therefore, I guessed, rather perversely came to distrust anything but faint praise. Better still, if praise was grudging and reluctant – as if the granting of it in some way *hurt*.

Allen's next film was *Crimes and Misdemeanours*, which Hollywood loved. I suspect this put him in a quandary. I, of course, was rather more straightforward in my response to criticism. Generally speaking, because I rarely carried the entire burden of a film on my shoulders (I was never a leading man – at least not on screen and never *that* kind of leading man – and did enough British movies to 'keep me honest'), I managed to dodge adverse comments. But I can't say that I'm one of those actors who disregard reviews or who, having read them, take no notice. I was once accused of having a voice that sounded like fingers being scraped down a window-pane. Bernard Levin said that in *The Homecoming* my Lenny had an appalling Cockney accent, and Mark Lawson mentioned the shrivelled size of my manhood when in *King Lear* I had to wade naked through a pool of cold water. Such things have stayed with me, so for various reasons I suppose they must have hit some kind of nerve. Still, I'm not sure that posh Levin was qualified to pass judgement on my accent, and even disregarding Lawson's own physical short-comings (the liver lips, the pudgy plasticine face, the old man's prematurely balding dome), I am not convinced that his no doubt enormous cock would not also have dwindled after a cold bath in front of several thousand people.

I would like to think that I don't take bad reviews to heart, though the above suggests that there are exceptions to the rule.

On the other hand, reviewers see films a year or so after you have completed work on them, so perhaps they can judge some things better than you. And in the theatre, critics can hit upon good things as well as bad, even giving clues about why a performance might be going well. Several times I have read a piece and thought, 'Mmm. Yes. I must work on that.'

But by this time – 1989 or so – I was beginning to regard myself as a film actor. Not 'primarily', but perhaps 'only'. *Vanya* excepted, it had been such a long time since I had worked with any kind of regularity on stage that I had even begun to cease being anxious about the possibility of any kind of comeback. Someone did ask me around this time what it would take to get me back in the theatre and I flippantly replied, 'A play by Harold Pinter written with me in mind.' A few years later it did happen more or less like that, but for the moment I was and thought of myself as a film actor. I felt very comfortable with film work. Theatre is hard work and angst-ridden and repetitive, and although movies can also be hard work, it is work of a different order and usually minus the angst. They suited my personal tendency to shrink away from responsibility and my professional preference for minimalist inflection and slight variations of tone. I was not like a 'star' who must become a kind of social construction and rely on being at least partially predictable. I made my living by being persuasively different in each role I attempted, and for the moment the screen felt the most convenient place to do that.

Besides, the work kept arriving, so there was no time for regret. After the *Iceman* breakdown I had worried about making a living away from the theatre, but events had now turned full circle. Pep seemed happy that I was at peace with myself. We had settled into married life very easily. She had become familiar to television audiences through the successful sit-com *Ever Decreasing Circles*, though she was also a fine theatre actress, championing and appearing in Rattigan's *The Deep Blue Sea* at a time when he was very far out of fashion. I went with her to Zimbabwe, where she played Donald Woods's wife in *Cry Freedom*. We stayed at the Sheraton in Harare and I divided my time between wandering round the set and being a tourist. I knew Richard Attenborough, the director, and liked Kevin Kline, who played the journalist Donald Woods, so the trip was relaxing and enjoyable. We also went on holiday to Mauritius a couple of times, bought a thatched cottage in Wiltshire, and behaved very much like a contented married couple, which, I suppose, is precisely what we were.

By this time, though there was never much doubt it would eventually happen, Pep had been embraced by my own family. The flat at Iverna – where I no longer lived but was still named as the sitting tenant – was a sort of large, neglected but warm sanctuary for Bee, Lissy and Barnaby (and many others besides), though Barnaby was about to move to Los Angeles, where he would eventually work at the House of Blues. Alice, Pep's daughter with Dan Massey, was a little guarded about me, her reticence caused by her age (a young teenager, she must have wondered about the small and rather grumpy man who had somehow elbowed his way into her life) and by my own in-ability to play the role of stepfather. But we were very at ease with our life, and whenever I was out of work or on edge, I would drive down the M4 to Wiltshire and mow the lawn or deliver one of the paintings that Pep had bought for the cottage.

And I worked. One of the first things I did after *Another Woman* was *Michelangelo*, a film directed by Jerry London and made for HBO in America. It wasn't very good. It was one of the few things I have done only for the money – and the money was particularly generous. The producer was Vincenzo Labella, a wonderful man who had also produced *Jesus of Nazareth*. I have no idea how much he believed in the project, but he gave the impression of believing, and for a producer that is at least half the battle.

I played Michelangelo's patron, Lorenzo the Magnificent, and seemed to spend a great deal of time on my deathbed talking in hushed, terminal gurgles about the devaluation of the local currency. In fact, there seemed to be hundreds of lines about the devaluation, but every time I suggested to Vincenzo that it seemed an odd subject for a man about to die, he would just smile and tell me, 'But Eeean. Is verri, verri him-portant. Is verri him-portant to geeve the audience thees in-formation. They will like eet ah lot.' He would then give me some justification of why they would like it a lot, most of which I forgot almost as soon as it was said.

He was the same when giving Pep and me a learned and entertaining tour of the local frescoes, characteristically combining acute academic knowledge with warm, playful enthusiasm. And it had also been like that when I was being fitted for costumes and there was an issue about turning a small Englishman into a Renaissance man of great prestige and power. I would try on a wig and Vincenzo would call out, 'Bigger, Eeean. Bigger hair. More hair.'

After the hair came the hat ('Bigger, bigger . . .') and finally the nose ('Bigger, bigger . . .') so that in the end I resembled a mutant Pinocchio figure. 'Wonderful, Eeean, wonder*ful*. Now you look the part, no?'

Though harmless good fun, the film, of course, disappeared. Apart from a handful of good things, most of the work I did for the next few years was undistinguished or mediocre. This is a matter of fact rather than of opinion. I suppose if you give yourself over wholly to making movies this is what happens. Projects are subject to all manner of pressures and strains which can dismantle their unity. As an actor, you start by selecting screenplays you like, go for the job, and hope that things will work out.

Steven Soderbergh's *Kafka* is a good example of the opposing elements at play in the making of a film. When I was asked to play Dr Murnau I immediately accepted. The film had all the credentials to be a popular and critical success, a kind of Holy Grail for all art. Soderbergh had just made *Sex, Lies, and Videotape* and even as a young director was already nudging the big time. Jeremy Irons, who was being hailed on both sides of the Atlantic for his portrayal of Claus von Bülow in *Reversal of Fortune*, had been signed up to play Kafka.

The screenplay by Lem Dobbs, which Soderbergh had admired and wanted to make into a film for a long time, tells the story of a character called Kafka who toils in an insurance office during the day but saves his mind for writing, which he does at night. His only friend at the office is mysteriously murdered and consequently Kafka is drawn into a world of sinister, bureaucratic conspiracy.

Of course, we'd all been there or thereabouts before. *Brazil* was still fresh in people's minds, Pinter had done a screenplay for an adaptation of Kafka's *The Trial*, and Richard Eyre had weighed in with a piece for television, *The Insurance Man*. *Kafka* was enormously popular in the 1980s, I suppose because the world perceived itself as being overrun by managers, administration and red tape. In my own modest way, even I had noticed that things were a little different. New signs were springing up all around our rural idyll in Wiltshire. Brown signs told motorists that they were entering a 'Historic Market Town', or in some cases merely a 'Historic Town'. Nearby Marlborough spent £150 updating its sign so that visitors were aware of its twin Gunjur in the Gambia. The *Marlborough Gazette and Herald* ran an article which reported that councillors thought the sign which merely announced the town as 'Marlborough' was 'a disgrace'. Signs seemed to be popping up all over the place telling us where we were, where we were going to, and what we should do once we arrived. One simply read 'Beware the bull', even though there was not (and never had been) a bull, prompting the thought that a bull would soon be purchased by the council in order for the sign to make sense.

So, I reasoned, Soderbergh's desire to film *Kafka* was based on sound enough instincts. And nothing actually went terribly wrong with the filming, but gradually you could sense the thing not working.

I liked Soderbergh a great deal. Rather preppy, willowy, somehow clean-looking and carrying with him an air of mysterious cleverness. He called on Pep and me at Stonor Road wearing a large and very smart raincoat, and Alice thought him the most beautiful man she'd ever seen. We got on well and he talked enthusiastically about working again on his next film, which was supposed to be about the birth of American football. Though Soderbergh was a mild-mannered, polite man, on set relations between him and Irons were tense. They always seemed to be arguing about the script. Irons was unhappy about it and as the star – which on the basis of von Bülow he clearly was – he wanted quite radical re-writes. Soderbergh was not yet sure enough of himself to either accommodate or fight Irons, and *Kafka* began to drift.

It became an immensely stressful film for Soderbergh to make. The weight of expectation, his difficulty in controlling a strong cast, and being away from home in the strange, albeit beautiful city of Prague, began to take a toll. He developed a number of nervous mannerisms, and a small tuft of white hair appeared on his face, as if the film was in some way administering small, sharply focused electric shocks to him.

As photographed by Walt Lloyd, Kafka was obsessed with images of bureaucracy gone mad, and this sense of being overwhelmed also became a reflection of what Soderbergh must have been feeling. Always owlish behind his glasses, he began to look stricken, his eyes apparently widening by the day.

Pale, wasted, leather-clad youths hung around the streets. They were about a year into Vaclav Havel's quiet revolution and wanted to see the West up close and measure themselves against it, to see, for example, if they'd got the right look. I think they expected Arnold Schwarzenegger or Tom Cruise to show up, cars to chase one another thrillingly through cobbled alleyways, and bombs to explode at regular intervals. And all we wanted to do was get the film finished and buy souvenirs, mostly big Russian officers' hats and medals which could be had by the yard.

At the end of the film, Kafka blunders into a place where hideous experiments are being conducted, which I (as the evil Dr Murnau) explain are to make people more controllable. The scene was played out inside a vast dome which housed a brain being focused upon by a huge lens. It was like the ending to a Bond movie and I played it pretty much as a Bond villain. At some point, Soderbergh turned to me, aware perhaps of the banality of this final setting and ruminating about his initial enthusiasm for what was a serious project, and wearily observed, 'It's all a crap shoot, isn't it?'

I don't think he meant it in the English way, i.e., 'The movie that we're shooting is crap.' His 'crap shoot' alluded to a game of dice and implied that the whole process of making a film was down to chance. But I wonder if he thinks that now, especially after the success of *Erin Brockovich*, *Traffic* and *Ocean's Eleven*.

After *Kafka*, I worked with another highly intelligent man, David Cronenberg. The difference between the two then was that Cronenberg was further along in his career and only interested in making films that were successful on his own terms. He knew what he wanted to do, knew too that there would not necessarily be a large audience for his work, and – perhaps most important – worked secure in the knowledge that nobody would be looking over his shoulder, telling him how to spend the budget. As such, his work had an integrity which in commercial cinema is a very rare commodity. With Cronenberg's ease of mind and assurance came a calm, relaxed, almost docile set. There was no sense of rush and quietly, peacefully, *Naked Lunch* unfolded before us.

Cronenberg was a very interesting person to work with, not least because despite being such a placidly avuncular academic, a decent family man, there was clearly another side to him. His hobby was racing cars, and his films were notoriously strange, often with undertones of sex, violence and a kind of cool dementia. *Naked Lunch* was no different, being a free adaptation of William Burroughs' apparently unfilmable novel. The plot is very difficult to explain, because a lot of it is a drug-induced fantasy and takes place inside the main character's head, though it did involve the use of fifty 'mugwump' creatures, typewriters that mutate into giant bugs with talking sphincters, giant centipedes, things that crawled out of inkwells, and a number of sci-fi blobs.

I played a character called Tom Frost, one half of an American literary couple (Judy Davis played my wife, Joan). Peter Weller played Lee, a sort of surrogate Burroughs, whose wife I may (or may not) have had an affair with. And then there was Roy Scheider, whose narrow face, broken nose, furtive eyes, impossibly metallic tan and ferocious facelift suggested that he was actually one of Cronenberg's creations rather than a very good character actor.

Occasionally, Cronenberg and I would exchange a few words about the work. He would tilt slightly forward and look at me from behind his enormous Dame Edna glasses, observing me as if I was a specimen, though always observing me warmly. And filming *was* in many ways like an experiment, with ideas being followed through to their conclusions without having to worry about the financial or intellectual consequences.

In the way that some people hum popular tunes, he liked to throw out ideas that had been running around inside his head, and once asked me whether I thought acting carried the same dangers as writing.

'In what way?' I replied.

'In the way that imagination and creativity are both natural – but also dangerous.'

'Dangerous?'

'Like a disease,' he continued.

'I don't know. I'm not sure that I use imagination when I act. Perhaps I do. It's mostly instinct.'

I didn't think I was much help. I thought he might be disappointed. He considered for a moment and then smiled.

'But surely by presenting an existence different from the one you're living . . . that's using the imagination?'

The way I acted – the way I was – meant that little imaginative substitution was needed. Pushing aside the life I was living was not too difficult; I had always assumed there wasn't actually a great deal to push aside.

'Mmm. Maybe,' I offered rather weakly.

Cronenberg, I think, is interested in areas of danger, and he considered writing to be one of those. Cars are another, as are questions of human frailty and decay. He is a remarkable man and I wasn't surprised when he later told me that his father had written pulp fiction and his mother was a musician. Genetically, he was strung out somewhere between them, a cultured sensationalist and a poet of the malformed psyche. He also possessed a good, wry sense of humour.

A few years later I worked with him again on *eXistenZ*, and for the part I was playing unearthed a strange middle-European accent. Cronenberg tolerated it well enough for the shoot (perhaps rather liking its alien, attention-grabbing quality), apparently quite amused by my performance. Then, right at the end of the shoot, he wrote a new line for the conclusion of the film in which the character I was playing admitted that he didn't know what he was saying. Who said Cronenberg didn't have a sense of humour?

A few months after *Naked Lunch* came *Blue Ice,* a film directed by Russell Mulcahy and starring Michael Caine. At the time, I remember reflecting how convenient and agreeable life had become. Work seemed to be arriving on a more or less regular basis. It was well paid. Though it was often hard work, discomfort and anxiety were rare. I was meeting and working with good, interesting people. And yet there was a sense in which I felt I needed something more. There was a steady rhythm to steady work, but I wondered whether it was enough. Occasionally I would worry when I heard that people thought I had entered some kind of unambitious comfort zone . . . and films like *Blue Ice* merely confirmed the feeling.

The film was produced by Caine himself (for HBO) and cost around six million dollars to make. It was an attempt to resurrect the kind of Harry Palmer character that Caine had played so brilliantly in the 1960s, and I gather the aim was to set in motion an entire sequence of Harry Anders films.

'Ian,' Caine told me, 'if this film takes off there'll be work for us all. If it doesn't, it'll go down the toilet.'

And that, more or less, is what it did, though I have noticed with amused and mild regret how frequently the movie turns up on television, like a bout of flu which proves very hard to shake off.

Still, even if *Blue Ice* had taken off, I'm not sure what kind of prospects it would have held for me. I was cast as Sir Hector, Anders's retired former boss at MI6, and was killed off in a final shoot-out. This involved me being hooked on to a crane, hauled sixty feet into the air and dangled over some docks. I recall the producer roaring with laughter when he saw the look of terror on my face as I was lifted off the ground for the first time.

'All right, Ian?'

'No!'

'You'll be fine.'

'I will not be bloody fine.'

'You look great.'

'I feel fucking awful.'

It made me think how little of this kind of work I had to do while making films. Because I tended to play character parts and was rarely (if ever) the star, I had been spared all sorts of horrors. Dangerous stunts, embarrassing bedroom scenes, the pressure of delivering an audience-targeted performance . . . I had missed them all. Up to this point, the only fearful act I'd ever been asked to do was ride a horse. I invariably fell off horses and they never travelled in the direction I wanted them to. A few years later, when making *The Emperor's New Clothes*, I caught my testicles underneath the saddle of a horse I was sharing with a very tall army officer. As the horse sped away, my balls slipped beneath the leather seat and the rhythm of the galloping horse set in motion an excruciating sequence of squeeze and release.

Eventually the horse was pulled up, I regained my testicles and fell to the ground in horrible agony.

'Can we go again, please?' the director asked.

'No,' I shrieked, 'we can not.'

But thus far I had not been asked to do much in the way of action or, come to that, sex. Caine told me that I was well out of it. We swapped stories about Roger Moore, a famous stunt coward, and he told me how Trevor Howard always stopped filming whenever there was a Test Match at Lord's.

In *Blue Ice*, the beautiful Sean Young insisted that all the crew dress only in their underpants during the filming of her bed-room scene with Caine. Caine told me he disliked nude scenes of any kind because they detracted from your eyes and your voice. Then he held up the padded cod-piece he was expected to wear to avoid any kind of genital contact.

'Not much passion in that, eh?' he chortled. Then he recalled a bed scene with Glenda Jackson in which she slid a sliver of false tooth into her mouth to hide the gap between her two top teeth. Caine was very good with stories – he had worked with so many people, and often gave the impression that while he was a serious professional, he thought acting in films could be a bit of a lark. 'Julie Walters once conned the whole crew into taking *their* clothes off during a bedroom scene,' he giggled. 'She told them it was a new Equity ruling or something.'

Although he's become something of an institution, I still feel that he's better as a character actor rather than playing the leading man. He may well disagree with this. Despite his relentless charm and his good humour, there is occasionally something guarded and cool about him, as though at any moment he's expecting to be rumbled for some unspecified crime. And he can be inscrutable behind those spectacles. He had, however, worked with Woody Allen (and, brilliantly, in *Hannah and Her Sisters*), and seemed to have kept up some kind of contact with him. I think he even told me that he was there on the occasion that Woody and Mia Farrow first met.

'Woody thinks you prefer more dramatic roles than the one you did in *Another Woman*,' he advised me.

'Did you enjoy working with him?' I asked a little sheepishly.

'He's brilliant,' Caine said.

'Did you get to read the script before you started shooting?'

'Yes.'

'What, all of it?'

'Yes.'

'Oh,' I said, trying not to sound too disappointed.

Then he told me how much he liked the very precise direction he was given, Allen's attention to detail, and the calm, almost churchy atmosphere on set. 'But Woody's more romantic than he lets on,' he continued. 'All that stuff about not liking the countryside and being in New York. He's got a whole landscape up on the roof of his penthouse. He likes walking there.' I must have looked dismayed. 'You've not been on his roof, Ian?'

'No. Just out for dinner,' I croaked. 'Once.'

Clearly he had encountered a very different Woody Allen from the one I had met.

Even though we didn't have a great deal to do with one another, I liked Caine, despite his being so different from me. Professionally, he never seemed to stop working, hoovering up projects as if each would be his last. This hit-and-miss approach, and the fact that he always gave himself an odds-on chance of doing something really good, suggested a kind of gregarious boldness which I did not possess.

There were also his close feelings towards his family, which I could never replicate. During the filming of *Blue Ice*, for example, he took time off to attend the funeral of his half-brother David in March 1992. The *People* newspaper had 'discovered' him quite recently, and by the time Caine found out about him he was sixty-seven years old and living in an asylum. His mother had apparently kept David a secret for over sixty years. He was moved to an asylum at an early age. The institution was called Cain Hill and I wondered what Mrs Micklewhite must have thought when, in ignorance of the name, Maurice had decided to become 'Michael Caine'.

The two half-brothers only had a few months together, but at least David found out that he belonged to someone and (judging from the way Caine behaved) was greatly cared for.

The ashes of David and Mrs Micklewhite travelled with him from house to house. At the time, I was reminded of my failure to visit my own brother's grave, my mother not attending my father's funeral, and my own bland feelings of inconvenience when they died.

I also recall playing around in my head with a theory about the acquisition of wealth and how it might be some sort of 'reply' to your parents. Now Michael Caine has a great deal of wealth (there's an apocryphal story of his doing a bad film for lots of money so he could buy a painting: 'Now *that's* art,' he's supposed to have said, meaning the painting, not the film), and I wondered whether there was any kind of link between tangible evidence of achievement and the strength of one's parental relationships. If so, I was afraid that my complete in-difference to acquisition and surroundings sounded a rather depressing, even weedy note.

When *Blue Ice* was released, critics did not so much savage the film as feel pity for it. It resembled, for example, 'a Fifties quota quickie' and embraced that 'familiar genre, the bad British thriller'. Though I was happy enough, and came out reasonably unscathed, being involved in such projects carried a tariff. Without the track-covering opportunities Caine allowed himself (to manage something memorable next time round), I found the lack of challenge gnawing at me. Without recognizing the origins of the itch, I now realize that I was perhaps looking for a way back to the stage.

16

BACK TO THE STAGE

By this time – the early 1990s – I was into my sixties and close to qualifying for a free bus pass. Since then, having passed the magic milestone, I have used the pass many times. I like travelling by bus. That or car, but rarely the Underground. As I've become older, I've also become less tolerant of enclosed, claustrophobic spaces. Ageing is to do with a decline in one's tolerance levels, as though growing old has the effect of provoking small annoyances and minor irritations until they become large annoyances and major irritations. As you grow older, you no longer feel the need to put up a cheery front to mask your aggravations. On all fronts, you have a lot less to lose.

Although I could imagine myself having panic attacks on the Underground and could recall with horrifying clarity having panic attacks on stage, I sensed that any other phobias were more or less under control. It's true that I don't much like heights and that I don't like being alone, but I can survive both.

When Harold Pinter called me and said that he had written a new play and would I like to be in it, I said, 'What's it called?'

'*Moonlight.*'
'What's it about?'
'A family.'
'A family?'
'Yes.' Pause. 'Yes?'
'OK. I'll do it.'

For a while I had been claiming that it would take a new Pinter play to get me back on stage, and now Pinter had written one. I had no excuses not to go back, though actually I did not need any. The thought of going back on stage did not worry me. I think it worried everyone else, though. In the circumstances, I actually felt quite serene and untroubled by the prospect.

Moonlight was staged at the Almeida Theatre in 1993. It was also the year I became a grandfather for the first time, Lissy having given birth to Talulah at West London Hospital in Hammersmith. I had never really imagined myself as a grandfather and felt badly equipped to play the role. My grandchildren habitually refer to me as Grumpy, which is, I suppose, affectionate enough, but also an indication of my grumbling ill temper and my inability to transform myself into the kindly white-haired Santa Claus figure I suspect they wanted but appreciated they were unlikely to get.

Grumpy, of course, is also one of the Seven Dwarfs, and by this time I felt I was becoming one of them, too. My size and the fact that I was almost the same height standing up as sitting down gave me a low centre of gravity, which meant that I did not so much walk as scuttle, and in trying to disguise the scuttle – predominantly by slowing things down a bit – did not so much scuttle as lollop, though even then I only managed to lollop in a scuttling sort of way. I had put on a bit of weight too, and from being 'impish' or 'sprightly' had now become 'stocky'. Rather than growing skeins of long, silvery hair, I was losing the stuff and becoming bullet-headed.

I was grizzled and grizzly, but I was still a grandfather. What did I feel about myself at this supposedly significant juncture? I suppose I felt quite good. At home, Pep cosseted me with a combination of good humour and practical affection. Like the cottage, Stonor Road was filled with paintings (she had a very good eye for art) and there were regular dinner parties. The cottage in Wiltshire became a sort of joint project and I was occasionally dispatched for the day to attend to some chore or other. Pep organized my life for me without ever giving the impression that she was actually controlling it or manipulating me. I felt loved and secure. Being a grandfather created a further sense of belonging and 'household', so when Pinter asked me about *Moonlight* I had my secure nest, and therefore had no hesitation in accepting the part. I had no reason not to.

And it *was* Pinter.

I think he was slightly irked that people had been saying that he hadn't written anything for fifteen years. We were a fine couple. I was panicky and he was blocked. Although I had been on stage since *Iceman* (*Vanya* and a benefit performance of *The Room* at the Haymarket Theatre in 1989 for the Terrence Higgins Trust), the observation had obvious substance so far as I was concerned. But Pinter had written six short plays and seven film scripts during that time. He had won an award for *A Kind of Alaska* and done *The French Lieutenant's Woman*.

'It's not as if I've been doing fuck-all in the last fifteen years,' he growled at me.

No, he hadn't been doing fuck-all, but I thought he had become more political. And more wary, perhaps. The press were often at him with jibes of being a 'Champagne Socialist' and 'An Angry Old Man', and at times he was understandably prickly. In the English way of doing things, there was some evidence of attempts to discredit him, and accusations of emotional ranting were quite common in the press.

However, he was always courteous and charming towards me, and the play when it arrived was not directly political at all. It was a personal piece about family relationships and death. I knew that his mother had died the year before, aged eighty-eight, though he was unsure whether the play had come from that. He never felt the need to explain his work to me (or anybody else), but I did get the sense that *Moonlight* was a kind of personal acknowledgement that he was getting older. We were more or less the same age, though I got the impression that he thought more about death than I did.

His father was still alive and must have been in his nineties; I think Pinter looked forward to visiting the old man, whose legs, by all accounts, were very weak, but who was in good humour despite his physical frailty and sudden loneliness. Pinter, I supposed, was more in touch with life than me, so it was logical that he would also be more sensitive about death.

In *Moonlight* I was to play the bedridden ex-civil servant Andy. Anna Massey was cast as Andy's wife Bel. She sits next to him doing embroidery, but the domestic intimacy is shattered by Andy's concern to find his lost sons, Fred and Jake. Though estranged from their father, they are also obsessed with him. Once I'd read the script and taken in its themes of dying and separation, seen how sharp and poetic Pinter's writing was, I knew that I had made the right decision about going back on stage. A date was set for September.

Although nobody directly alluded to my *Iceman* crack-up, it must have been a worry. Perhaps a collective decision had been taken whereby no one would mention 'Ian's little problem', a bad smell that everyone hoped had gone away. At any rate, there was no need to remind me of it. People were thoughtful without being impertinent.

As rehearsals drew near, I felt fine. Pep must take a lot of the credit for this. In addition to having already provided a safe nest from which I could operate, she became absolutely the reason why I was never to feel that the decision to go back on stage was flawed. Apart from the delicate cajoling and the unconditional support, there was also her own work. She had, for example, recently done Rattigan's *The Deep Blue Sea* and been Vita Sackville-West in *Vita and Virginia*, and was showing herself to be a really wonderful actress. Though I don't think there was ever any sense of competition or jealousy between us, I do remember stopping to think what good work she was doing.

Nor, since *Blue Ice*, had my own film career been a triumphant one. I had done, for example, a film called *The Hour of the Pig*, set in the Middle Ages, in which a pig was brought to judgement in a court of law. I played Albertus, a cynical priest, though I seem to remember that much of the time was spent avoiding Nicol Williamson. The film was decent enough; with the exception of Colin Firth it was packed full of older, established actors who lent their familiar mannerisms to a project that might otherwise have resembled something like *Carry on Canterbury Tales*. Thus, Donald Pleasance did some eye-rolling, Michael Gough dusted down his lofty drawl, and I went through my repertoire of furtive glances.

In *Loch Ness*, which starred Ted Danson (from the American television series *Cheers*) and Joely Richardson, but whose rolling hills and general landscape shots made it fodder for the Scottish Tourist Board as much as anything else, I played a man known only as Water Bailiff, a kind of custodian of the loch. The film was directed by John Henderson, a very pleasant, amiable man with whom I also did television work on *The Borrowers* and *Alice Through the Looking Glass*. I didn't much mind the part, though the film was quite forgettable. Though I knew Henderson and liked him, I had daily difficulties referring to him as 'Hendo', which was how he preferred to be addressed. I seemed to spend ages rowing a small boat around Loch Ness, something I was not very good at. Despite the swimming lessons at Wassall, I was still timid of water. I was also at the mercy of the loch's very changeable weather systems and grew to hate climbing into the boat.

'OK, Ian?' Henderson would shout.

'Fine. Yes. Hang on a minute . . .'

'Trouble with your *rollocks*?' Hendo roared.

'No. Yes. Almost there.'

'Weather looks *dodgy*,' Hendo guffawed.

'Thank you, John.'

'Mind your *rudder*,' Hendo cackled.

'Yes. Thank you, John.'

In addition to all this, there always seemed to be a small group of Nessie watchers hanging around, observing my discomfort, pointing, and when the occasion demanded, which was quite often, sniggering. 'All that money he's being paid,' you could hear them thinking, 'and he can't even learn how to row a boat.'

Filming was a pleasant enough experience, though since *Blue Ice* something was clearly gnawing at me. Though I had also been involved in Kenneth Branagh's version of the Frankenstein story and Nick Hytner's *The Madness of King George* – both perfectly respectable projects with good roles for me, especially in *King George* – I was beginning to feel the need to do important work again – or at least, *differently* important.

Pep came to join me in Scotland and we had a bad argument (my fault), at the conclusion of which she slapped me. This happened in the car and I recall noticing a car loaded with German tourists behind us observing events with great interest. Although the slap had stung me, I had more or less asked for it and no great harm had been done. Still, with such an attentive audience I couldn't resist milking the moment and putting on a display of pained surprise and reacting as if I had just been horsewhipped.

Why the performance? Because I couldn't resist an audience? Because I *needed* an audience? Or perhaps because I needed some kind of reassurance? Making up is all the sweeter for following a falling-out. And the presence of the German spectators was a further encouragement, maybe even part of the restorative. My performance arose naturally from the sense, maybe the conviction, that everyone was not a solid identity but an actor trying to play himself.

Something similar had happened ten years or so before this. I had been to see Sarah-Jane in pantomime and was driving home behind her when her car was involved in an accident and flipped over. Rather than being immediately frightened at what I was seeing, my mind somehow slowed everything down so that I witnessed the smash in slow motion, and a kind of three-dimensional slow motion at that. I observed the accident and was apart from it, aware of everything yet curiously unaffected. In the event, Sarah-Jane was fine, and I remember a rather sheepish policeman poking his head through the open window of my own car and asking Pep for her autograph. Afterwards, when I confessed my response to Sarah-Jane, she said it must be something to do with the actor in me – monitoring events, aware of everything, and being absolutely absorbed by them.

At the time of the Loch Ness incident, I could not say I was actually irritated by the work I had been doing in the cinema and for television. Some of it, after all, was good – and I had been good. And yet, though I did not acknowledge it (and with characteristic inertia was awaiting deliverance), I did need a different sort of challenge. A quick review of my recent CV, Pep's work, the inner knowledge that I was ready for a return to the stage, the call from Pinter . . . I had become or was becoming restless. Eventually, going back on stage became the sole answer to a question I had not yet asked of myself. I had become content to the point of complacency, mired in the absolute straightforwardness and convenience of my life. Samuel Johnson said: 'It is so very difficult for a sick man not to be a scoundrel,' and I was close to becoming one. Or at least becoming difficult to live with.

Habitually, work was the only means I had to soothe myself. I needed challenge and variety and quality to prevent the blurring of myself, the inconsequential drift of character.

David Leveaux directed *Moonlight*. He was personable, highly intelligent and completely focused. I was treated with invisible, unselfconscious concern. After rehearsals, usually over a drink, David would occasionally check that I was 'feeling OK' or 'doing all right' – a sort of cosy shorthand for confirming my psychological state – and I could not have wished for a better director.

Going to rehearsals and doing the play seemed perfectly normal. So normal, in fact, that like the onset of absolute quiet, noticing its relative uneventfulness would actually have been unnerving. There was a diverting strangeness in the fact that Anna Massey was cast as Andy's wife Bel. She was, after all, Dan Massey's sister and my wife's ex-sister-in-law. The exceptional circumstances were further enhanced by Dan then marrying Pep's younger sister. Pep and Anna had retained a good friendship, so the situation was not as embarrassing as it might have been. And it was fascinating to work with Anna, a fine actress and an interesting, eccentric woman. She is a very particular person – particular, for example, about cleanliness and such things as dogs not being in the room whilst people are eating. These Howard Hughesian traits are somehow a part of her acting manner, allowing her performances a sense of self-contained, tight enclosure, though suggesting at the same time an aching, unconsummated desire to be someone else. Thus, she is instinctively brilliant at managing to portray contrasting moods and states of being, implying two things at once.

And as Bel, she was terrific. For much of the play, she becomes the object of Andy's scorn and derision, especially with regard to her apparent inability to make contact with his lost boys. 'What a wonderful woman you were,' he says, and 'All that famous rationality of yours is swimming about in waste disposal turdology.' In order to protect herself from her husband's scatological jibes, Bel re-invents Andy as a more romantic persona, though you are always aware that she understands why she is modifying her view of him. Anna's natural sense of equivocation is comic, sad, touching, and infinitely suggestive.

For a while, I felt awkward at the prospect of having to spend the entire play in a bed, though I knew that Pinter's stage directions asked for this with final, monosyllabic certainty ('ANDY in bed') and there would be no flexibility about it. A part of me wanted to make use of my energy and stride around the stage.

'There's no chance, is there?' I once asked David Leveaux.

He looked at me with benign concern, perhaps worried that if I wasn't allowed out of bed I might go to pieces.

'No. You're on the edge of extinction. The play is partly about dying alone. The bed's all part of that,' he answered amiably but conclusively.

It helped that the rest of the cast – including a young Michael Sheen and Dougie Hodge – were so good. During rehearsals I had assumed my accustomed role of 'good company man', dispensing notes without the slightest intention of actually taking responsibility for anything I might say, and delighting in the presence of two young men who were clearly going to be very good actors.

On the first night (which was 7 September 1993), I walked on stage and climbed into bed. Earlier, Pep had reassured me that everything would be fine. How many times had she done so in the weeks leading up to that night? I had learnt my lines and, like a small schoolboy being tested on his homework, had run through them with her. Then I waited for Bridget to speak, the opening words of the play coming from Andy's daughter, who might, David Leveaux had explained, actually be speaking from beyond the grave.

'I can't sleep. There's no moon. It's so dark.'

My throat felt dry, though beyond that I was strangely, almost serenely calm. There didn't even seem to be the usual nerves, whose intensity is often needed to drive a performance forward. I was as composed as I can ever remember being, relaxed to the point of complete self-possession. I had no worries. I had once again found some kind of self-definition.

Bridget was now talking about Bel and Andy. 'They need to sleep in peace and wake up rested. I must see that this happens. It is my task.'

I thought of Pinter's own estranged son Daniel, and wondered again how much of *Moonlight* was directly autobiographical. There is certainly a streak of covert but none the less acute pain running through the play. I did not have the nerve to ask Pinter directly about this, but quickly gathered that he did not give the autobiographical angle much credibility.

My own son Barnaby had recently gone to America, where he intended to stay. He had been a child actor in *The Lost Boys* and *Omen III: The Final Conflict* (incidentally, scripted by Andrew Birkin), but had decided that acting was not for him. America was a chance for him to make a life for himself. Since he'd moved there, I found myself feeling closer to him. We were quite alike, both physically and in terms of character, and I often wondered whether he felt dispirited by the proximity of a 'successful father', a category into which I suppose I had fallen. And what of Pinter's son? How dispirited must *he* have been? I was not always a good or attentive father, though I could not have contemplated a sense of permanent dissociation. Once, I had pulled Barnaby out of school and shouted at him for not taking the dog for a walk. He must have been about fourteen years old. Afterwards, we didn't speak for a long while. Pinter's image of a family dislocated but still very much a part of each other is, of course, an archetype. During rehearsals, he had told me that Andy was not only alone, but that he 'seemed to deny the existence of more or less anybody else'.

'It is my task,' Bridget says. 'Because I know that when they look at me they see that I am all they have left of their life.'

And how far would I be able to grieve if I lost one of my own children before I died? Instinctively, I think back to the relative lack of feeling at the death of my own parents. Then, in the same split second, all such thoughts evaporate. I must speak. My mind empties completely and its chambers are flooded by a sense of the rhythm and shape of Pinter's language. I know the words, though I don't feel that I have to give them a specific meaning or interpretation. I understand exactly what is required, as though I'm actually responding from some place deep within myself. My calm is overwhelmed by an inexplicable, unwilled sense of vigour which is quickened by the sudden shadow of Andy's loneliness and past longings. I do not know where any of this comes from, or how the emotions are generated.

Bridget's opening speech ends. The faint light around her, which has marked out her stage territory, becomes even more faint. I say, or rather snarl, 'Where are the boys? Have you found them?'

And that's it. For the next eighty minutes or so I am oblivious to anything but Pinter's words, which are anchored deep within my mind and swim effortlessly, intuitively to the surface whenever necessary.

Encouraged by the success of *Moonlight* at the Almeida and

then the Comedy Theatre, the play was taken to Dublin in 1994 as part of a Pinter festival. Karel Reisz took over from David Leveaux, and Pinter himself directed *Landscape*. Then *Landscape* alone was staged at the Cottesloe. This is a short two-hander which barely lasts thirty minutes. By then, Pep was playing opposite me.

It would be delightful to report that such a run expressed my sense of joy at returning to the theatre, 'coming home', if you like. But the truth is that even though I was grateful for the opportunity, and in particular enjoyed *Moonlight*, most of what I experienced merely confirmed my preference for film. Not all film work but, all things considered equal, the medium of film. Apart from the first few performances of *Moonlight*, I felt this for much of the time, and at times felt it quite strongly. I had grown to prefer the process of making films and quickly began to resent the repetition which is an inevitable part of stage work.

Landscape did have its attractions, however. Its brevity appealed to me, and not only because I had come to approve of short plays. Earlier in the year, Deborah Warner and Fiona Shaw had successfully staged Beckett's *Footfalls* at the Garrick, showing that it was possible to offer 'brief theatre' in the West End. I was beginning to wonder whether long plays (even Shakespeare's long plays) were deserving of an audience's time and trouble. The two hours' stage traffic did seem an awful lot to sit through and often the poor quality of the productions made the whole thing a painful, numbing experience. Pinter's own *New World Order* had, in 1991, come in at only six minutes, and I liked the idea of an audience spending longer on its journey than it did in the auditorium – a different sort of two hours' traffic.

And I enjoyed working closely with Pinter, as opposed to merely working with his words. Even though he could be tough, he was also very supportive and cajoling, flexible and gentle when he needed to be, and not at all dogmatic or prescriptive in his reading of lines. There was something about him that invited you to impress him, an air of something that was maybe paternal or authoritarian. At one point during rehearsals there was a great deal of noise coming from the crew, and I knew this irked Pinter, who always demanded absolute concentration.

Without thinking, I shouted, 'Can't you stop that fucking noise? We're trying to work.'

Pinter looked at me, adjusted his spectacles, and said quietly, 'Quite right, Ian. Quite right.'

I had said it only because I knew he would have said it, or at any rate wanted to say it. Whenever we worked together I felt we were somehow on the same wavelength, as though we naturally understood one another. I'm not certain how true this might be of us as people, but as actor and writer, it was absolutely so. 'You put on my shoe and it fits!' as he once said to me.

I found *Landscape* a difficult piece. Though it only lasted thirty-five minutes, I was worried about forgetting my lines. Pep not only had to worry about her own character, of Beth, but also I was asking her to appease my own anxieties and foibles. Back home at Stonor Road, we would sometimes discuss things across the kitchen table, talking about, for example, a line that needed playing more forcefully, or some word that required a different emphasis.

And the play itself was staged in a kitchen, across a table on which there was a teapot and a teacup. It comprises the two interwoven monologues of a married couple, Duff and Beth. She doesn't appear to hear his voice and he is infuriated by her impenetrability as she retreats into idealized memory. Originally heard on the radio in 1968, it was an ideal companion piece for *Moonlight*, but also held up well enough on its own.

Pep's sensuous delivery and unspoken emotional remorse was well suited to the mellifluous phrases with which she responded to Duff's harsh, occasionally brutal rasps. And she was brilliant at suggesting Beth's willed obliviousness, the doubleness of Pinter's intentions, her eyes both myopically blank and full of scorching power. Even though the two characters appear not to communicate or even see each other, Pep said that I had taken on something of Pinter's stare, 'which drills into your mind'.

All of the work with Pinter was well received, and everyone was kind about my apparent 'bravery' in going back on stage – though in truth it just felt like cowardice at having not gone back earlier. And I couldn't have done it without Pep, who supported me, I think, more than I understood at the time. Though we managed *Landscape* all right, I got the impression she couldn't have acted with me again, that the burden of looking after me on and off stage was simply too great. Although we also acted opposite one another in *The Borrowers* (as a loving couple called Pod and Homily), that was for television and was an altogether different thing. We came across then, by all accounts, as an affectionate, eccentric, essentially cute partnership. Pinter does not allow the same kind of amiable frivolity; I am sure that our relationship reflected a little of each work's ambience.

Despite getting through the play, I did realize that I was not actually 'cured'. A friend of mine who was a doctor gave me an examination and said that although he wasn't worried about my physical health, my central nervous system was very weak. I knew that I was unlikely to desire a full-time return to the stage.

I suppose my ideal existence would have been with a healthy diet of film work punctuated by 'suitable' but infrequent jobs in the theatre. In this respect, the two years from 1993 to 1995 worked very well for me. As well as the Pinter, I was also able to do Stanley Tucci's *Big Night*, the Sidney Lumet film *Night Falls on Manhattan*, and *Mary Shelley's Frankenstein*, which was Kenneth Branagh's project.

I had worked with Branagh a few years before, on *Henry V*, and thought him an inspiring man, a powerhouse of ambition. However, I had not until that point appreciated quite how driven he was. He used to get up at five a.m., and his driver would drop him at Hanger Lane, from where he would run to Shepperton Studios. On arrival, he would work out furiously in the gym and then emerge glistening and toned on the set, ready to act, ready to direct, clad in not much more than a pair of tights. I believe that several pre-torso scenes had already been shot and rejected. Though the film then became a movie about Branagh's body, I liked him a great deal. He was funny and witty, but (a little like Pinter) carried with him a vague but certain air of threat. In addition, the technical team he had assembled were extremely loyal, and such allegiance would not have been granted unless it had been earned.

The monster was played by Robert de Niro, who had to endure four to five hours of make-up and could only work every other day as he had to let his skin recover from the glues which were used to disfigure him. He looked a little like an overbaked potato covered in stitches, and scooted around on a pair of roller blades which were hidden beneath his costume.

Although I had met de Niro before, during *Brazil*, I was still slightly in awe of him. Certainly he had an intimidating presence, but there was also the sense of de Niro as a living legend, which he now carried with him with an easy, un-selfconscious swagger. Branagh was also wary of him. He had to act with *and* direct de Niro, and the great man's reputation for being difficult had preceded him. De Niro preferred to work by making a whole series of takes, each a slight variation on the preceding one. This, he claimed, gave the director choice, but it gave the editor a headache and tended to slow filming. After *Henry V*, when some had rather absurdly claimed that Branagh was the new Orson Welles, he had been given a large budget, but even this could have been vulnerable to a long sequence of de Niro takes.

Fortunately, the monster's costume was so uncomfortable and cumbersome that de Niro must have come to the conclusion that his normal practice would not apply. Branagh would say something like, 'Lots of eye contact, Bob . . . I'd like to see the soul inside that collection of cuts and bruises you're carrying around.' And de Niro would just do it, quickly, efficiently, convincingly, and entirely without fuss. As Branagh saw that he did have control of his movie, after all, so his confidence grew and his natural frenetic energy began to illuminate the whole production. De Niro trusted his director, and the two of them often disappeared into Branagh's mobile editing suite to watch the dailies, chatting and laughing like two old drinking pals.

I had a scene with de Niro, and ironically it was me, the steady, reliable Holm, who was to cause delays. I played Victor Frankenstein's father, and at one point, immediately after I have been scared to death by the sight of the monster climbing through the window, I have my eyes closed by de Niro. I was so nervous of acting with him that I kept closing them before his bandaged fingers could do it. After the sixth or seventh take, I was showing no sign of being able to keep my eyes open and de Niro was becoming agitated. He turned to Branagh and said, 'This guy keeps closing his eyes before I can do it. What can we do about this?'

'Ian,' Branagh asked politely, 'problems?'

'No. I'll be fine.'

'Mmmm,' frowned de Niro.

I wanted to tell him that I was a trained Shakespearean actor, an accomplished if slightly nervy stage performer, and had even been nominated for an Oscar for my film work ... and that of course I could keep my eyes open. Which is eventually what I managed to do. At the rap party, de Niro apologized for his impatience and congratulated me on my 1964 *Richard III*, which he had seen on tape.

Despite the obvious and strenuous efforts that went into the making of *Mary Shelley's Frankenstein*, the finished product was something of a travesty, especially when judged against James Whale's original, where Frankenstein is less a man of action and more of a lonely aesthete. Branagh's blood-soaked frenzy of cinematics tried almost too hard to make an impact. It was an interesting example of a talented man not quite sure of himself and trying to compensate through exaggeration. The result was something which didn't do him justice.

Compare that with Stanley Tucci's *Big Night*, made with a tenth of the budget and shot in only thirty-five days. The action centred around two Italian restaurants in the 1950s and was a subtle but sharp, funny examination of consumerism and art. I played the devious Pascal, the producer of safe, commercialized cuisine, who is successful because he pays attention to the market rather than the quality of his food.

Big Night did very well in America and received very good reviews over here. However, despite the obvious differences between it and *Mary Shelley's Frankenstein*, I enjoyed working in both. In theatre, the sense that you are acting in something not very good is more immediate, the effects on the cast more instantly corrosive. Certainly I have been on film sets (for example *Jesus of Nazareth*) where the slow drip of anguish eventually undermines and splinters morale, but in general bad work is punished most miserably in the theatre. Despite Pinter, *Moonlight* and *Landscape*, despite Frankenstein, I still felt most comfortable on the film set. But despite *that*, I had still been discussing for two years the possibility of doing *King Lear* at the National Theatre.

'Richard Eyre is directing,' I said to Pep.

'That's good,' she replied. I was afraid that after *Landscape*, though she had held up very well, the effort of dealing with me on and off stage had exhausted her. She knew how difficult I could be when out of work – but *King Lear* was more than 'work'.

'It's very long,' I said to Pep.

'Very long,' she agreed, though without betraying too much reservation.

'It's *the* play, as far as Shakespeare is concerned.'

'Then I suppose you'd better do it.'

'Yes. I suppose I ought.'

And I knew when I accepted Eyre's offer that this would be a real test of my nervous system.

17

KING LEAR

I had worked with Richard Eyre before, liked and admired him, and never had any doubts about him doing an excellent job. I was surprised, however, at the intensity of his approach to *King Lear*. He told me that he had always wanted to do the play, and that for him the timing was now absolutely right. During the early stages of our talks he said *Lear* was a highly charged, emotional piece of work and that 'the arias could not be ducked'. In other words, the ferocious, elemental conflicts between Lear and nature would have to be played at full throttle – even though he was keen to use the Cottesloe, by far the smallest of the three stages at the National, and thereby emphasize the domestic nature of the drama.

'Our parents cast long shadows over our lives,' he admitted to me early on (echoing the opening words of his autobiography), and I nodded back in what I thought was an agreeable enough manner, even though I had never quite understood why so many people did carry their fathers and mothers around with them for so much of their lives. Eyre's own father, I already knew, had been a very autocratic man with whom he had endured a difficult relationship. Apparently Eyre Senior had never showed any emotion until his stroke, at which point he was prone to bouts of uncontrollable crying. And like Lear, his self-control became thinner as he weakened. Like Lear, he wanted to know his offspring better, but left it too late. Like Lear, there was a streak of vanity running through him.

Though he was far too intelligent and sensitive to source a production of *King Lear* directly from personal circumstances, it was clear that the fierce, concentrated energy behind Eyre's direction was at least influenced by his own experiences of 'family'.

I thought that, actually, he was like most other people in this respect. That is, other people *did* carry their parents within them all their lives. I was the odd man out. Beyond my lack of height and a handful of readily identifiable physical characteristics, I felt and still feel absolutely unconnected to my father and mother.

Eyre talked as well about the aftershock of losing one's parents, and how as their memory dims one wants to draw them closer and discover more about them. As he phrased it, to find out more about himself ('know who I am') by finding out more about them. Though this was not an emotion with which I could readily identify, I could see why it might have been important, and in what ways it might have been useful to *King Lear*.

The casting of Michael Bryant as Lear's Fool was significant as it emphasized the revelatory urge that had always been a part of their relationship. Eyre felt that the Fool was Lear's alter ego, and as Bryant and I were more or less the same age, there would be an immediate sense of correspondence. As played by Bryant, he was a sharp-tongued Cockney who was granted incredible licence to acquaint his king with some uncomfortable home truths. It helped that he was one of the longest serving and most respected members of the National's company, someone, incidentally, who refused almost all television and film work because he believed that 'proper acting' was done on the stage. He was perfect casting as the Fool, instinctively embracing the air of entitled, cussed, complementary otherness which was required to puncture Lear's pride. Although he was always wonderful to work with, and very generous with his advice, I occasionally felt that Bryant was slightly, if impishly, scornful of my film work – 'armchair acting', he would have called it – and I wondered if this had also been a factor in the casting.

Like Pinter, Eyre was discreet when it came to seeking re-assurances about my mental state. I had done *Moonlight* and *Landscape* with surprisingly little trouble, though my nerves at that time had been steadied by exceptional circumstances: the right plays, Pinter, brevity, novelty, and, of course, Pep.

A few years before, Eyre's production of *Hamlet* had been jeopardized when Daniel Day-Lewis felt unable to continue, disappearing from the stage in the middle of a performance, never to return. Eyre talked about this with me, which I suppose may have been a way of indirectly addressing his fears about my own state. His unselfish, understanding charity towards Day-Lewis convinced me that if I ever needed help then he would be someone I could trust.

'Dan's problem wasn't really with the ghost or the ghost of his father,' he said, 'but with everything else the play deals with.'

I agreed. Though the subject was not necessarily uncomfort-able for me, I didn't feel I had much to contribute beyond muted understanding. Day-Lewis and I are entirely different, as uncomplementary as it is possible to be. He is volatile and electric and explodes from within roles, often after saturating himself in character, whilst I prefer to work through intuition and in a much less premeditated way.

Eyre also said, 'Mothers and fathers, suicide, death, love . . . you know, *everything*. *Hamlet* touches on the lot, and I think Dan was knocked out by it all. He battled with the issues until they just overwhelmed him.'

'No need to worry about me on that score,' I replied jauntily. 'Issues don't really affect me.'

Though I appreciated the weighty matters upon which *Hamlet* and *King Lear* dwelt, I could say with confidence that I would not be undone by any deep thoughts I might have about them. My problems were altogether less solemn, less issue-based, and generally much closer to home.

I think that Eyre's experience with *Hamlet* was also one of the motivations for performing *King Lear* in the Cottesloe. He said that, after a very good rehearsal period, staging it in the vast open spaces of the Olivier had somehow drained it of substance. From the very beginning, he was adamant that we should use the smaller space, saying that above all else he wanted to retain the tremendous intensity of the play. He felt that consequent problems of scale were lesser issues which could be overcome, whereas loss of concentration could not. In fact, he claimed that he would never do Shakespeare on a big stage again, 'because you have to come on twice'.

As well as Michael Bryant, Eyre had assembled a brilliant cast, with David Burke playing Kent and Timothy West as Gloucester. Throughout rehearsals, the production gathered terrific momentum and everyone was optimistic that we had something quite special within our grasp. Eyre had been there before with a promising *Hamlet*, but this time he was determined not to let the potential slip away. He became even more forceful and dynamic as the opening night approached, handling individual actors with great sensitivity while still preserving a strong sense of 'company'. Paul Rhys, for example, who played Edgar, demanded a disproportionate amount of rehearsal time, apparently wanting every single word and nuance explained. Eyre saw that this needed to be done –

actors have different ways of travelling to the same destination – indulged him, and was rewarded with a fine performance.

A couple of weeks or so before we opened, the press interviewed me about the production. By and large, I have avoided such things. Over the years my media invisibility has been construed as reluctance and occasionally linked to my nervous disposition, and I have even been labelled as something of a recluse. This has rather suited me, though in fact my backwardness was often nothing more than a lethargic lack of enthusiasm for doing publicity. It is true that those who prefer doing it, for whatever reasons, do tend to find their ways to microphones or the front covers of glossy magazines, or wherever.

Many interviewers wondered if playing Lear was something I had looked forward to during my career. I could honestly say that, no, I didn't feel that way, and for that matter did not feel it much about any part.

'Even Prospero?' one asked. Journalists are always looking for digestible soundbites, and creating questions to which even a simple 'yes' or 'no' is a little loaded.

'*Especially* Prospero,' I replied, emphasizing my long-standing aversion to *The Tempest*.

Prospero is one of those parts with which actors tend to end their careers, a mutual signing-off, as it were. Perhaps the sense of 'end' is one of the reasons I don't much want to do it, but I tend to think it's more to do with my lack of respect for it as dramatic theatre. I have never seen a good production of the play – or at least one which has transported me – and at the time of writing have turned down several offers to do it.

Nor had I ever wanted to do Hamlet, another part for which journalists in particular felt I should have had a yearning. In 1989 I had been cast as Polonius in Zeffirelli's film of *Hamlet*, and the experience merely reminded me that I would always have felt awkward in the prince's role. Mel Gibson played Hamlet and Franco Zeffirelli, who was recovering from a car accident and had found solace in drink, didn't do much more than keep the camera close by his lead man. He had invested a fair amount of his own money in the project and reasoned, I suppose, that he would stand a better chance of making it back if the film was to feature a star turn. And actually, though many suspected the worst, Gibson was fine. He had magnetic, slightly mad eyes and spoke his lines with a measured, almost respectful conviction. In addition, he was willing to ask for and act upon advice. Several times he sauntered over and said, 'Hey, you're more used to this kind of language than me. We should talk about it . . .' And though *Romeo and Juliet* is a lesser play, I am more pleased not to have missed playing Romeo, though again I could not say that even that was a part I really *wanted*.

One interviewer seemed mildly startled that I didn't have some kind of game plan for my career, and didn't believe that I hadn't always wanted to play Lear. But with characteristic indolence, I have had no sense of professional direction and just go by instinct. Other people tried to make something of the parallels between Lear and myself, especially the fact that we both have three daughters. However, as far as I was concerned, there was no conscious cross-referencing between life and art and the two things remained entirely separate.

More interesting, for me at least, was Lear's descent into madness. My childhood years had been spent living alongside the vast Gothic asylum which my father ran, and I had grown up with derangement. I now realized that lunacy had become a fact of life for me. It held no stigma and I never even considered it to be much of an illness. If anything, it was rather fantastical. Not actually normal, though far from unacceptable, and never anything much more than curious.

This, I think, was not only the result of my prolonged proximity to the asylum, but also because my father never talked about it, though in truth we rarely talked about anything. Thus, madness was merely a fact, folded into our rather humdrum, middle-class existence, and as much a part of it as our Sunbeam Talbot or even Gooch the chauffeur. And the inmates themselves – or rather, the ones I could see – were generally unfussy, oddly preoccupied creatures. Remember Mr Anderson, for example, the man who spent his days steering his wheelbarrow from one end of the asylum's garden to the other, obsessively picking out each crumb of soil from it, never satisfied until the barrow was completely emptied. But I never saw straitjackets, or heard sinister moaning, or witnessed any of the other clichés about lunacy.

It was also significant that by playing in the farm on the other side of the asylum building, my whole childhood set-up attained a kind of bucolic idealism. Of the farm, the asylum and home, it increasingly seemed to me that 'home' was the most uncomfortable place to be. I was there to be seen – seen sometimes, that is – but never, ever heard. On occasions, for example watching through closed windows as the adults played tennis, I desperately wanted to join in. However, tennis parties – and most other parties – were out of bounds to me. I suspect that I grew up believing that tennis was actually a stranger activity than anything practised inside the asylum. I was the one who began to feel like an inmate, cloistered away and forbidden contact with the outside world.

Madness therefore held few terrors for me. And the fact that I had been diagnosed as having a weak central-nervous system, in addition to actually having cracked up, only made it more familiar, even homespun. The effect of all this on my playing of Lear, I think, was to allow me to consider those passages where he is raging against the elements as nothing more than a ferocious extension of character. In other words, I did not feel a need to 'play' madness, perceiving it as extreme though not necessarily unnatural behaviour.

What pushes people over the edge and into these extremes is altogether more difficult to fathom. The *Iceman* meltdown was terrifying because its source seemed to be somewhere close to the very centre of me. Aware that in some fundamental way I was under attack, my system responded by closing down completely. This, I suppose, is as extreme as it gets. I can also recall, while at Rada, pushing someone into the gutter and trying to strangle them. I have no idea why it happened, other than thinking that I was provoked beyond reason, or at least beyond my reason. A single moment of uncontrolled violence is perhaps not much for an entire lifetime; in fact, life has tended to direct me towards its mirror image of willed passivity, suppressed impatience and grumpy inertia. On the other hand, there are probably a few walls which still bear the imprint of my frustration finding expression; I wonder if that's the kind of thing people mean when they refer to my acting as being like 'coiled violence'. Generally, I prefer to live simply and to turn away from anything that might cause aggravation. My moderation is a refusal to be burdened and perhaps exasperated even by small irritations, less I am vexed or 'perturbed in the extreme'. The tight packaging on CDs, the small print on an A–Z map and the retrieval of messages from my mobile phone cause me disproportionate bouts of annoyance.

Still, Richard Eyre and I both agreed that Lear's outbursts should be as loud and highly charged as possible. In some productions these 'arias' are ducked and in their place are substituted all kinds of apologies for madness – nervous tics, mumbling, and so on and so forth. But at these moments Lear is operating right on the edge and he needs to be at full throttle. In preparation for the important moments where this occurs, I was sent to a gym to develop my perineum, which as I soon learnt is situated somewhere between a man's testicles and his anus.

Apparently it was from this region that I would discover the power to deliver Lear's element-defying speeches. The trainer who had been hired to help had a brutal but effective system which involved all kinds of stretching and pulling. When I told Pep, she misheard and asked why I should be entitled to *per diems*.

The other royal madness I had been involved with, a few years before, was Nick Hytner's film *The Madness of King George*, the title of the Alan Bennett play from which it was adapted (*The Madness of George III*) having been changed for the US market. Americans, apparently, would want to know about the first two films in the series.

George's madness was rather different from Lear's, as his odd, confused behaviour was provoked by the hereditary disease porphyria. I played Willis, the king's doctor, whose character underwent something of a transatlantic sea change in making the journey from stage to film. At the National, Willis's contribution to George's naturally occurring remission is played down, but in the film he is given more credit for the healing process. Americans place far greater faith in therapeutic ventures than the English, and Willis was, if nothing else, at least enterprising. I therefore played him as a cross between a male nanny and a rather sinister social worker.

The Madness of King George was in fact a hugely enjoyable film to make. Nick Hytner had directed the stage play and was making his first film. Small, nervous and thoughtful, he strolled round confidently in brown brogues and chinos. He was also bright, sharp, artistically ambitious, and very quick to learn. He knew exactly what he wanted and within two or three days had slipped the second assistant director (who had been briefed to chaperone Hytner's first efforts at making a movie) and taken complete charge.

Nigel Hawthorne had, I think, just been outed and was

outraged at the invasion of his privacy, though he was so sure of the King George role that there were few difficulties in gearing his stage performance for the camera. Earlier, he had taken the villain's role in Sylvester Stallone's *Demolition Man*, to prove to American doubters that he could cut the mustard on the big screen. Rupert Everett played the absurdly pompous Prince Regent, and did it very well, while two of my favourite actors (John Wood as Thurlow and Geoffrey Palmer as Warren) were also cast. Wood in particular is capable of such subtlety, and always appears to be so grounded and intelligent, very different from my own more instinctive approach. And Palmer's timing – especially his comic timing – is so wonderful that he is able to inject all sorts of strange, surreal possibilities into his scenes.

The play implies that monarchy and lunacy share common frontiers, that there is something pathological about the exercise of power. Some have even gone so far as to say that the history of madness is the history of power. There is something in this, though I would refine the notion and say that madness is more closely associated with the *loss* of power or authority – or the fear of losing it, of things moving beyond one's control. We are all, in Swift's phrase, in 'a perpetual possession of being well deceived', which allows the whole business to become more domestic and less exclusive to royalty.

And Lear's madness is, of course, both – he is a king who has lost control of his kingdom and in the process seen his grip on domestic matters disintegrate. Richard Eyre told me that as he grew older, he found his sympathies actually moved *away* from Lear. Something of this was reflected in the programme notes, which claimed that what we thought of the play and the king depended upon our own age. Eyre growing older had in some ways brought him literally closer to the king, though this diminished distance also prompted him to feel less pity for the ailing Lear and to identify more with his 'wronged' children. He began, in short, to understand where the old man was coming from. Lear's predicament was now observed with a knowing, penetrative gaze.

We therefore put a lot into the first and pivotal scene of the play and wanted to suggest that Lear was playing a game with his daughters. He thinks he is having a bit of fun and asks each one to tell him how much they love him, all the time waiting for his favourite, Cordelia, to join in. When she won't play, he over-reacts and begins to lose his sense of perspective. From there, the momentum is irresistible, and it is pretty much downhill all the way, right up until the moment he faces the elements.

The energetic impetus is, I think, one of the reasons why I did not have any nervous problems with *King Lear*. If Eyre was anxious about me, he did not show it. Everything about the production seemed so sure-footed. Every night I referred to it as 'climbing on board the juggernaut' or 'climbing Everest', but certainly *climbing*, and there was a real sense of the verse and the drama pulling you forward with great compulsion and urgency. After each performance I would feel drained and exhausted, though consumed in a very different way from a Pinter play. With Lear there was a physical weariness that was similar to the feebleness one experiences after extreme exercise. But the discipline and stillness that Pinter's work demands is somehow more taxing, sapping your mental reserves and testing your subconscious.

I gave one interview (I think to the *Evening Standard*) where I said, perhaps rather glibly, that doing Lear wasn't that difficult, that the king was merely a little impulsive, loses his land, then goes mad. 'It's quite easy really,' I remember saying, possibly in a conscious echo of Olivier's words to Laughton about the same play nearly forty years earlier. And on one level I really did believe that it was quite straightforward. Unlike in Pinter, I didn't have to think too much about the lines or analyse what was happening. It all seemed quite without guile and relatively uncomplicated. The teasing of family, the loss of position, the madness, and the production's internal momentum; it appeared entirely logical and sensible. All I had to do was learn the lines, allow the rhythm of the words to push me forward, and be 'me', sort of gremlin-like. As Hugh Hudson once observed, when I play monarchs, I have a tendency to strip away the regality and veneer and find the ordinary person, the Everyman, to whom the audience can relate.

My only worry was that the grizzled beard I had grown would make me look like Captain Birds Eye gone loopy. It was one of those productions in which a lot of beards were grown, and during some scenes the audience – which was packed in close to the action – must have felt it was surrounded by a tribe of stocky, hoary, bullet-headed old men.

Taking my clothes off during the storm scene was my own idea. As the play is about a once-great man dissolving and stripping off, it just seemed the obvious thing to do. I don't think it was evidence of any new insight into the play, more that I was an actor willing to do it. It was the first time I had taken my clothes off on stage and I have to say that it felt entirely impersonal. I did not, as it were, feel that I was revealing anything of myself. Ian Holm had long ceased to exist by the time I appeared. Neither was I aware of the audience taking sharp gulps of breath or giggling in an embarrassed manner.

Usually speaking, men from the United Kingdom find it very difficult to take their clothes off in front of men, in front of women, and especially in front of men and women. Even though I am an actor, and people assume that in some way I am immune from feelings of embarrassment and self-conscious physical awareness, I always assure them that this is certainly not the case. Still, the only awkwardness I felt was during the interval when, off stage, I stood naked, myself again, and had to be smeared with mud by a couple of stage hands. Though they were delicate in placing the sludge, discreetly averted their eyes, and even made polite conversation about the way the play was going, we all understood that this was a very embarrassing moment. Nobody likes to have his balls smeared with sludge by a complete stranger in more or less full view of twenty other complete strangers. But back *on* stage . . . that was different.

Acting at the National provided its own distractions. I didn't much like it. The acting space was fine, but the miles of corridors, the steady, relentless hum of bureaucracy, the 'works canteen' cafeteria, the unavoidable sense of many other things going on simultaneously, even the concretized look of the place . . . all of it seemed very untheatrical. As I'd reflected when performing in *Landscape* two years previously, you had to think twice to remember that you *were* in a theatre, though maybe this momentary dislocation was somehow soothing to my nerves. It also reminded me of a backhanded remark that Peter Brook once made about Peter Hall when they were jointly running the place: 'Peter's so good with the memos.' And when we talked about the National, or rather I grumbled and he listened, Richard Eyre would recall that he'd once quoted another of Brook's pronouncements to Albert Finney, who was similarly disgruntled with the building. 'A theatre should be a musical instrument,' Brook had said. 'Yes,' replied Albert, 'and who'd make a violin out of fucking concrete?'

Meanwhile, Richard Eyre's production rolled forward like a well-oiled machine. Tim West has never been better and bristled with patrician authority, while all the work with Paul Rhys was paying off. Barbara Flynn, Amanda Redman and Anne-Marie Duff were outstanding as Goneril, Regan and Cordelia, precisely capturing Eyre's intention of making the audience identify with Lear's mistreated children. Their parts were crucial in establishing the convincing balance he wanted between the intimate violence of family life and sheer, elemental unfairness. 'I gave you all,' says Lear, to which Regan spits back, 'And in good time you gave it.' Goneril is unsteady, Cordelia weeps uncontrollably. His daughters know they are unloved, and when he comes to live with them he is embarrassing. He rages and weeps and and breaks down in public, and then he abuses their servants. Any pity Goneril and Regan might have had for him is transformed into contempt.

Though I never *don't* read reviews, I rarely allow them to get too far under my skin. For one reason or another, this time I was slightly more attentive to them. Perhaps this was to do with some residual anxiety about being on stage again, maybe a little to do with the awareness that this was a major production. A few critics did not think that the production managed to transcend the claustrophobia of playing *King Lear* on a small stage and emphasizing the inability of parents and children to love selflessly. However, in general it was received with enormous acclaim. Benedict Nightingale, reviewing it in *The Times*, went so far as to say it 'may be the best *Lear* I have seen'. A frail John Gielgud came to see the transfer to the Old Vic and congratulated me. Richard Attenborough brought Tony Blair, and a year later I was awarded a knighthood. In addition, I won the *Evening Standard* Drama Award, the Critics Circle Theatre Award, and the Olivier Best Actor Award. *King Lear* was very good to me, an undoubted career highlight.

Before the reviews and the awards, Richard Eyre had been cautious about the production. From the rehearsal period he knew he had created something special, and yet he also understood this was no guarantee of success. There had been an early scare when the *Evening Standard* Hot Tickets section had announced that Eyre's production of *King Lear* should provide 'a suitably doomy contrast to the irresistible feel funky factor of his *Guys and Dolls*'.

'Why are they bringing *that* up?' he asked, perhaps anxious that some sort of weird, misleading comparison was being drawn between two entirely distinct projects.

In general, though, his attitude to critics was quite cheerful, or perhaps cheerfully resigned. He has been Director of the National Theatre, so he knows all about being in the firing line and being held accountable to the press. I found it interesting to talk to him about this, especially since (with a few exceptions) I have tended to slip too much attention. He once reminded me of Christopher Hampton's observation that theatre people are bound to feel about critics as lamp-posts do about dogs, though I also knew that, like all of us, he was incapable of being entirely unaffected by reviews.

Eyre is a deeply sympathetic and protective man who wants to stand guard over cast and crew without jeopardizing the integrity of his productions. He is also a cautious, self-doubting person, aware of an actor's scepticism towards directors, and very private about what occurs during rehearsals, as if what happens there is some kind of shameful secret.

He did not have to worry on any account, though of course he was worried about everything. His natural inclination to doubt – provoked by his father, developed by the inevitable trials of his career, and marinated by his time as Director of the National Theatre – was in this case unfounded. *King Lear* was both a critical and popular success. Eyre had achieved an almost entirely successful union of text and design, character and actor, play and audience, something which all directors aim for but few achieve. His only regret, and one that I share, is that the play was seen by relatively few people. The run at the Cottesloe could not satisfy public demand (though there was also a tour to Istanbul and Salonika). It seemed a pity, but on the other hand I don't suppose I could have held myself together for a long, punishingly tautological run.

Quite recently, I saw Tim West's *Lear*. They were in the middle of a gruelling tour which included matinées. I don't know how they did it. Everyone looked exhausted. Over the past years, Eyre and I have talked on occasions of resurrecting *Lear*. 'I think there's a bit more work to do on the storm scene,' he might say, or 'Perhaps the opening could do with more snap.' I think we're both glad that nothing has happened. The prospect of achieving perfection is tempting, but of course unrealistic and un-attainable. And as Eyre also pointed out to me, the best advice he's ever been given about running a theatre is to make sure you have a good restaurant, as people care more about eating than plays.

18

SIR BILBO BAGGINS

As I've suggested, *King Lear* was the core of a series of works which at that time led to a number of awards or award nominations for me. I am quite flippant about such things and often wonder what all the fuss is about. Though mildly (but never absolutely) cynical about such things, I am yet to turn one down. There is no great mystery behind my serial acceptance of awards and honours. Flattery, an undeniable sense of personal achievement, the need for a wider recognition of that achievement, good manners, and the sense of wanting to avoid the even greater fuss that a refusal would inevitably bring on.

Captains of industry and government servants assume they will be rewarded, though actors – and, I suppose, writers and dancers and artists – by and large do not. I knew someone who worked in the Foreign Office and resigned because he was unhappy in his job. Within a year, his wife had left him. Deprived of their trophy son, his in-laws were furious, and more or less told him he'd brought it on himself. All he'd had to do was keep his nose clean and hang on for another twenty years and he'd have certainly bagged his OBE. Such automatic procedure is unheard of in the arts.

When I heard in 1998 that I had been awarded a knighthood, I felt that it was, in part, an acknowledgement of my work. It was not something for which I had been waiting, or which I necessarily expected. The curiously non-committal letter arrives a while before the ceremony, and it gives you the chance to refuse the award, being worded in such a way that you could do so without loss of face to either party. The implication is somehow that if you don't want the knighthood then, despite the letter, you probably won't be offered one. Apparently, a surprising number do refuse. I accepted because it felt like an accomplishment and because accomplishing things was why I had become an actor in the first place.

Pep asked me what being knighted meant.

'I don't know. A trip to the palace.'

'Anything else?'

'Apparently we can get married in St Paul's Cathedral.'

'We're already married.'

'There's a medal,' I muttered hopefully.

She nodded attentively.

'And then I suppose I'll be *Lady Penelope*,' she finally said.

Nine years earlier I had been awarded the CBE and the Queen – smaller even than you expect her to be, though more horsey than anticipated, and wearing an indelibly grumpy expression – had said to me, 'You do mostly films now, don't you?'

It felt like an admonishment (i.e., you've stopped proper acting, haven't you?), and betrayed at the very least some ruthlessly digested research. Her straightforward question, if indeed it was a question at all, admitted knowledge, concern, allegation, and perhaps even pity. I was almost keen to see her again after Pinter and *King Lear*, hoping perhaps that she might twinkle at me and say how pleased she was that I was back on stage.

The actual process of being knighted is, of course, something of a cattle market. Beyond the dubbing, there is no contact with the Queen. There are simply too many dubbings (around two thousand) and the day passes in a blur of deteriorating expectations and mounting, impatient boredom. Those who get the sword early on (and I was one of these) have to resume their places in the crowd immediately, while the others simply have to wait their turn.

There is no rehearsal, though nearly everything is worked out in the most precise manner, and explained in the short talk which precedes the ceremony. There is a clear instruction, for example, about the placement of your left foot when kneeling before Her Majesty. When the moment comes you move forward, shadowed by the usher dressed in funereal black, take a step past the Queen, turn, nod your head ('Nod only,' we were told. 'Under no circumstances must you *bow*'), then go down on your left knee. We were led to believe that the usher was there in case someone fainted from nervousness. Despite such careful consideration, we were not told how long we should remain on our knees. After the sword's sequence of light taps had been completed, I stayed down too long, uncertain what to do next, awaiting direction. The Queen said nothing, though she coughed lightly and emitted a small but distinctly impatient sigh. I rose to my feet and shuffled back to my place amongst the audience.

It struck me afterwards that patronage is never far from being patronizing. Why do people like me need to be loved and treasured by the establishment? As I said, I like to think that my knighthood was recognition for something worthwhile, though I suppose there is every chance that it was nothing of the sort. The writer V. S. Naipaul – though actually *Sir* Vidia Naipaul, which does make a difference, though I'm not quite sure of what kind – accused the nation of imposing an 'aggressively plebeian culture' on the Prime Minister, so perhaps Mr Blair was not much moved by my Lear, but had listened more attentively to his children, who might have seen me in *The Borrowers* or *Loch Ness* or maybe the Luc Besson film *The Fifth Element*. On the other hand, Auden once wrote about the Arts improving under a Sovereign who despised culture. So who knows what lies behind the dishing-out of knighthoods?

Mention of *The Fifth Element* reminds me that earlier in the same year I had also been nominated for that film (amongst others) in the London Film Critics' Circle Awards. The others were *The Sweet Hereafter*, *Big Night* and *Night Falls on Manhattan*, and I find it inconceivable that any informed nomination could have judged Besson's film their equal. I do remember, however, being pleasantly surprised by Bruce Willis's competence and professionalism in *The Fifth Element*. I supposed he had been cast precisely because of his cocksure but entertainingly ordinary screen persona, but he clearly wanted to move beyond the limits he'd created. Besson, though, wanted the vest and the torso, and insisted on the pleasing smile Willis had perfected in the television series *Moonlighting*. During one scene, Willis said, 'I haven't done that smile for a while – but if that's what you want . . .' Then he'd perform his trademark expression, his raised eyebrows automatically ascending into the space left by his receding hairline.

Willis was also very generous, often throwing lavish parties at his rented home. One morning – I can't now remember whether I was arriving or leaving – I observed with horror that there was a not insignificant number of dead fish floating on top of the pool. As I bent down to get a closer look, I saw that they were not fish at all but a flotilla of used condoms.

In other ways *The Fifth Element* was a very uncomfortable film to make. This was partly because of Besson's continual encouragement of me to 'overdo' my role as Father Cornelius. Usually the model of restraint, I was gradually impelled to become increasingly indulgent. I was not alone. Gary Oldman (who played Zorg) sported a set of Bugs Bunny teeth that provided only a slight distraction from the Bowie–Hitler hybrid he had become. Besson claimed that he had been thinking about the film since he was sixteen, and I felt the whole project was in some way self-gratifying. Leggy models in futuristic air-hostess outfits lolled round the set and Jean-Paul Gaultier provided the costumes, as well as strolling around and spraying everyone with something from his new range of perfume.

Milla Jovovich played Leeloo, a sort of human waif whose mixture of naivety and ambition wasn't too far removed from Milla's own character. She quickly acquired the nickname Band Aid because her outfit was little more than a bikini bandage. Besson and Jovovich became man and wife (or man and waif) soon afterwards, and their affair was a matter of public display. His on-set manner was equally conspicuous. As director, he would frequently walk on to the set without saying 'Cut!' and walk amongst the actors while dispensing advice. It was a kind of confused, fluid interventionism I had never before experienced, and it only contributed to my feeling of ghastly unease about the project.

Having said that, I am sometimes hailed by strangers who might shout something like, 'Yo! Father Cornelius!' and then tell me that *The Fifth Element* was the film that changed their lives. I have no answer for this other than to say that perhaps Besson knew what he was doing better than I do. His boast that the film would become the new *Bladerunner*, ripped off and copied for the next fifteen years, may not be as facile as I first suspected.

On the other hand, I felt Atom Egoyan's *The Sweet Hereafter* to be fully deserving of the praise it received. Unusually – for reasons I've spoken of – I played the lead in this film. Not the conventional kind of lead – middle-aged, cynical, in receipt of frequent distraught phone calls from a neglected junkie daughter – but a lead none the less. My character, Mitchell Stephens, arrives in a small Canadian community which has been traumatized by a school-bus accident that wipes out most of its children. Stephens's job is to persuade the bereaved parents into a lawsuit against the bus company.

Egoyan is one of the best directors I have worked with. He is extraordinarily bright and, like fellow Canadian David Cronenberg, is more or less trusted to pursue his own projects in his own way. As well as being intelligent, Egoyan can also be very funny, and when I experienced nerves and for a while felt that I could not do justice to the part of Mitchell Stephens, he was both supportive and sensitive.

This was the first time I had been scared during a film. At one point, I recall, I was even weeping at the hopelessness of it all and Egoyan had to take me in his arms. I think a number of factors contributed to my nervousness on this occasion. While I was making *The Sweet Hereafter*, I was also commuting to Ohio to do a few scenes for Danny Boyle's follow-up to *Trainspotting*, *A Life Less Ordinary*. The irregular absences from Egoyan's set made me feel like an outsider whenever I returned, and as I generally enjoy being a part of a film's entire production process, the switching between movies may have panicked me.

It didn't help that the team Egoyan had gathered around him was brilliant. There was an obvious sense of intimate camaraderie between them, and the actors knew their characters frighteningly well. Though everyone made me welcome, and there was no method-influenced suspicion towards me off set, it was easy to feel like an intruder. It is also possible that something of Mitchell Stephens's interloping hung in the air.

Egoyan nursed me through and conjured from me, I think, one of my best film performances. When *The Sweet Hereafter* was released in 1997, I was nominated for and received several awards. Egoyan – who is acutely but not bitterly aware of existing in Hollywood's shadow – won an Oscar nomination for his direction, though (absurdly, predictably, inevitably) lost to James Cameron and *Titanic*. Of the two directors, I know which one I would back to eventually make a masterpiece. Keep an eye out for his son, too; only a small child at the time of writing, though when I saw him, already a protégé.

Egoyan also directs for the stage and is a great admirer of Pinter and Joe Orton. Apparently, he cast me as Stephens after seeing the 1973 film of *The Homecoming*. He told me he liked the curious combination of sympathy and menace that he observed in the role. Being an Englishman also meant I was automatically considered as being outside the shattered community.

During one scene, Stephens is on a plane and finds himself sitting next to Allison, a childhood friend of Zoe, his junkie daughter. The encounter compels him to go over the gradual breakdown of his relationship with his daughter and to describe the complex, unresolved feelings he has for her. Though I expected Egoyan to cut in at any point, he allowed me to go on talking, treating it as a single shot.

When he did stop me, he apologized. 'Sorry, Ian. I don't want to cut in, but I have to.'

'Was it all right?'

I knew it was.

'It was riveting. I was tempted to keep going.'

'I know.'

'It seems a shame to disturb your delivery. It was meticulous.'

Occasionally I am asked about the performances or moments of which I'm most proud. This long take in *The Sweet Hereafter* would be a strong contender. Its concentrated stillness and intensity reminded me a little of Pinter. As Stephens recalls a moment when he had complete control over his daughter's life, he is by contrast preparing the viewer for his present helplessness – in his job and as a father. As a parent, husband and lawyer, his life is passionately unresolved. Egoyan had ushered me to such an intuitive understanding of Stephens's role that his uncertainty and rage (the sympathy and the menace Egoyan had seen in *The Homecoming*) were effortlessly reproduced.

Another quality of his directing was his habit of saying precisely what he thought. Rather than voicing the usual bland encouragements ('Good ... Terrific ... Excellent'), he was specific ('*Very* subtle ... *So* compelling ... Extremely *potent*'). Such things make an actor trusting and appreciative.

It is ironic, if unsurprising, that while I could do such '*very* subtle' work in *The Sweet Hereafter*, it is the fashion photography and comic-book visuals of *The Fifth Element* that more usually provoke recognition and claims of a life-altering experience. I wondered whether the same might be the case for *Lord of the Rings*, when I was cast as Bilbo Baggins in Peter Jackson's epic trilogy. The film would inevitably involve a great deal of merchandising to help recoup the $300 million outlay for making all three films back-to-back, and Bilbo's character would not be exempt. Part of me shuddered at the prospect of being translated into twelve inches or so of rubberized doll, no doubt not looking much like myself – though still similar enough to cause disquiet.

I was already very familiar with *Lord of the Rings*, not from reading it, but from having played Frodo in the Radio Four dramatization of the book twenty years previously. Michael Hordern played Gandalf in a grand, rather old-fashioned way, and the rest of the cast boasted an exciting collection of talent. The adaptation lasted for weeks, and when its twenty-first anniversary coincided with the release of the first part of the film version, it was re-released on compact disc.

It was made, I suppose, at a time when the BBC took risks and there used to be more opportunity for unconventional work. Though I have done plenty of television and radio work, my understanding of what goes on in the BBC is limited. All I know is that the quality of the parts I have been offered has deteriorated. So has the work. And so has the quantity of work. There may well be all kinds of reasons for this, but people like Richard Eyre, who should know, tell me that the required and pragmatic reforms at the corporation could have been carried out without losing its sense of a common purpose – i.e., working towards a collective good. He says that now there is little sense of the vision and continuity he believes are needed to transform moderately good work into something of real excellence.

I think this is a fair point. Certainly many of the projects I did for the BBC had been characterized by a sort of amiable conviction that what was being done was somehow 'worthwhile' and had nothing to do with making (or saving) money, or management initiatives, or whatever. When Pep and I did *Macbeth* for the World Service, it seemed as if the project came together more from a series of happy coincidences than any organizational strategy. I also recall working with the dictatorial Jane Morgan on *The Mill on the Floss* and admiring her nononsense approach, which meant we were all treated like slightly naughty schoolboys. Not, actually, a bad way of approaching actors. And then there was the exhausting, semi-Proustian experience of reading Wilkie Collins's *The Woman in White*, by myself, over twenty-four takes, with nothing more than a chair and an Anglepoise lamp. Much of the radio and television work I have done was characterized by what could be called a 'common vision', where the primary aim was making programmes of good quality. There was a collective sense of endeavour, of people working for or towards something they believed in. I do not think this is now the case.

By the time I thought all this, I was into my sixties. Actually quite well into my sixties, and therefore in danger of all sorts of curmudgeonly complaining ... not only about the BBC, but about fresh vegetables, the state of the Health Service, the demise of the Cox's Orange Pippin, traffic, crime, the loss of the good old days, and the inglorious present. I once read that you can't be angry without causing damage to yourself. By and large I don't get angry, but not getting angry doesn't mean that you don't *notice*.

This was also the time when, despite being a grandfather several times over (after Talulah, Lissy begat Poppy, then Sarah-Jane begat Archie and Ellie, and Jessica begat Tierney and Caris), I was again on the point of divorce. Pep and I had separated, not without some difficulty, and one of the more agreeable things about signing up for *Lord of the Rings* was that it would put some distance between us and allow some kind of respite.

Matthew Bramble, in Smollett's novel *Humphrey Clinker*, has something to say about the ageing process and the way in which it alters one's perception of life. He says, 'the impetuous pursuits and avocations of youth have formerly hindered me from observing those rotten parts of human nature, which now appear so offensively to my imagination'. I thought of this while I was reading the book during the flight to New Zealand, where the filming of Tolkien's book was to take place. Part of my problem, I considered, was that the more rotten parts of human nature did not appear offensive to my imagination. Perhaps they should have done, though the pursuits of youth still interested me.

At any rate, *Lord of the Rings* proved to be a fabulous distraction. Nothing had quite prepared me for the scale of the project and the apparent creation of an entirely new world. Although I was only there for a couple of months, actors like Ian

McKellen (who was playing Gandalf) and Christopher Lee (Saruman) were there from beginning to end, a period of eighteen months. Elijah Wood (Frodo), Sean Astin (Sam), Billy Boyd (Pippin) and Dominic Monaghan (Merry) had been there so long that they sported tattoos of pledged brotherhood, replicating in real life the intimate Hobbit fellowship they reflected on the screen.

Outside this constructed little bubble of Middle Earth, the rest of the world was going frantic. There had, apparently, been a kind of internet hysteria about the casting of the movie. Scholars, children, parents, anyone who had ever read a book . . . all seemed to have an opinion about *Lord of the Rings*, regarding it almost as personal property which was merely on temporary loan. In one poll, it had recently been voted Book of the Century, beating James Joyce into a relatively distant second place. I wondered why it exerted such a fierce grip on people – though, generally speaking, not on me – and came to the rather ungallant conclusion that it was something to do with the chasteness of the world view it offered. Though good and evil were pitted against one another, this was a comparatively straightforward conflict, not much complicated by sexual tension. With the exception of Arwen and Galadriel, *Lord of the Rings* is mostly male. I did notice, though, that Saruman's eye (which amongst other things sucks the souls of those who are tempted by the Ring and is clearly shown on the cover of the books) had become an all-consuming vaginal slit.

Presiding over this Brobdingnagian event was the director Peter Jackson, who looked like Stephen Poliakoff on a particularly bad day. He was a woolly little man with a crinkly, grow-anywhere beard and a bandy, slightly concertinaed shape. He always wore shorts and operated a rota system with what seemed to be just two short-sleeved shirts. There was no doubt he was a good director, though I did wonder how this affable, slightly eccentric man had come to be entrusted with the simultaneous direction of three major movies which, if they had gone wrong, would certainly have sunk the studio. But in fact he was absolutely the right choice.

His quirky nonconformism was buttressed by a stubborn, visionary streak; he had already insisted on the trilogy being filmed at one and the same time. This was so there would be no chance of money 'running out' for the second and third parts; the *Superman* movies had been done in much the same way. One night I sat down in my hotel room in Wellington and watched videos of a selection of Jackson's other films. The first was *Bad Taste*, a distasteful low-budget gore movie that appeared to be quite serious whilst also poking fun at itself. This, I thought, was a good sign for someone who was now attempting to stage a story in a fantastic yet believable world. The second was *Heavenly Creatures*, about an adolescent girl who persuades a friend to help murder her mother. And the third was *Braindead* – another 'shocker' – which ends with the hero's mother transforming herself into a giant moloch and swallowing him up her uterine canal. Somewhere amidst all this plausibly rendered hocus-pocus I began to understand precisely why Jackson was the right man for the job. Possibly the *only* one.

He had boundless energy; often we would have to wait for his return from another set – frequently by bicycle – before we could begin filming. There was always a backlog, and Jackson would keep in contact with everyone via his mobile phone, finishing one take and then rushing off to catch up with something different happening somewhere else. This was not a film where deep delving into character motivation was required, so by the time he turned up, everyone was ready to go. Jackson knew exactly what he wanted and would watch a scene unfolding with purposeful concentration. If he said 'Good,' then you knew it would have to be done again. He was actually a shy man and kept things pretty simple, trusting his team and the actors to do their jobs while he somehow held the whole thing together. 'Good . . . Good . . . Yep . . . *Very* good . . . Go again . . . Very good. . . . Very *good* . . . We can probably do one more . . . *Excellent!*' Then you knew you'd got it, and off he went.

Although he was very focused, there was also a boyish restlessness about Jackson, as if he was somehow itching to join in. Sometimes this compelled him to work very close to actors, and occasionally his frizzy face would appear about ten inches away and he'd say, 'This is where I want the camera. Right here.'

On one of the few occasions when Jackson was still, we had a conversation about the logistics of making three films at the same time, and he said, 'It's like running a war.' Sometimes there were as many as nine other sets to consider, and some of them were hundreds of miles apart. Even with a helicopter to supplement his bike-riding, there was no way he could be everywhere. On those occasions he had to allow others to direct scenes, and then sit in front of a bank of television screens while the rushes were fed through to him. It seemed a ridiculous way to make films, but Jackson seemed to have got the balance right and, like a music-hall plate-spinner, had grown to know instinctively when one part of his act needed attention and when another could be left alone for a while.

He claimed to me that the toughest but most satisfying part of the work was filming Bag End, Bilbo's home. The average height of a Hobbit is only three and a half feet, and to create this illusion on screen was extraordinarily complex – or seemed so to me. Some of the dialogue between McKellen (as six-foot Gandalf) and me (as three-foot-something Bilbo) involved computer trickery, but also two different-scale sets were built. In the first, a normal person would seem like a Hobbit, because the doors were a couple of sizes too big and the ceilings were a good height. In the second set, which was much smaller, McKellen was always in danger of banging his head on the ceiling, and the doorways were all so small that he had to crouch to go through them. There were also a number of short and tall stand-ins wandering around, who doubled for the Hobbits or other characters and were used for over-the-shoulder shots, or wide shots when the actors' faces were not visible. Acting in Bag End – both big Bag End and little Bag End – with this weird collection of people, and being trailed by twenty or thirty crew members, all banging their heads and lugging equipment through the hot, cramped spaces, was often an ordeal which only the Hobbit-like Jackson approached with much enthusiasm. He, I think, derived great satisfaction from mastering the problem.

Despite the grand scale of the enterprise, nothing was left to chance and there was almost obsessive attention to detail. My ring pocket, for example, was kept full of stones when it was hung up so that it looked baggy and used. Every morning, the Hobbit feet took an hour to put on. There is a scary moment in the film when a crazed Bilbo makes a grab for the Ring and his face is suddenly transformed into a sickening, Ring-affected grimace. Lots of photos were taken of me looking as frightening as possible, then a sculptor created a spooky caricature which replaced my real face for just a couple of frames. When the movie came out, this was my grandchildren's favourite moment; they would ask me to 'Do Bilbo!', at which point I would cause them to scream by suddenly adopting his chilly expression.

I had never worked with Ian McKellen before – or even met him, I think – and found him utterly charming and generous. He was always very kind, at one point observing how well he thought I had done something and saying that I had set a standard to which he could now aspire. I knew that he had said much the same to Judi Dench when they did *Macbeth* at

Stratford, and perhaps he had said it to others. Some have said that he flogs the charm a bit too much, but I never thought his remark was influenced by stagy affectation or doubted he was anything but genuine.

We talked a little and I discovered that he had visited Stratford on a school trip in 1955 ('the Annual Senior Stratford Camp'), just at the point when I had started there. Like me, he loved Olivier's flamboyance and recalled the thrilling leap he had made from the archway at the end of *Coriolanus*. He could even remember cycling to one of our cricket matches, and recalled Peggy Ashcroft refusing to admit that she'd been caught and Glen Byam Shaw fielding in a deckchair. Reassuringly, he could not recall any of my own performances, either on stage or on the cricket field.

McKellen is seven or eight years my junior, and although he too had been fired by Olivier's acting, it was interesting to note how different we had become. Despite being a calculating actor – systematic, fastidious, thinking about every facet of his per- formance from make-up to text – there was also something of the showman in him, perhaps a faint trace of his admiration for Olivier, and it was this combination which made him such a charismatic, magisterial, though wry Gandalf.

I knew that, in the past, McKellen had occasionally been annoyed by the perception that to get a decent stage part actors often had to make their names *outside* theatre. This, I felt, had led to some uneasy, fidgeting performances whenever a camera came near to him, as if he was determined to impress. But in the recent *Gods and Monsters* he was quite brilliant, very at ease, and at last able to trust his ability and (importantly) his presence.

Though we sometimes wondered at the strange world we inhabited for the making of *Lord of the Rings*, its première at Leicester Square Odeon on Monday 10 December 2001 (a day I'll never manage to forget) left us in no doubt that something extraordinary had happened.

'A whole host of stars will be there,' we were informed.

'Who?' someone asked.

'Cliff Richard for definite,' came the reply. And indeed he was.

We were instructed not to give autographs, otherwise simply getting into the building would have taken too long, though Sean Bean missed the briefing and held things up by signing for anyone who asked. Girls were screaming, 'We love you, Elijah!' Someone shouted at me, 'Watcha Baggins!' There were two days of interviews, with fifty interviews each day. I was presented with a pre-retail Bilbo doll, which I thought made me look like Doctor Who, though someone else (who claimed its chunky sleekness resembled a sex toy) renamed it 'Dildo Doll'.

I still receive between twenty and thirty fan letters every week, some just addressed to 'Bilbo', and I was only in a handful of scenes. Goodness knows how many McKellen gets. I am hardly famous – certainly not on a Tom Cruise scale, for example – but in a small way I somehow acquired a tiny corner of celebrity pie. Now, taxi drivers stop and ask me if I would mind signing an autograph for their sons or daughters. Children call me Bilbo. And one person said to me, 'Are you Ian Holm? *Wow!*' This is all very odd, though because I'm so old and celebrity won't – can't – last for very long, it's perfectly manageable. My head was not altogether unturned, I have to admit, though I know that I'm not a movie star and will never have a movie-star life.

Immediately after I had finished my part in the filming, I took a holiday in New Zealand. It is probably the most beautiful place I have ever visited. To breathe the air is to remember what air is *really* like. And yet as I stood on one of its breathtaking mountains overlooking one its wonderful lochs, and considered the scale and variety of the landscape, I also felt very mortal. *Lord of the Rings* showed Bilbo as both younger and older than my true age, and at the appropriate times I was therefore made up to look relatively youthful and then virtually senile. I did not recognize the younger Bilbo, but the older version was very identifiable. He was quite close to Ian Holm. I was alone, and being alone made me consider myself at uncomfortably close quarters. I was losing, for example, all trust and ease in my body. The back I had injured while falling from a lorry during National Service was now causing me considerable pain. I didn't think that I was getting fat, or was particularly over-weight; it was more that my body was just turning *into* fat. And knowing these things sometimes made God's creation look worthless.

19

HOMECOMING (II)

At the beginning of 2001, I was more or less single, approaching seventy, trailing four ex-wives, and though a serial grandfather, still feeling fit and aching to perform. Actors, by and large, do not have a choice about such things. They never retire. Work gives up on them before they give up on the work. And for me, whose existence was animated by not much more than the playing of roles, continuing to work was imperative.

Generally, when people reach this kind of age they are settled in habit. The important relationships in their lives have been long established and there is a sense of life being contemplated in tranquillity. One becomes grandfatherly – a little self-indulgent, kindly enough, though perhaps mildly impatient of the way things have changed, and finally deserving of a sedentary life. But my grandchildren's fond euphemism for me alluded to a truth. I was – I *am* – grumpy. My children have often reminded me of this, nudging me whenever I overstep the mark, and sometimes nudging me quite hard.

After separating from Pep, after sixteen years together, I moved into a modest flat near to Gloucester Road. There was an element of urgency in this. The recent deterioration in our relationship had accelerated to the point where I quickly needed somewhere to live. It was the first time I had been alone for many years. I kept a few of the paintings we had collected together. I bought a television that was so advanced its screen was able to detect movement and swivel round accordingly. One day a sofa, a chair and a bed were delivered. Another day was spent watching wooden slatted blinds being installed. There wasn't much else.

I asked Sarah-Jane's partner Paul to help with alterations and decorating, mainly to the kitchen. For a while, I was distracted by the works and would call him up to ask about a door knob which needed fitting or a cupboard which didn't look right. It all came at a time when I wasn't working, and in the absence of such stimulus I indulged the habit of countering my own emptiness by devouring some other existence.

Sarah-Jane and I went out for a meal, during which she took issue with my phone calls and much else besides. She talked of how she and Jessica sometimes felt that they were from the family I had left behind, and said that I had grandchildren who would like to see more of me. Rarely can understatement have been deployed with such acuity.

When Sarah-Jane was fourteen she had written to me saying that she didn't want to see me again. This would have been when she was feeling at her most sensitive about my separation from her mother, though it had occurred ten years or so earlier. It must also have been around the time that Bee and I were breaking up. The apparent repetition stirred uncomfortable thoughts and memories. I think she felt her father was ridiculous. By the time Sarah-Jane and I eventually resumed our relationship, she had, I think, become resigned to my ways and decided that little would ever change – though sometimes, when it was felt that my behaviour demanded it, I would need reprimanding.

This most recent dressing-down developed into a consideration of my present circumstances. Sarah-Jane reminded me that without work or Pep's good-humoured ironizing, which gave some kind of acceptable form to my manner, I was in danger of falling prey to any number of passing fads or obsessions.

'Like ornamental door knobs,' I suggested.

'Exactly,' she confirmed. 'You're like a child.'

'In what way?' I asked, though aware of sounding quite like a child when I said it.

'For example, you can't *not* say what's on your mind.'

She was right, and I understood that without work to fill my time – to engage me – I was a rootless nuisance. Although the roles hadn't yet dried up, I was aware of the cameos becoming smaller, and despite *King Lear*, I didn't relish being on stage for long periods. Though I had done *From Hell*, *Joe Gould's Secret* was the last film to hand me a substantial role. I liked the story (about an intelligent, Harvard-educated man dropping out, becoming a trampish bum and being invited to modish Manhattan parties as a cute eccentric) and I liked working with Stanley Tucci, who directed the film and played the other leading role. It was, I think, a good film, though a good *art-house* film, and despite Tucci and I working hard on publicity, it didn't do much business. This was due in part to the studio, which had acquired the movie after the initial backers encountered financial problems, not being much interested in it.

During the shoot for this film, my nerves had returned, though they had been managed with the aid of beta blockers and various medications. On this occasion, I wasn't unduly anxious or surprised by the attack. It had started when Tucci asked me to improvise scenes and concoct credible 'street' behaviour for a hobo. I could see perfectly well what was behind his thinking – it is difficult to script that kind of dereliction – but I disliked it intensely and felt unable to do his bidding. On this occasion, Pep was unable to help me because her ex-husband Dan Massey had died and she had her hands full back in England. I felt that my nerves had tangible origins and a set of particular circumstances; it didn't *feel* the same as before.

But I felt obliged to take the part, not least because it was a big role. And how many more of those would I be offered? As I write, I am considering a film which concerns a seventy-three-year-old man who, sometime in the 1960s, buys a 1920s Indian Streamliner motorcycle and determines to break the world land-speed record. The record stood at over two hundred miles per hour, and the machine was built with a top speed of only fifty-four m.p.h. The film involves a lot of mechanical tinkering, a journey to the salt flats in America, and – inevitably – the successful completion of a lifetime's ambition. It's a true story. It's the only considerable part I have been offered for a year or so. I am obliged to consider it.

In so many ways, therefore, the offer to play the old patriarch Max in the 2001 revival of *The Homecoming* was manna from heaven. In 1967 Pinter had told me that one day I would play Lenny's cantankerous father. As a relatively young man I'd laughed at the preposterousness of the idea, but thirty-four years later Michael Colgan put together a Pinter Festival at the Lincoln Center in New York, which also featured a number of plays besides *The Homecoming*, one of which was a new work, *Celebration*, which had been premièred at the Almeida.

For a number of reasons, I was keen to take the opportunity. Chief amongst these was the renewed involvement with Pinter himself. I still considered *The Homecoming* the best of his plays, though when I told him as much during rehearsals – Robin Le Fevre directed, but the author made a number of appearances – he reminded me of what I had said to him when the part of Lenny had been first offered to me in 1965.

'What was that?' I asked.

'You said, "Well, I don't much like the play, but it's a good part so I'll do it." '

'Did I really?'

'You did.' Pinter beamed, with his usual chummy menace.

A schedule was put together whereby we would do a mini-rep season in New York. The other pieces would play alternate nights, while *The Homecoming* would have a straight run which would last a week. In addition, the production would be taken to the Gate Theatre in Dublin and then the Comedy Theatre back in London. It brought to mind Tom Stoppard's quip about Pinter's apparent interest in having the theatre named after him, only for Stoppard to remark that it would be easier for the playwright to change his name to Harold Comedy.

In 1967, American audiences had initially received *The Homecoming* with dumbfounded disgust, but this time round we were greeted with ecstatic acceptance. In the interim, American audiences had thought about the play, come to recognize it as a work of genius, and were now prepared to pay their respects. There was a blood-vessel-bursting eulogy in the *New York Times*, standing ovations, and even – something I've not experienced before or since – a couple of entrance rounds. These were very disconcerting. As the lights went up and I hobbled on stage, all coiled anger and disappointment, an explosion waiting to happen, I was met by a warm and then relatively thunderous round of applause. Used to working for applause rather than being granted it before the work was done, I wondered what I should do next. For a moment, I considered whether there was any point in continuing. After all, things could only get worse. How could I live up to the ovation? And should I acknowledge the applause, appearing gracious yet thereby dissolving the sense of irascibility which I felt was necessary to Max's first appearance? With characteristic lack of commitment I did a bit of both, halting just long enough to indicate that I heeded the acclaim, but also trying to stay inside the character I had developed. The effect, I felt, was unfortunate and perhaps rather graceless. Stopping in the middle of the stage, I must have looked like an old man realizing that he was about to break wind.

About ten days before the play opened in Dublin, despite the absence of personal crises and the general feeling of confidence that we had created a very fine production, I began to experience another nervous reaction. Though I knew that my problem had not simply dissolved, I had assumed after *King Lear* that it was manageable. Or at least, after *Joe Gould's Secret*, capable of being contained. But one morning I woke up and felt that I couldn't do the play. I lay in bed – sweating, still, afraid. Eventually I forced myself to get up, though by the time I reached the theatre my hands were shaking and my heart felt as if it was about to erupt inside my chest. I called Lissy and she tried to calm me down. Alarming memories of *The Iceman Cometh* only made things worse, and it wasn't long before I was once again holding on to furniture and leaning on doorways, terrified that I would pass out. By this time my skin had become a damp waxy hide and my hands were uncontrollable, shuddering with an almost supernatural ferocity.

And once more I experienced the sense of being close to some kind of meltdown, my body slowly disentangling itself from any form of control I might be able to exert over it. I was drowning in dread. And at the back of my mind I could hear something – not exactly a voice, though more insistent than an echo – which reminded me over and over of what acting means, of the terror involved in letting yourself down and disappointing others. It was as if I recognized the arrogant hopelessness and futility of being able to interest an audience. In my mind, each one of its members had assumed an overwhelming individuality and they were represented as a collection of hard-to-please characters rather than a single unit. The problem of actually *entertaining* them seemed impossibly magnified.

And, of course, Pinter's meticulous language hemmed me in, contributing to the sensation of claustrophobia, disallowing variation, prohibiting relaxation. Each word, each rest, had its own organic purpose. Years before, at Stratford, during one of Olivier's stage crises, I had watched him making up lines in *Titus Andronicus* as a way of jolting his performance back to life. 'The birds are flying o'er the lee,' he twittered, 'and – lo! – the breathy wind hath come again.' Fat chance of making things up in Pinter. Even the small daily deviations in performance that an actor needs in order to transform recital into acting were, in this writer's case, necessarily minuscule. A slightly different stress here, a shorter exhalation of breath there . . . in the best possible way, Pinter folded you absolutely into his world.

Lissy helped me through it. Once more, I was put on medication. I managed to make it on to the stage for the previews, and though I walked off it again during one of the first performances, I was at least able to pull myself together, turn round and return to my bewildered stage family, who out of necessity were experiencing one of Pinter's longer pauses.

It helped that the cast was so good and seemed so committed to the play. Ian Harte, for example, had been experiencing difficulties playing Lenny, bringing a number of odd accents and stresses to his performance. He is a very fine actor, though for some reason it just wasn't working. When he asked me for advice I think I talked a great deal about Lenny's charm. Despite everything else, Lenny is a captivating fellow, and this is what makes him so magnetic. I admired Harte's persistence in being able to chisel a good performance out of his frustrations. It was also interesting to observe Lia Williams updating Vivien Merchant's cooler, more removed portrayal of Ruth. By contrast,

Lia's performance was full of animated ruthlessness and she completely slayed Max's family.

Pinter and I are very friendly with one another, though I could not say we are friends. Our relationship depends on the maintenance of a certain distance. Still, he has come to be one of the important threads which runs through my life. Not quite part of the sunshine or candlelight, but an abiding presence, like a fire burning deep in a ship's hold. Though he is so much more than an autobiographical writer, he does, I think, work from life as well as from his own subconscious, and Max and Lenny are to some extent projections of Pinter. They are, like him, at once aggressive, funny, sensitive and bullish. In practical and theatrical ways, our lives have therefore been curiously, almost intimately related. Now he has become rather grand, though not necessarily aloof, which is something else altogether. Joan Bakewell has said that he understands 'the significance of his own life', so why shouldn't he be a little dignified?

I have a great regard and fondness for Pinter, a partiality now perhaps leavened by nostalgia as it seems possible (if not likely) that *The Homecoming* will prove to have been one of my last stage roles. I am no longer capable – mentally or physically – of performing long repertory-style runs, and it seems clear that despite my apparent calm during *King Lear* four years earlier, I am still vulnerable to panic attacks. It is getting to the point (if it has not already been reached) when neither I nor a potential employer would want to invite the risk of another on-stage crack-up.

In 2002 I was rehearsing for a new play at the National Theatre, *Mappa Mundi* by Shelagh Stevenson. This should have been a perfectly appropriate production. The director Bill Alexander and the cast – which included Tim McInnerny and Lia Williams – were excellent. So was the role I would have played – an old man called Jack, on the verge of death, but intimately and savagely embroiled with his family. It was a good part in a fine play. In addition, there would be no long run and no tour, thereby calming my dread of repetition. The theatre knew it was taking a gamble, but everyone involved said they were willing to take the risk. I rehearsed the play very happily until about two weeks before the opening night. At that point I began to experience the familiar symptoms of inner tightness and shallow, hurried breathing, the harbingers of my anxious condition. This time, though, I knew that medication and soothing words would not see me through. Very quickly, I made a decision to drop out of the production. It was, of course, extremely awkward. Fortunately, Alun Armstrong was able to take my place. Though I didn't see the production, by all accounts he made a very good job of it.

Earlier, I had been thrilled by the writing and the character I was invited to play. I was keen to do it, though perhaps misguided, and doggedly underestimated my physical strength. When I began to feel tight inside, my body understood that it was unable to cope with the strains that fighting through the anxiety would inevitably impose. I had only just recovered from radiotherapy for cancer of the prostate. Physically, I was still quite weak.

This was my first encounter with serious illness, though its timing – in respect of my age – should not have been a surprise. Throughout the rest of my life, however, the usual sorts of ailments had occurred at unconventional times. As a young boy, I had somehow missed mumps and chickenpox altogether; all the usual experiences of childhood – occasional sickness, unselfconscious happiness, the naive sensation of unlimited possibility – seemed destined to pass me by. In most respects, I skipped boyhood, though I did eventually get a sort of mumps when *The Homecoming* was filmed in the early 1970s. Even this late entry into the world of childhood was then diagnosed as an infected perotic gland. I had to take cereals through a straw, and filming – much to the annoyance of the movie's insurers – had to be postponed for two weeks.

Chickenpox caught up with me a few years later, while I was making *Inside the Third Reich* in Vienna. I caught it from Lissy and woke up one morning to find not only my face covered in spots and pustules, but also parts of my body, my arms, and even (so I discovered) my testicles. I was, like Bottom, utterly transformed, and was quarantined inside my room. I remember feeling very ill indeed, as though life itself was coming to an end, and that given the choice, I would rather die than carry on living. Food was left for me on a tray outside the room. Apart from Bee, who kept vigil and traipsed the streets asking in shops for baking soda to rub over my infected parts, only two people dared to visit. One was Robert Stephens, who showed no fear at all about my predicament, and the other was Tom Bell. Both would come to see me on a regular basis, never merely putting their heads round the door, but staying to gossip, tell me what was happening on set, and sometimes to read an English newspaper which they'd managed to find.

Ten days later, I emerged from my cell, pock-marked, blotchy, heavily made-up, and once more became Heinrich Himmler. Stephens took me out for a celebratory slice of chocolate cake at one of Vienna's many famous cafés and I asked him why he had taken the trouble to visit me while everyone else kept their distance.

'Dear boy,' he said, 'you looked so *miserable*. I couldn't *not* come.'

'But you might have caught something,' I said.

He laughed. 'With my looks, do you think anyone would notice?'

Though Stephens told me that as a child he had suffered from chickenpox, I later discovered this to be untrue. He had actually taken quite a risk in coming to visit me.

By nature, I am a hypochondriac. This may or may not be of relevance to my anxiety attacks, but I am instinctively impatient with imperfections in the mechanics of my body. I dislike it intensely when my knee aches or my back gives me a twinge, when things don't work as they ought. I think I was a particularly bad patient during the bouts of mumps and chickenpox – disobliging, bad tempered, a real burden. Yet when I discovered the cancer, I reacted in a relatively calm and even rational manner. I never thought I would die, for instance, although for most of my life even a runny nose had sent me into a gloom-laden frenzy of self-pity.

I woke up one morning in September 2001 unable to pee. I knew that this difficulty was being caused by an enlarged benign prostate. My urologist, Roger Kirby, had identified the problem a few months earlier. With medication, he said, you could keep the swelling down. 'We tend to try and leave that sort of thing alone.'

'What do you mean,' I asked, ' "*leave that sort of thing alone*"?'

I was worried by his nonchalance, the kind of medical nonchalance which suggested to me the masking of some other, more serious problem.

'I mean we'd rather not operate. If it's possible.'

'You mean it's possible?'

'We'll see how things go.'

So I had taken the medication, grumbled through occasional bouts of painful compression, and told myself that even though it was a 'very common condition in males', I would be exempt from its more extreme manifestations.

That was until I couldn't urinate. It's difficult to describe the sudden, inundating shock and terror that occurs when you can't perform a basic function that you've been performing without difficulty for seventy years. My first and in retrospect rather bizarre response was to look at my face in the mirror. Everything seemed as it should be. Even the by now familiar distortions caused by Time's mudslide were somehow encouraging. Reassured, I returned to the toilet and tried again. Still the same. A distressing build-up of pressure with apparently no hope of release.

I began to panic. It felt quite literally as if I was about to explode. I wondered what was happening to all the stuff that wasn't coming out.

It was a bright Saturday morning. I called Lissy and she drove me to Roger Kirby's clinic. The bed wasn't ready. The catheters didn't work. I remember there was a large poster detailing in vivid colours the various kinds of urological cancer – kidney, prostate, testicular, bladder. Mockingly, it was situated near to the toilets. Roger Kirby told me that he would have to operate on Monday morning.

Afterwards, he told me that he had found cancer behind the prostate.

'I've taken quite a lot out, but I would advise radiotherapy,' he said cheerfully.

'Do I *need* radiotherapy?' I asked.

'It's up to you, of course. But I'd certainly advise it.'

He showed me an X-ray, the ridge of darkness around the prostate. The cancerous growth. It would be best if that wasn't there. It could spread. At the least, it would keep coming back. I felt strangely occupied, as if I'd been invaded. Of course I needed radiotherapy – to relieve the pressure, the alien activity.

Like most people, when I was a child I assumed that I would become brave simply by virtue of being older. Adults didn't cry or complain about trips to the dentist or make lame excuses about avoiding unpleasantness. The mention of radiotherapy –

different, I know, from chemotherapy, but sinisterly related – revealed the absurdity of such assumptions.

I saw my GP to discuss the practical details of the procedure. 'Where should I go?' I inquired.

'Think about America,' he said. 'Don't go here. Go to America.'

'Can I think about it?'

'Certainly. Think about it, by all means – *then* go to America.'

He explained that America was where the best private treatment was available, and that as I was in any case 'going private', I might as well go there.

'What happened to the NHS?' I asked without much seriousness.

'There are simply too many of us,' he said, meaning too many patients, 'and you'd have to wait too long. Still, it's better than it was. In the old days they didn't wait, they just died.'

So I went to New York. Being a cancer patient became another role, a part to be played; I surprised myself and others by approaching it with directness and a matter-of-fact sense of reality. By and large, I just got on with it. The treatment took place in the Presbyterian Hospital in the Upper 160s. Regular taxis didn't go that far, so I would make the subsequent journeys in a mongrel collection of battered old Lincolns, Buicks and Chevys. Very few of the drivers spoke English. Very few of them could actually drive. They were renegade, gypsy drivers, probably illegal, trying to make a few dollars in the least conspicuous manner.

The first visit to Dr Petrylak took place at about nine in the morning. He wore highly polished Gucci shoes, was indeterminately young, and generated the well-groomed, well-tanned, well-scrubbed warmth of expensive, godly reassurance. His handshake was encouragingly strong. Soon, he produced the X-rays, nodding his head and stroking his chin, then smiling positively at me.

For the next forty-two days (excluding weekends) I made the trip up to the Presbyterian Hospital, lay on a bed beneath something which resembled a giant washing machine, and was subjected to a daily fusillade of radiotherapy. In a way that later reminded me of being piped aboard a ship, there were three short blasts on each side of my body, climaxing with a single sustained salvo on the prostate itself.

Dr Petrylak took a back seat for much of this procedure, overseeing the treatment from a polite distance but delegating much of it to Dr Schiff, who possessed the same strong, warm, clean hands. He warned me to be careful of eating, as my bowel movements would now become loose and frequent. I shouldn't be surprised if I started to develop breasts. It was likely that I would lose my pubic hair. I would be prone to hot flushes.

'Anything else?' I asked.

'You'll most probably lose your sex drive.'

'I'm seventy,' I said.

'Whatever. You'll still lose your sex drive. We've *fried* your prostate!'

Because I have a naturally slow metabolism, none of these things happened immediately. At one point I thought I might escape the side effects altogether. By the end of the treatment – in April 2002 – my only souvenir was what looked like a severe case of sunburn on my right buttock.

For weeks, months, there was nothing; and then, as Dr Schiff had warned, hot flushes and trips to the toilet became a way of life. I returned to the mirror. There were the breasts. It was if they had sprung up overnight, or if not sprung up, then sagged down. And not exactly breasts, but lumpen, hollow pouches of flesh. Soon after, I became a pubic Kojak.

I was sustained in New York by a small, liberal, close-knit group of people with whom I shared an apartment block in New York's Village. Of almost parodic constitution (a teacher, a writer, an artist, a gay couple, and so on and so forth), they made me feel entirely at home and made me an apparently intimate part of their lives. Despite feeling quite ill, and never less than enfeebled, and despite enduring the hypochondriac's nightmare, I was calm. Inside, something had taken over, enabling me to get myself to New York and through the treatment. People called and asked if I was all right. With uncharacteristic stoicism, I would reply that I was fine. My subconscious was dealing with a problem from which my conscious mind would have taken flight.

With respect for my subconscious thus enhanced, I even went to therapy. The generosity of the Village community extended to concern over my spiritual wellbeing. They concluded that I had 'issues' which needed 'addressing', so they fixed it for me to see Dr Marsha Brenner, a wise, grey-haired therapist who offered me the chance to 'talk' on an irregular basis. I was able to sustain the visits because they seemed more like chats with a friend than an intense procedure (Dudley Moore used to go twice a day!) and because, I suppose, I quite liked talking about myself. At various times people had told me that I could be 'childlike', that I had arrested development in adolescence, that this accounted for my 'difficulties' with women, that my occasional seizures were a little like a childish rage, even that any skill I might have as an actor was related to a childlike tendency for absorbed wonderment. It's all very interesting. But at my age, do you really want to know who you are?

The only other time I had been – so to speak – in the psychiatrist's chair was before the production of *King Lear* in 1997, when worries were voiced about the possibility of me having another nervous attack. The man I went to see specialized in phobias and said that if I wanted to do the play then I would. He talked of Dreaded Objects and pointed to a chair, asking me to imagine it represented something I hated.

'What do you hate?' he asked.

'Spiders,' I said.

'Well then. There you are. The chair is a spider. If you walk towards it, one step at a time, soon you'll be in a position where you can grasp it.'

'The chair?'

'The chair as spider.'

Dr Brenner didn't want me to walk towards anything. In fact, she wanted me to lie down during our sessions, even though I felt uncomfortable doing so. I needed to see her in order to communicate and interact. Kindly, firmly, she told me to stop performing.

But she raised an interesting point. I felt that I had taken up acting in part because I didn't want to be known or have a fixed 'identity'. Dr Brenner told me of a senator who came to see her, jabbed a finger at his body and whispered, 'There's nothing there.' I am also worried that there's nothing there. That's why I have to find something. I also think too much self-analysis (maybe *any* self-analysis) ruins an actor. Talent should be trusted. Figuring out where it comes from merely dissipates ability.

'But who is this person who is doing the acting?' Dr Brenner asked me.

'I don't know,' was my enduring reply.

I like New York and I liked being there during my radio-therapy sessions. At one point, when an apartment became available, I considered moving to the Village, but laziness, the difficulty of work, and the distant drone of being British pre-vented any kind of decisive action. This despite the impression that England was long sickening, despondent, and somehow without much to offer. In the end, though, I just didn't get around to it. Then the treatment ended, I came back to London, and the feeling subsided. As usual, I tended to float with events rather than influencing them.

Does this mean that I have profited from life and am therefore content to trust it? And if I have profited, then why can't I leave it satisfied? On the other hand, if life has given me nothing, then why do I still desire it?

Even my faint brush with death raises questions of this kind. Once raised, they can never be withdrawn or erased.

Pinter once said to me that being an actor was hard, maybe the hardest thing.

I used to think the hardest thing was living through an African famine or mining in Siberia. Now – nearly ten years after the question was initially asked – what do I think? Facing your own blankness every day and waiting to infuse it with some other, more meaningful yet second-hand state; finding the hints, shapes and patterns of another life which will grow inside you; living life without knowing who you are; living with too much regard for yourself; living with *no* regard for yourself; the struggle to put across the complexity of another character; the anxiety of disappointment; the terror of rejection; the fanciful absurdity of the theatrical world, the false friendships, the indifference, the spite, the jealousy, the underhand dealing; the obscure reviewers who either have an agenda or are merely stupid; the rewarding of the talentless; the cold-shouldering of the talented; the money that is automatically siphoned off to the inept but photogenic; people who buy you drinks and seem to be interested in you or may even like you but really just want to use you; the money and the time lavished on anything that panders to 'target audiences' (is anyone *not* between the ages of fourteen and twenty-five?); the parties where people come up to you and say, 'Aren't you that bloke from *Minder*?'; the sense that what you do means nothing; people who say that it must be nice being an actor because you don't have to get up in the morning and even when you do work it's only for a couple of hours in the evening; the contempt of those you respect; the contempt of those you don't respect; being given the brush-off and told that you're not what they expected – just a small man with bad breath; being honest and not being believed ('Well, you're an actor, aren't you?'); being honest and told that you're only hiding behind your honesty; feeling immortal yet worthless; publicity; the loneliness of not knowing who you are; the British film industry; not being Bilbo Baggins; not getting parts; *getting old* and not getting parts; the prospect of not going on the stage again; being in Scorsese's latest (about Howard Hughes) but listening to de Caprio insisting that even off set everyone calls him 'Mr Hughes'; improvising; method acting; being interviewed by some twenty-five-year-old publicist who has only got the job because of contacts and who starts by apologizing for not having seen the movie or play or even having had time to read the press release.

And now? I feel compromised by my brush with mortality and my diminished sense of invulnerability. Perhaps I feel some guilt at parts of my life, can no longer have 'no regrets'. Inhabiting the moment, moving on and putting things behind me no longer seems an easy option. In addition, though, I have recently found love once more.

The early stages of the courtship were conducted across a room, while she did me in oils.

'You're very good at being still,' she told me.

'I like being still,' I replied, meaning I liked proving that I was good at being still. In fact, spending hours in make-up, being in plays by Pinter, and actually not much minding the sustained focus of a close-up had prepared me quite well for portrait-sitting. Also, I suppose, I enjoyed being the centre of someone's attention.

Sophie is the artist's name. We met at a party given by a mutual friend. In only a few weeks we had arranged that she would paint my portrait. The liking we already had for one another escalated into something more passionate, perhaps as a consequence of those motionless, intense encounters. As 2003 drew to a close, I knew that I wanted to spend more time with Sophie. I was introduced to her friends and family, and she was welcomed by mine. I had found romance again, a little late and unexpectedly, perhaps, but no less urgent or joyous for that.

We went to Venice to look at paintings, staying in an apartment belonging to one of her friends. She also accompanied me to America for the making of the movie about Howard Hughes, and chatted (with informed enthusiasm) to Scorsese about films. And then, very suddenly and while in Los Angeles – not quite on an impulse though not quite without one either – we got married. On arrival at the hotel I had approached reception and asked (impishly and without serious intent) about the possibility of making marriage arrangements. The desk directed me to the Events Manager, who informed me that I could of course get married at the hotel. It would cost sixty-seven dollars. All I needed was cash or a credit card and some ID.

And a few days later that was more or less what happened, though in more barmy circumstances than the businesslike Events Manager could have imagined. Sophie and I were married while forest fires were raging round Los Angeles, so that the backdrop was one of black, billowing smoke and intense, colourful flames. The next day we discovered that one of the film sets we were using had been destroyed by the fire.

The reception was held in the back garden of one of my eldest son's friends – Barnaby was by now absolutely rooted in California with a job, a house and a girlfriend. He sprayed 'Just Married' on our car in spongy white foam and loaded a large, almost vulgar cake into its boot. On arrival at his friend's house, the cake fell out of the boot and Barnaby caught it moments before it hit the ground.

It seemed that the wedding was flirting with the bizarre, its shimmer of unreality enhanced by the intense, dreamy heat which even at night didn't abate and caused Sophie to head up to the hotel's pool in the early hours. Even now, several months later, she and I cannot quite believe what happened, the unanticipated, fantastic nature of the event lending it the quality of hallucination.

A month or so before Sophie and I were married, I gave an interview about *The Emperor's New Clothes*, in which I suggested that work was more important than love. I think what I meant was that I am generally impatient with love and have often sought refuge in what has been, for me at least, the apparent reliability, the durability, of work.

So, returning to Pinter's observation, is acting the hardest thing? I would still say, 'It's hard enough – though not, of course, the hardest thing.'

IAN HOLM: A SELECTIVE CV

Theatre

1956 Season at Worthing Rep.
       Love Affair (Lyric Theatre, Hammersmith)
1957 *Titus Andronicus* (European Tour and Stoll Theatre)

Three seasons at Stratford. Plays appeared in include:
1958 *Much Ado About Nothing*
       Romeo and Juliet
1959 *Othello*
       Coriolanus
       A Midsummer Night's Dream
       King Lear
1960 *The Merchant of Venice*
       The Taming of the Shrew
       Twelfth Night

In January 1961, became a long-term contract artist with the RSC
and appeared in London and Stratford in the following plays:
1961 *The Cherry Orchard*

Ondine
The Devils
Becket
The Taming of the Shrew
1962   *A Midsummer Night's Dream*
Measure for Measure
The Taming of the Shrew
Troilus and Cressida
1963   *The Tempest*
Edward IV
Richard III
1964   *Henry IV*
Henry V
Edward IV
Richard III
1965   *The Homecoming*
1966   *Henry IV* (I and II)
Henry V
Twelfth Night
1967   *The Homecoming* (Music Box, New York)
Romeo and Juliet
1970   *The Friends* (Roundhouse)
A Bequest to the Nation (Haymarket Theatre)
1972   *Caravaggio Buddy* (Traverse Theatre, Edinburgh)
1973   *The Sea* (Royal Court)
1974   *Other People* (Hampstead Theatre)
1976   *The Iceman Cometh* (Aldwych)
1979   *Uncle Vanya* (Hampstead Theatre)
1989   *The Room* (Pinter Benefit at the Haymarket)
1993   *Moonlight* (Almeida Theatre and Comedy Theatre)
1994   *Moonlight* and *Landscape* (Gate Theatre, Dublin)
Landscape (National Theatre)
1997   *King Lear* (National Theatre)

2001   *The Homecoming* (Gate Theatre, Pinter Festival in New York, Comedy Theatre)

Television
1964   *The Wars of the Roses* (dir. Peter Hall)
1974   *Napoleon and Love* (dir. Reg Collin)
1977   *Jesus of Nazareth* (dir. Franco Zeffirelli)
1978   *Flayed* (BBC Play of the Week)
       The Lost Boys (dir. Rodney Bennett/BBC)
1979   *The Misanthrope* (dir. Michael Simpson/BBC)
1982   *We, the Accused* (dir. Richard Stroud/BBC)
1985   *The Browning Version* (dir. Michael Simpson/BBC)
       Mr and Mrs Edgehill (dir. Gavin Millar/BBC)
1988   *Game, Set and Match* (dir. Patrick Lau/Granada)
1989   *The Endless Game* (dir. Bryan Forbes/TVS Films)
1990   *Stuff of Madness* (dir. Mai Zetterling/HTV)
1991   *Uncle Vanya* (dir. Greg Mosher/BBC)
       The Last Romantics (dir. Jack Gold/BBC)
1993   *The Borrowers* (and 1994; 2 series; dir. John Henderson/BBC)
1995   *Landscape* (dir. Harold Pinter/BBC)
1996   *Roald Dahl's Little Red Riding Hood* (dir. Donald Sturrock/BBC)
1997   *King Lear* (dir. Richard Eyre/BBC)
1998   *Alice Through the Looking Glass* (dir. John Henderson/Channel 4)
2000   *The Last of the Blonde Bombshells* (dir. Gillies MacKinnon/BBC-HBO)

Film
1968   *A Midsummer Night's Dream* (dir. Peter Hall)
       The Fixer (dir. John Frankenheimer)
       The Bofors Gun (dir. Jack Gold)

1969 *Oh! What a Lovely War* (dir. Richard Attenborough)

1970 *A Severed Head* (dir. Dick Clement)

1971 *Mary, Queen of Scots* (dir. Charles Jarrott)

1972 *Young Winston* (dir. Richard Attenborough)

1973 *The Homecoming* (dir. Peter Hall)

1974 *Juggernaut* (dir. Richard Lester)

1976 *Shout at the Devil* (dir. Peter Hunt)

      Robin and Marion (dir. Richard Lester)

1977 *The Man in the Iron Mask* (dir. Mike Newell)

      March or Die (dir. Dick Richards)

      Holocaust (dir. Marvin Chomsky)

1978 *The Thief of Baghdad* (dir. Clive Donner)

1979 *S.O.S. Titanic* (dir. William Hale)

      Alien (dir. Ridley Scott)

1980 *All Quiet on the Western Front* (dir. Delbert Mann)

1981 *Time Bandits* (dir. Terry Gilliam)

      Chariots of Fire (dir. Hugh Hudson)

1982 *The Return of the Soldier* (dir. Alan Bridges)

1984 *Greystoke* (dir. Hugh Hudson)

      Laughterhouse (dir. Richard Eyre)

      Dance with a Stranger (dir. Mike Newell)

1985 *Brazil* (dir. Terry Gilliam)

      Wetherby (dir. Richard Eyre)

      Dreamchild (dir. Gavin Millar)

1988 *Another Woman* (dir. Woody Allen)

1989 *Henry V* (dir. Kenneth Branagh)

1990 *Hamlet* (dir. Franco Zeffirelli)

1991 *Kafka* (dir. Steven Soderbergh)

      The Naked Lunch (dir. David Cronenberg)

1992 *Blue Ice* (dir. Russell Mulcahy)

1993 *The Hour of the Pig* (dir. Leslie Megahy)

1994 *Mary Shelley's Frankenstein* (dir. Kenneth Branagh)

      The Madness of King George (dir. Nick Hytner)

Loch Ness (dir. John Henderson)

1995 *Big Night* (dir. Stanley Tucci)

1996 *Night Falls on Manhattan* (dir. Sidney Lumet)

1997 *The Fifth Element* (dir. Luc Besson)

A Life Less Ordinary (dir. Danny Boyle)

The Sweet Hereafter (dir. Atom Egoyam)

1999 *Simon Magus* (dir. Ben Hopkins)

eXistenZ (dir. David Cronenberg)

The Match (dir. Mick Davies)

2000 *Esther Kahn* (dir. Arnaud Desplechin)

Joe Gould's Secret (dir. Stanley Tucci)

Beautiful Joe (dir. Stephen Metcalfe)

Bless the Child (dir. Chuck Russell)

2001 *Lord of the Rings: The Fellowship of the Ring* (dir. Peter Jackson)

From Hell (dir. Albert and Allen Hughes)

The Emperor's New Clothes (dir. Alan Taylor)

2003 *Lord of the Rings: Return of the King* (dir. Peter Jackson)

Awards

1965 *Evening Standard* Actor of the Year for *Henry V* and *The Homecoming*

1967 Tony Award for Best Supporting Actor in a Drama for *The Homecoming*

1968 BAFTA Award Best Supporting Actor for *The Bofors Gun*

1979 RTS Best Actor Award for *The Lost Boys*

1981 BAFTA Award Best Supporting Actor for *Chariots of Fire*
Cannes Film Festival Best Supporting Actor for *Chariots of Fire*

1982 Oscar Nomination for *Chariots of Fire*

1987 Ninth Annual ACE Winner Actor in a Theatrical Special for *The Browning Version*

1989 Awarded the CBE

1993 *Evening Standard* Actor of the Year for *Moonlight*
Critics Circle Theatre Award for *Moonlight*

1995 BAFTA Nomination Best Supporting Actor for *The Madness of King George*

1997 *Evening Standard* Best Actor Award for *King Lear*
GENIE Best Actor Award for *The Sweet Hereafter*
National Board of Review best cast ensemble for *The Sweet Hereafter*

1998 Critics Circle Theatre Award for *King Lear*
Olivier Best Actor Award for *King Lear*
London Film Critics' Circle Awards nomination for *The Sweet Hereafter, Big Night, Night Falls on Manhattan* and *The Fifth Element*
Chicago Film Critics Award Nomination for Best Actor for *The Sweet Hereafter*
Best Male Performance 1997 Toronto Film Critics Association, *The Sweet Hereafter*
Awarded Knighthood

1999 Honorary Doctor of Letters, University of Sussex

LIST OF ILLUSTRATIONS

The photos without credit have been kindly supplied by family members. Others are as follows:

Midsummer Night's Dream: Brian Seed / Lebrecht Music Collection; Henry Bayton: The Raymond Mander and Joe Mitchenson Theatre Collection; *Titus Andronicus*: Photographer Angus McBean, Copyright Royal Shakespeare Company; *King Lear*: Photographer Angus McBean, Copyright Royal Shakespeare Company; *Twelfth Night*: Tom Holte Theatre Photographic Collection, Copyright Shakespeare Birthplace Trust.

Henry V: Tom Holte Theatre Photographic Collection, Copyright Shakespeare Birthplace Trust; RSC discussion group: Michael Stroud / Express / Getty Images; *Oh! What A Lovely War*: bfi Stills.

The Iceman Cometh: © Donald Cooper; *Shout at the Devil*: TONAV PRODUCTIONS / THE KOBAL COLLECTION; *Holocaust*: Mirrorpix; *The Lost Boys*: BBC.

Uncle Vanya: John Haynes/The Raymond Mander and Joe Mitchenson Theatre Collection.

Napoleon and Love: bfi Stills; *Time Bandits*: bfi Stills; *The Emperor's New Clothes* (both): Ch4 Films/Mikado Films/RAI Cinema/Kobal.

Chariots of Fire: 20TH CENTURY FOX/ALLIED STARS/ENIGMA/THE KOBAL COLLECTION; *Greystoke*: bfi Stills; *Alien*: Aquarius Collection; *Mr and Mrs Edgehill*: BBC; *The Borrowers*: BBC; *Laughterhouse*: GREENPOINT FILMS/THE KOBAL COLLECTION; *Moonlight*: © Donald Cooper; *Frankenstein*: Aquarius Collection.

Richard Eyre and Ian Holm: TopFoto.co.uk/HENRIETTA BUTLER/ARENA IMAGES; *The Homecoming*: TopFoto.co.uk/MARILYN KINGWILL/ARENA IMAGES; *King Lear*: © John Haynes; Sophie and Ian Holm: © Tom Bloom.

Ian Holm at the National Theatre: © Steve Pyke.

INDEX